The Revolutionary Thoughts of Kwame Nkrumah

The Revolutionary Thoughts of Kwame Nkrumah

Kwame Nkrumah

inkani

© Inkani Books, 2024

This edition published May 2024

ISBN 978-1-7764215-5-8

Edited by Efemia Chela, Nkhensani Manabe and Vijay Prashad

Text set in Source Serif 4 by Frank Grießhammer for Adobe

Inkani Books
2nd Floor, South Point Corner,
87 De Korte Street
Braamfontein,
Johannesburg,
South Africa,
2001

Inkani Books is the publishing division of The Tricontinental Pan Africa NPC

inkanibooks.co.za

CONTENTS

ABBREVIATIONS

AALC Africa-American Labour Centre

AATUF All-African Trade Union Federation

AFL-CIO American Federation of Labour and Congress of Industrial Organisations

CPP Convention People's Party

ECA Economic Commission for Africa

FAO Food and Agriculture Organisation

GNTC Ghana National Trading Corporation

IASB International African Service Bureau

ICFTU International Confederation of Free Trade Unions

ILO International Labour Organisation

MRA Moral Re-Armament

MPLA *Movimento Popular de Libertação de Angola* (Movement for the Liberation of Angola)

NATO North American Treaty Organisation

NLC National Liberation Council

OAU Organisation of African Unity

RDA *Rassemblement Democratic Africain* (African Democratic Assembly or African Democratic Rally)

TUC Trades Union Congress

UGCC United Gold Coast Convention

UGFC United Ghana Farmers' Council

UN United Nations

UNCTAD United Nations Conference on Trade and Development

UPA *União das Populações de Angola* (United People of Northern Angola)

USIA United States Information Agency

WFTU World Federation of Trade Unions

Foreword

My father died in exile in 1972, six years after the coup d'état against his democratically elected government. The coup was physically led by the officers of the Ghanaian army and police, but – in fact – the coup was engineered by the United States and the United Kingdom. These countries could no longer tolerate Kwame Nkrumah's attempt to build the sovereignty of Ghana and the integrity of the African continent through a pan-African project that had created such institutions as the Organisation of African Unity.

The coup came when Nkrumah was on a visit to revolutionary China and Vietnam, and significantly, the year after he published his monumental work, *Neocolonialism: The Last Stage of Imperialism*. It presented a powerful critique of the global political and economic system that had emerged after the formal end of colonialism in Africa and other parts of the world. Robert Smith, of the US State Department, said that the book was 'simply outrageous.... We were blamed for everything in the world.' US aid to Ghana was cancelled and the US began an economic war to undermine the Pan-African and Ghanaian project.

In 1989, Smith said that the book might have contributed in a material way to my father's 'overthrow shortly thereafter.' It was not the book itself that spurred the coup. What angered the US and its allies was that the ideas about state sovereignty and the need to fight against the neocolonial structures. It exposed the true nature of the Western agenda towards Africa, which was to continue to control access to its abundant resources, on which much of their wealth and progress was built. Nkrumah's critique of neocolonialism challenged the prevailing Western narrative that colonialism had ended, and that former colonies were now free to chart their own course. His argument that imperialism had simply taken on a new form after the end of colonialism was seen as a direct challenge to Western interests, and to the dominant neoliberal economic model that was being promoted by Western powers at the time.

In addition to Nkrumah's vision of building a continental project of Pan-African unity and dignity, it was his awareness that there was a compelling need to educate the African masses to understand the structures that inhibit progress and of the organisational needs of the present that sealed his fate. These thoughts – these revolutionary thoughts of Nkrumah – were what the western powers found dangerous enough to determine to remove him from power and to derail the agenda to achieve true economic and political independence for Africa. And, unfortunately, up to date, these ideas have not been studied in the way they must be if we are to restore both the sovereignty of our countries and of our continent. Indeed, until this collection, by incident or by design, Nkrumah's books are remarkably difficult to find on the African continent.

Therefore, this volume, *The Revolutionary Thoughts of Kwame Nkrumah*, is not only timely but will form part of a larger revival of the debate around reclaiming Africa's place in the world order and the tenets of socialism and pan-Africanism. I am very pleased with the African Union of Left Publishers, Inkani Books, Militant Books, and others for working with the Socialist Movement of Ghana to create this important volume which will bring my father's insights in a condensed form to a new generation. I hope that it will be the basis not only for discussion, but also for the advancement of the revolutionary thought of Nkrumah, ultimately leading to the true social, political and economic independence of Africa he so valiantly fought for.

Professor   November 2023
Francis Nkrumah   Accra, Ghana

Foreword

The Socialist Movement of Ghana (SMG) is more than honoured to be associated with the publication of this volume, of selections from Nkrumah, by the African Union of left Publishers with Inkani Books, Militant Books and others. For us, this work could not have come at a better time given the intensity of the search for answers to the many problems which confront the working people of Africa and the world.

The fact that today, the peoples of Africa who stay on the richest continent in the world suffer excruciating poverty and under-development needs to be explained. The forces behind the senseless expenditure of billions of dollars on the building of weapons of mass destruction in the face of hunger, illiteracy, disease, and many other forms of deprivation must be exposed for who they are. It is also extremely important that progressive and revolutionary forces around the world find the space and theory necessary for uniting our struggles as a condition for the defeat of imperialism and capitalism.

SMG is convinced that the works of Kwame Nkrumah, a pan-Africanist and Marxist intellectual provide sufficient insights into the national liberation struggles of peoples of Africa, the fervour for the building of a united Africa under the banner of scientific socialism and global working class unity. We fully endorse this great work in the knowledge that it will lead to a better understanding of the works of Nkrumah and significantly contribute to the liberation of our world from the clutches of neo-colonialism, imperialism, and capitalist exploitation.

Kwesi Pratt Jnr.,   September 2023
Secretary-General of   Accra, Ghana
the Socialist Movement
of Ghana

The One Who Could
Not Be Contradicted:
An Introduction

In 1935, Kwame Nkrumah (1909–1972) arrived in London to procure his visa to study in the United States. On the streets of the capital of the British Empire, Nkrumah heard a newspaper seller excitedly shout, something unintelligible. He looked over at the newsstand and saw a placard that read, 'MUSSOLINI INVADES ETHIOPIA.' Ethiopia was one of the few countries on the African continent that had not been colonised by the West. Nkrumah, who was born in the coastal village of Nkroful in the Gold Coast and had been influenced by his education at Achimota School but mainly by his contact with the National Congress of British West Africa (founded in 1917), reacted strongly to this news. Nkrumah recalled his reaction in his autobiography, written in 1956:

> At that moment, it was almost as if the whole of London had suddenly declared war on me personally. For the next few minutes, I could do nothing but glare at each impassive face wondering if those people could possibly realise the wickedness of colonialism, and praying that the day might come when I could play my part in bringing about the downfall of such a system. My nationalism surged to the fore; I was ready and willing to go through hell itself, if need be, in order to achieve my object.[1]

Nkrumah, in his mid-20s, bristling with anger and determination, had already defined himself as an enemy of colonialism. He was clear about the importance of anti-colonial nationalism not only for his native land but for all of Africa, and indeed for the colonised world.

BEFORE NKRUMAH

From the late 15th century, European traders entered the gold business, which is why they named this large swathe of Western Africa, the Gold Coast. Greed transformed basic commerce into violence, as the Europeans set up forts along the coastline and shifted from the trade in gold alone to the trade in gold and

---

1   Kwame Nkrumah, *The Autobiography of Kwame Nkrumah* (Edinburgh: Thomas Nelson and Sons, 1957) p. 29.

human beings, and later yet into the palm oil and cocoa trade. For the next 400 years, Europe leached the wealth of the Gold Coast, its residents forced to work in conditions and at wages that prevented the social development of the various communities from Pulmakong, in the north, to Axim, in the south. Minimal amounts of the vast wealth of the Gold Coast went into education and health care, little indeed was used to develop the infrastructure of the interior of the country. People in rural Ghana saw their livelihood oscillate at the rhythms of the world prices for gold, humans, palm oil, and cocoa.

Colonialism produced its antithesis, which emerged from within the dynamic of Ghana's history. Despite a long history of trying to overcome the sovereignty of the people of Ghana, the Europeans faced significant challenges. The Ashanti Empire held fast through four Anglo-Ashanti Wars (1823–1831, 1863–1864, 1873–1874, and 1895–1896) until the territory became a British protectorate in 1897.[2] The resistance by the older powers moved from frontal combat to legal battles, with the formation of the Gold Coast Aborigines' Rights Protection Society to confront the British attempt to seize land through the Crown Lands Bill (1896) and the Lands Bill (1897).[3] Men such as John Mensah Sarbah (1864–1910) and Joseph Ephraim Casely-Hayford (1866–1930) were professionals (lawyers and journalists) who argued that African identity was tied to the land, and the detachment of land would undermine the African sense of self.

In 1903, Casely-Hayford published *Gold Coast Native Institutions: With Thoughts Upon a Healthy Policy for the Gold Coast and Ashanti*, which made the case for self-government.[4] Casely-Hayford's son, Archie, joined Nkrumah's Convention People's Party in 1951 and served in Nkrumah's government as Minister of Agriculture and Natural Resources, Minister of Communications, and then Minister of the Interior. These early nationalists, many of them constrained by their belief in the virtuousness of the British Empire, set the terrain for Nkrumah and his peers.

In 1914, Casely-Hayford and the Nigerian doctor Akinwande Savage discussed the formation of a National Congress of British West Africa (NCBWA), which was created three years later. The NCBWA drew from earlier initiatives, illustrated by the role of men such as Kobina Sekyi, a lawyer and the grandson of the Chief Regent of the Cape Coast. As a former president of the Aborigines' Rights Protection Society he refused to wear European clothes and only wore Ntama cloth or Batakari (the latter Nkrumah wore as he declared independence in 1957).

---

2   Although this was not the last war, since Ashanti forces fought the British in the War of the Golden Stool in 1900, retaining their royal symbols despite the erosion of their power.

3   S. K. B. Asante, 'The Neglected Aspects of the Activities of the Gold Coast Aborigines Rights Protection Society', *Phylon*, vol. 36, no. 1, 1975.

4   Casely-Hayford, *Gold Coast Native Institutions: With Thoughts Upon a Healthy Policy For the Gold Coast and Ashanti*, London: Sweet and Maxwell, 1903.

When Nkrumah was teaching at the Roman Catholic Junior School in Axim in 1931, he visited S. R. Wood, the secretary of the NCBWA. Three years later, Wood travelled to London to make a petition to the colonial authorities. At that time, Wood met the remarkable pan-Africanist and communist George Padmore (1903–1959), exemplifying the linkages between the various strains of anti-colonialism of that time. In August 1935, when the Italian invasion of Ethiopia inflamed Nkrumah, pan-Africanists (such as Padmore), African student organisations (including those built through the initiative of the NCBWA), and British communists set up the International African Friends of Abyssinia.[5] Wood was on its executive committee (along with Jomo Kenyatta, future president of Kenya, and Peter Millard of British Guiana who was one of the key figures with Nkrumah to organise the 1945 Pan-African Congress); Wood was present in London to receive Haile Selassie in June 1936.

Nkrumah went from London in 1935 to study at Lincoln University, a historically black college in Pennsylvania. Apart from his studies, Nkrumah involved himself in a range of political activities, including developing his own pan-African sensibility alongside Nnamdi Azikiwe (1904–1996), who would become the first president of Nigeria in 1963. Nkrumah and Azikiwe experienced the grotesqueness of Jim Crow racism (including being refused water in the American South) and entered into the world of African-American political organisations, whose work mirrored that of groups such as the NCBWA.[6] 'My aim was to learn the technique of organisation from these groups', he later reflected.[7] Both Nkrumah and Azikiwe wrote for their college newspapers and in the Black press (such as the *Baltimore Afro-American* and *The Crisis*), and met important figures of the Black liberation struggle in the US. During this time, Nkrumah read widely, searching for a theory to best explain the horrendousness of colonialism:

> I concentrated on finding a formula by which the whole colonial question and the problem of imperialism could be solved. I read Hegel, Karl Marx, Engels, Lenin, and Mazzini. The writings of these men did much to influence me in my revolutionary ideas and activities, and Karl Marx and Lenin particularly impressed me as I felt sure that their philosophy was capable of solving these problems.[8]

Nkrumah was impressed by the impact W.E.B. DuBois (1868–1963) and Marcus Garvey (1887–1940) had on the African-American population. DuBois, one

---

5   George Padmore, *Pan-Africanism or Communism? The Coming Struggle for Africa*, London. Dodson, 1956, p. 151.

6   Nkrumah, *The Autobiography*, p. 43.

7   Nkrumah, *The Autobiography*, p. 45.

8   Nkrumah, *The Autobiography*, p. 45.

of the great revolutionary thinkers, had been present in London during a Pan-African conference in 1897 that had been organised by the West Indian lawyer Henry Sylvester-Williams, and it was DuBois who nurtured the flame of Pan-Africanism through four subsequent conferences (in Paris, 1919; in London, Paris, and Brussels, 1921; in London and Lisbon, 1923; New York, 1927). Garvey's slogan 'Africa for the Africans' took these Pan-African ideas to the masses, evoking the possibility of a strong anti-colonial consciousness. By 1945, when Nkrumah returned to London, he had been prepared for the intense political activity that would absorb him for the rest of his life.

THE SOCIALIST PAN-AFRICANIST

A month after his arrival in London, Nkrumah was busy with Padmore, R. Ras Makonnen (1909–1983), and Peter Abrahams (1919–2017) building the Fifth Pan-African Congress to be held in October. The lead organisers of the congress came from across the world of the Black Atlantic: Nkrumah from the Gold Coast, Abrahams from South Africa, Padmore from Trinidad, and Makonnen from British Guiana. Over 200 delegates came to the congress and endorsed both the United Nations Declaration of Human Rights and the doctrine of African socialism. The final declaration contained a *Manifesto to the Colonial Workers, Farmers, and Intellectuals of Africa*, drafted by the key organisers, including DuBois and Nkrumah. The tone of the text carries the sensibility of anti-colonial Pan-Africanism that inspired them and explains Nkrumah's orientation:

> We believe in the rights of all people to govern themselves. We affirm the right of all Colonial peoples to control their own destiny. All Colonies must be free from foreign imperialist control, whether political or economic. The peoples of the Colonies must have the right to elect their own government, a government without restrictions from a foreign power. We say to the peoples of the colonies that they must fight for these ends by all means at their disposal.

> The object of Imperialist Powers is to exploit. By granting the right to Colonial peoples to govern themselves, they are defeating that objective. Therefore, the struggle for political power by colonial and subject peoples is the first step towards, and the necessary prerequisite to, complete social, economic, and political emancipation.

> The Fifth Pan-African Congress, therefore, calls on the workers and farmers of the Colonies to organise effectively. Colonial workers must be in the front of the battle against Imperialism. Your weapons — the Strike and the Boycott — are invincible.

This Fifth Pan-African Congress calls upon the intellectuals and professional classes of the Colonies to awaken to their responsibilities. The long, long night is over. By fighting for trade union rights, the right to form co-operatives, freedom of the press, assembly, demonstration, and strike; freedom to print and read the literature which is necessary for the education of the masses, you will be using the only means by which your liberties will be won and maintained. Today there is only one road to effective action—the organisation of the masses.

Colonial and subject peoples of the world—Unite!

This manifesto contains many political advances: the need to break with the view that colonialism has any benefit; the requirement of political independence as the first step to sovereignty; the necessity of organising the masses – led by the workers – to be the only instrument of this anti-colonial struggle; and the recognition that political power must be the instrument to build economic democracy.

As he was helping organise the Pan-African Congress, Nkrumah began to draft a text on imperialism (that resembled the dissertation that he had begun at Lincoln, 'The History and Philosophy of Imperialism, With Special Reference to Africa').[9] This text – *Towards Colonial Freedom* – argued that 'the basis of colonial territorial dependence is economic, but the basis of the solution of the problem is political. Hence, political independence is an indispensable step towards securing economic emancipation.'[10] Against the liberal nationalists who merely wanted political independence, Nkrumah needed to show the real nature of imperialism and argue for economic democracy alongside political sovereignty. His assessment of imperialism that appears in *Towards Colonial Freedom* builds on Lenin's 1916 text, *Imperialism: The Highest Stage of Capitalism* and on WEB DuBois' 1915 'The African Roots of the War':

The colonies are thus a source of raw materials and cheap labour, and a 'dumping ground' for spurious surplus goods to be sold at exorbitant prices. Therefore, these colonies become avenues for capital investments, not for the benefit and development of the colonial peoples, but for the benefit of the investors, whose agents are the governments concerned. That is why it is incoherent nonsense to say that Britain or any other colonial power has the 'good intention' of developing her colonies for self-government and independence. The only thing left for the colonial people to do

9   Ama Barbara Biney, 'Kwame Nkrumah: An Intellectual Biography', London: School of Oriental and African Studies, Ph.D., 2007, p. 47.

10 Kwame Nkrumah, *Towards Colonial Freedom. Africa in the Struggle Against World Imperialism* (London: Heinemann) 1962, p. 6.

is to obtain their freedom and independence from these colonial powers.[11]

To that end, Nkrumah laid out a three-part agenda:

1. Political Freedom, i.e. the complete and absolute independence from the control of any foreign government.

2. Democratic Freedom, i.e. freedom from political tyranny and the establishment of a democracy in which sovereignty is vested in the broad masses of the people.

3. Social Reconstruction, i.e. freedom from poverty and economic exploitation and the improvement of social and economic conditions of the people so that they will be able to find better means of achieving a livelihood and asserting their right to human life and happiness.

From at least 1945, Nkrumah had made three decisive breaks from many of his contemporaries in the Gold Coast struggle. First, he laid out the view that political sovereignty without a socialist orientation would merely exchange one set of tyrants with another. This demand for economic freedom is articulated clearly in the three-part agenda that appears in *Towards Colonial Freedom* and then laid out precisely in *Neo-Colonialism* (1965).[12] Second, that political sovereignty for the Gold Coast was necessary but not sufficient. Nkrumah had seen in 1935 that Ethiopia's political independence was not a guarantee of either political power or social democracy. A proper Pan-African perspective required the independence of the entire continent, not just one part of it. In his 1957 independence speech, Nkrumah said, 'Our independence is meaningless unless it is linked up with the total liberation of the African continent.' Anti-colonial leaders of his time all understood the necessity of regionalism and internationalism, which is why 29 African and Asian countries went to Bandung, Indonesia in 1955 to pledge themselves to a global anti-colonial agenda.[13]

Third, it was clear to Nkrumah early in his political career that, as he wrote in *Africa Must Unite*, 'the social effects of colonialism are more insidious than

---

11 V. I. Lenin '*Imperialism: The Highest Stage of Capitalism*', January-June 1916, *Collected Works*, vol. 22, Moscow: Progress Publishers, 1964 and WEB Du Bois, 'The African Roots of the War', *The Atlantic*, May 1915.

12 This is a view shared with Frantz Fanon, *The Wretched of the Earth*, New York: Grove Press, 1963.

13 The idea of Pan-Africanism has within it the strong tendency towards internationalism rather than parochialism. See Issa Shivji, 'What is PanAfricanism?', *Interventions no. 1*, September 2023, Tricontinental: Institute for Social Research.

the political and economic. This is because they go deep into the minds of the people and therefore take longer to eradicate. The Europeans relegated us to the position of inferiors in every aspect of our everyday life.'[14] Nkrumah, who had experienced racism in the US, in Britain, and from colonial officials in the Gold Coast, understood that it was only when the validity of inferiority 'was questioned that the stirrings of revolt began and the whole structure of colonial rule came under attack.' For that reason, the anti-colonial movements need to fight the idea of inferiority head on and post-colonial nations needed a robust, anti-racist educational policy with literacy at its centre. In sum, these three departures shaped Nkrumah's political orientation when he returned to the Gold Coast in 1947.

TOWARDS FREEDOM

When Nkrumah got off his ship at Takoradi, the immigration official took his passport and said, 'So you are Kwame Nkrumah.' Nkrumah felt that was that. He would be arrested. But that did not happen. The official, an African, called over other workers and they shook Nkrumah's hand energetically. They said that they had heard about him and were 'waiting anxiously for my arrival day after day.'[15] When Nkrumah travelled to meet the political forces and deliver speeches, he discovered that the mood in his country had altered. There was no longer a belief amongst large sections of the people in the possibilities of advancement through the British colonial regime.

In December 1947, a group led by Paa Grant – a merchant from Sekondi-Takoradi – formed the United Gold Coast Convention (UGCC) in Saltpond 'to ensure that by all legitimate and constitutional means the control and direction of Government shall within the shortest time possible pass into the hands of the peoples and the Chiefs.' Nkrumah quickly discovered that the UGCC 'lacked the support of the masses and of some of the chiefs.'[16] A year later, he was invited to take on the post of general secretary of the UGCC. While Nkrumah recognised that the body was 'backed almost entirely by reactionaries, middle-class lawyers, and merchants', he nonetheless saw its utility. [17]The UGCC was the first instrument that Nkrumah joined to 'organise the masses', in accordance with the *Manifesto* from 1945.

The tide of history accelerated soon after Nkrumah arrived back home. Chief Nii Kwabena Bonne III formed the Anti-Inflation Campaign Committee to tackle

---

14 Kwame Nkrumah, *Africa Must Unite* (London: Heinemann) 1963, p. 32.

15 Nkrumah, *The Autobiography*, p. 67.

16 Nkrumah, *The Autobiography*, p. 70.

17 Nkrumah, *The Autobiography*, p. 62.

high inflation in the Gold Coast. The committee informed the colonial Chamber of Commerce and the United Africa Company (a subsidiary of Unilever) that if prices were not brought down, they would start a boycott campaign. The boycott began on 26 January 1948, but was ended on 20 February after the colonial government intervened because they saw that it had captured the imagination of the people. The committee's campaign had tested the anti-colonial possibilities in the Gold Coast, and it had found the people ready. The day the campaign ended Nkrumah spoke in Accra on 'The Ideological Battles of Our Time.' The response to that speech, he later wrote, showed that 'the political consciousness of the people of the Gold Coast had awakened to the point where the time had come for them to unite and strike out for their freedom and independence.'[18]

A week later, a spur showed how far the people were willing to go. Men who had fought in Britain's armies across the world took the lead. Soldiers from the Gold Coast who had fought in the First World War (WWI) returned home with grievances about their treatment. They formed the Gold Coast Ex-Servicemen's Union in 1919. This group was revived by B.E.A. Tamakloe in 1946 and grew rapidly due to the racism experienced by the almost 30 000 Gold Coast troops who served the British Empire in Asia and the Middle East.[19] The group's newspaper, *Ex-Service*, catalogued the failure of the British colonial regime in their treatment of these ex-servicemen.[20]

In February 1948, their Union led a march to Christiansborg (Osu) Castle, the headquarters of the colonial regime. The police fired on them, killing two people. This incident provoked widespread protests around the country. The UGCC was found wanting, which Nkrumah had predicted, but he backed this upsurge from below. It had indicated to him that a sharper organisation was necessary to advance the demands of the people. Nkrumah's support for the upsurge was the reason why the colonial state arrested him, for the first time, and held him for a few months.

When Nkrumah left prison, he moved decisively to set up a more radical platform. First, he founded the *Accra Evening News*, which reported on the state of the public dissatisfaction with the colonial regime.[21] Second, he helped set up the Committee on Youth Organisation (CYO) as the youth wing of the UGCC, but which quickly went beyond the UGCC to demand 'self-government now'; the CYO drew in what Nkrumah knew were the three most radical sections of the Gold Coast society – market women, ex-servicemen, and students. For

---

18 Nkrumah, *The Autobiography*, p. 76.

19 For one account, see Isaac Fadoyebo's memoir about his time in Burma. *A Stroke of Unbelievable Luck* (Madison: University of Wisconsin) 1999.

20 David Killingray, *The Colonial Army in the Gold Coast. Official Policy and Local Response*, 1890-1947 (London: School of Oriental and African Studies) Ph. D., 1982.

21 The *Accra Daily News* was not the only paper. Nkrumah also set up regional papers, such as the *Morning Telegraph* (Sekondi) and the *Daily Mail* (Cape Coast).

the CYO and UGCC, Nkrumah travelled up and down the length of the Gold Coast, holding mass meetings and incubating a new national liberation culture (including the adaptation of old religious songs into liberation songs with new lyrics). 'All leaders of West African political thought and action are stigmatised as agitators,' he wrote, which is precisely what he had become.[22]

Nkrumah knew by early 1948 that the UGCC would not last. The strains of the new radicalism of the people of the Gold Coast were reflected in political disagreements within the executive. Rather than split the UGCC, Nkrumah hastened to build a mass base with CYO and through the *Accra Evening News* so that the new organisation would be able to transcend, rather than split, the UGCC. In June 1949, the UGCC's executive expelled Nkrumah and the CYO. Ready for this, Nkrumah and the CYO leadership formed the Convention People's Party (CPP), which drew in the mass base of the UGCC that Nkrumah had helped to build.

'You personally must try to break down that perilous apathy that has taken hold of some members of the community through long years of imperialist domination', Nkrumah wrote the next day.[23] Apathy would be broken by 'positive action', which Nkrumah defined in his first major political pamphlet written and published in the Gold Coast (*What I Mean By Positive Action*, 1949).[24] Grounded in his assessment of the 'non-violence' that had shaped the Indian freedom struggle, 'positive action' was nonetheless a call for political unrest in all spheres of life – from writing anti-colonial articles in newspapers to economic boycotts. No tactic was left out since different tactics would draw in different people and the point was to draw in the entire Gold Coast population against the colonial regime. The CPP announced a Positive Action Day on 8 January 1950. It turned into a general strike. Nkrumah was arrested on 20 January and sentenced to three years in prison. With the realisation that Nkrumah and the CPP had captured the spirit of the country, the colonial state announced a concession – an election in February 1951 to elect a legislative council *for* the colonial state.

The CPP decided to contest these elections despite their limited scope. It was an excellent test of the CPP's political power. The party won 34 of the 38 seats (UGCC won three seats). From prison, Nkrumah ran in this election for the Accra constituency, which he won with 90 per cent of the vote. He was released from prison and became the prime minister of the new government.

---

22 Kwame Nkrumah, 'Agitation', *Accra Evening News*, September 1948.

23 Kwame Nkrumah, 'You', *Accra Evening News*, July 1949.

24 In a cheeky move, Nkrumah lifted the term 'positive action' from the colonial state's Watson Commission, which wrote that the Gold Coast needed to be managed by the 'positive action of the government'. Colonial Office, *Commission of enquiry into disturbances in the Gold Coast*, 1948.

From 1951 to 1957, Nkrumah led a government in the Gold Coast, which was still under British rule and the CPP along two axes during this period: first, to continue the struggle for full independence, when Ghana was born on 6 March 1957, and second, to build the basis for the future Ghana. The key issue from 1951 till the coup against Nkrumah in 1966 was education. When Nkrumah returned to the Gold Coast in 1947, the literacy rate in the country was only ten per cent. That is why the CPP had pushed an Accelerated Development Plan for Education (1951), which sought to hastily modernise national education by decentralisation of control of education to local councils and by the abolition of tuition fees as a spur for universal primary education.

Without an accelerated education programme, Nkrumah recognised his project would fail because he needed to build an educated population to run the civil service (which remained in the hands of the British till 1957) and to develop the economy. The educational policy was not just for the cities, but for rural areas, where Nkrumah had driven to build the UGCC and later the CPP, and where he had joined the unrest over land rights and with anger amongst the people about the colonial disregard for their health and education.

Two years after he became prime minister, the colonial state was forced into accepting a new constitutional process that called for full independence, preceded by another election in 1953 for an enlarged parliament, and for devolution of power to this assembly. On 11 July 1953, Nkrumah gave what is perhaps his most important speech, which was later called 'The Motion of Destiny.'

> Our demand for self-government is a just demand. It is a demand admitting of no compromise. The right of a people to govern themselves is a fundamental principle, and to compromise on this principle is to betray it ... According to the motto of the valiant *Accra Evening News* – 'We prefer self-government with danger to servitude in tranquillity'. Doubtless we shall make mistakes as have all other nations. We are human beings and hence fallible. But we can try also to learn from the mistakes of others so that we may avoid the deepest pitfalls into which they have fallen. Moreover, the mistakes we may make will be our own mistakes, and it will be our responsibility to put them right. As long as we are ruled by others we shall lay our mistakes at their door, and our sense of responsibility will remain dulled. Freedom brings responsibilities and our experience can be enriched only by the acceptance of these responsibilities.

When Nkrumah finished this speech, 'members jumped to their feet. They cheered, clapped, and sang the party song. They made such a noise that the crowds waiting in the street outside heard, and they too began to cheer.'[25] In the elections held in 1954, the CPP won 72 out of the 104 seats, and it won a clear majority again in 1956 that led to the final declaration of independence the following year.

In 1957, the movement led by Nkrumah attained the first of their goals: political independence, a significant feat. Now, Nkrumah had to deepen the work that had already begun in 1951: drive an agenda for education and for science and technology, build infrastructure, and diversify the economy. The commitment to socialism was clear. In the Second Five-Year Plan, Nkrumah's government called for a policy agenda to 'abolish disease, poverty, and illiteracy.' That was the priority. To do so, the government had to intervein in the economy to modernise agriculture and industry as well as move toward worker and peasant control over their own productive processes. Ghana – as a new post-colonial state – had few resources to drive a strictly socialist agenda. The country would need to attract investment, and because of the character of the world system, this borrowing could likely come from the Western bond holders and from Western countries.

'We want industry in Ghana,' Nkrumah told parliament on 4 March 1959, 'and we are always ready to make reasonable arrangements with any government, institution, or individual who can bring a sound proposition to us. In short, we intend, as in the past, to follow a common-sense and practical approach to industrial development.' Ghana needed new factories (to process oil and flour and to make cement), it needed new infrastructure for power and transportation, and the country required its own communications infrastructure (a new television station, for instance). Building infrastructure – such as the immense Volta River Project – was both expensive and complicated, and the government struggled to complete this project given the low levels of literacy due to the malice of colonial rule.

Nkrumah understood this reality and recognised that the subjective antidote to this was to create a strong party, the CPP, and to strengthen political education amongst its cadre. The political project of building a conscious population and a vital cadre was the basis of building an advanced economy. This included the building of a new civil service ('It has always been my conviction that after any political revolution, non-violent or violent, the new government should, immediately on coming into power, clear out from the civil service all its old leaders').[26]

But to strengthen the party and to build expertise would require an immense effort, an effort against the seductions of corruption for a poor population now confronted with the country's resource wealth and with multinational

---

25 June Milne, Forward Ever. The Life of Kwame Nkrumah, London: Panaf Books, 1977, p. 27; Nkrumah, *The Autobiography*, pp. 187-205.

26 Nkrumah, *The Autobiography*, p. 146.

corporations willing to bribe to get their way, and an effort against the minimal education facilities built by the colonial state. These are not easy tasks – to divert a substantial part of the social wealth into education and to build a moral compass within the party and in the state bureaucracy to overcome the temptations of corruption. Ghana, like most Third World countries, found these barriers very difficult to overcome.

A new consciousness could not just be imported into the new society. It had to be built and the foundation had to be on sources of knowledge on the continent: traditional African thought, Islamic thought, and Western inheritances (in the lead, Marxism). Modern socialism, from Marxism, would animate the old socialist communitarianism of African traditionalism and the Islamic idea of the egalitarian community (*ummah*). These issues gripped Nkrumah when he wrote his book *Consciencism* (1964) and in a speech he gave in Cairo two years after that:

> We know, of course, that the defeat of colonialism and even neo-colonialism will not result in the automatic disappearance of the imported patterns of thought and social organisation. For those patterns have taken root and are in varying degree sociological features of our contemporary society. Nor will a simple return to the communalistic society of ancient Africa offer a solution either. To advocate a return, as it were, to the rock from which we were hewn is a charming thought, but we are faced with contemporary problems, which have arisen from political subjugation, economic exploitation, educational and social backwardness, increases in population, familiarity with the methods, and products of industrialisation, modern agricultural techniques.[27]

Several speeches in this volume contain Nkrumah's assessment of the need to build a new Ghana from the Gold Coast that had emerged out of colonial rule. The material conditions that presented themselves laid out significant constraints against which he had to build mass projects at the same time as dealing with the counter-revolutionary tendencies within Ghana, egged on by the imperialist forces.

BUILDING AFRICA

The Berlin Conference of 1884–85 had divided the African continent amongst the many European colonial powers (the only countries that were not colonised were Ethiopia and Liberia, which is why there was such a strong reaction in 1935 when Italy invaded Ethiopia).[28] From early into his political career, Nkrumah

---

27 Kwame Nkrumah, 'African Socialism Revisited', *African Forum*, vol. 1, no. 3, 1966.

28 Liberia had been shaped by African-Americans and by the American Colonisation Society, keeping it within the sphere of influence of the US.

was committed to the orientation of Pan-Africanism, which meant not merely a consciousness of African identity but the necessity for African liberation projects and later post-colonial African states to work in concert with each other to produce a united Africa.

In December 1951, Nkrumah brought together the forces involved in the 1945 Fifth Pan-African Congress to meet – for the first time – on the African continent. It was fitting that they met in Kumasi, the capital of the Ashanti Empire, and it was equally fitting that Azikiwe and Padmore were amongst the delegates. The meeting pledged to defend the new state in the Gold Coast and to 'cultivate friendship of States interested in the destiny of Africa.'[29] Here were two elements of Pan-Africanism: defence against imperialism and the need to forge African unity.

After Ghana was formed in 1957, Nkrumah went further, holding two complementary conferences in Accra. The first, in April 1958, was the Conference of Independent African States, which brought together the continent's eight independent states, and the second, in December 1958, was the All-African People's Conference, which assembled the national liberation organisations that were still fighting the colonial rulers. The unity of the states was hastened when France penalised Guinea for its vote against the 1958 referendum to join the French Community. Nkrumah invited Guinea's Sékou Touré (1922–1984) to work with him to create a union of Ghana and Guinea (Mali joined this process in 1960). At the People's Conference, Nkrumah met with Patrice Lumumba (1925-1961), the leader of the *Mouvement National Congolais* and discussed the entry of the Congo into this union when it would eventually win its independence.

Out of these two conferences and the discussions Nkrumah had with post-colonial states and national liberation movements emerged the Organisation of African States (OAS) in May 1963. The OAS adopted a number of the important lines of march developed by Nkrumah, such as to coordinate the work of the post-colonial states to enhance the life of African people and to fight for the eradication of colonialism (through a Liberation Committee that would work out of the OAS's Addis Ababa headquarters).[30]

At the All-African People's Conference, Nkrumah met Lumumba, and a highly respected intellectual from Martinique and Algeria, Frantz Fanon (1925–1961). In them, Nkrumah saw the future. If Lumumba's movement succeeded in Congo, this strategically important country could provide the base for the freedom of Africa, and if Fanon's sharp wisdom about colonialism, violence, and the pitfalls of national liberation could be digested, then

---

29 'Congress of Kumasi: Nationalists Meet in the Gold Coast to Lay Plans for West African Co-operation', *West African Review*, February 1954.

30 Georges Nzongola-Ntalaja, 'Pan-Africanism since decolonisation: from the Organisation of African Unity (OAU) to the African Union (AU)', *African Journal of Democracy and Governance*, vol. 1, no. 4, 2014.

nothing could stop the entire continent. Nkrumah cultivated Lumumba, helping his fledgling movement with material and ideological support, and then sent Ghanaian officials to assist Lumumba when he became the prime minister of the newly freed Congo in 1961.

At the end of the All-African People's Conference, Fanon felt that all parts of the African continent would be free by 1960. There was bravery in this. 'Independence is never granted,' Lumumba told the *Chicago Daily News* in July 1960. 'We won our independence by our own blood and effort.'[31] Congo won its freedom as Fanon predicted, and Algeria won its independence in 1962, a fight in which Fanon participated actively, affirming his hopefulness. These were not just the words of Fanon and Lumumba, but ideas that had a mass character.

In 1962, Maria Dulce Almada Duarte (1933–2019), a member of the *Partido Africano para a Independência da Guiné Cabo Verde* (PAIGC), told the United Nations that 'the Cape Verdean people are more and more aware that the country's poverty is a myth' – they lived in a rich country whose social wealth was being leeched by Portugal, and with the end of Portuguese rule the people would flourish.[32] Amilcar Cabral (1924–1973), the leader of the PAIGC, set up training camps in Ghana, with Nkrumah's permission, to advance Duarte's findings. When his guests left Accra, Nkrumah mused, 'The African Revolution has started in earnest.'[33]

In the intervening years, the reality of what Fanon called the 'granite block' set in.[34] This granite block was the rigid socioeconomic order that would concede a few things but refused to alter its basic structure of domination over property and privilege. Lumumba's democratically elected government was overthrown by a Belgian-US-British-engineered coup, supported by sections of Congo's elite. It was intolerable to allow a sovereign nation to control the Shinkolobwe mine, where the US procured the uranium to bomb Hiroshima and Nagasaki in 1945. Lumumba was then assassinated brutally in 1961. 'Long live Congo! Long live Africa!', Lumumba wrote in his final letter to his wife Pauline.[35]

His mentor, Nkrumah, watched from Accra, desolate. There was nothing he could do. Four years later, the British ambassador to Ghana, A. W. Snelling wrote, 'On the whole, it is in the interest of Britain that Nkrumah should cease to rule

---

31 Patrice Lumumba, *The Truth About the Monstrous Crime of the Colonialists*, Moscow: Foreign Languages Publishing House, 1961, p. 57.

32 Maria Dulce Almada, 'Cape Verde: Slaves, Poverty and Aridity', *The African Liberation Reader*, vol. 2, ed. Aquino de Bragança and Immanuel Wallerstein, London: Zed, 1982, p. 30.

33 Susan Williams, *White Malice: The CIA and the Covert Recolonization of Africa*, New York: Public Affairs, 2021, p. 50.

34 Franz Fanon, *The Wretched of the Earth* (New York: Grove, 1963) p. 109.

35 Williams, *White Malice*, p. 375.

Ghana.'[36] The US had already set in motion plans to overthrow him. They hated his defence of freedom on the continent and felt aggrieved that *Neocolonialism: The Last Stage of Imperialism*, was such an indictment of imperialism in Africa.[37] Robert Smith of the US State Department later said that the book, published in October 1965, was 'simply outrageous... We were blamed for everything in the world.' US aid to Ghana was cancelled as a consequence. The book, and Nkrumah's politics, would be his downfall. Smith revealed in 1989 that the book might 'have contributed in a material way to [Nkrumah's] overthrow shortly thereafter.'[38] In 1966, Nkrumah was ejected from power while he was on a trip to the People's Republic of China.

By 1966, the coups in Congo and Ghana prevented the left from retaining power. Other lesser-known coups – against Louis Rwagasore of Burundi in 1961 and against Modibo Keita of Mali in 1967 – also defined a continent of coups.[39] These coups, many of them undertaken by militaries on behalf of the imperialists, were studied carefully by the South African communist Ruth First in her 1970 book *The Barrel of a Gun: Political Power in Africa and the Coup d'État*, which argued that these coups – now almost a familiar sight – came because the military was a holdover from the colonial period, other state institutions were weak, and radical forces were too fragmented to drive an agenda.[40] Colonialism had not produced the kind of liberal institutions that would have power over the military, and the postcolonial attack on the left disoriented the mass bases that might have prevented a military takeover. Mostly, the military entered with a whisper in the ear from a Western ambassador.

Nkrumah took refuge in Guinea, where in 1968 he wrote his account of the coup, called *Dark Days in Ghana*. 'Further examples of CIA activity and the work of other foreign intelligence organisations in Africa could be given. They would provide material for a book of their own'.[41] But even here, having been overthrown in a coup, clear-eyed about imperialism and exiled in Guinea, Nkrumah wrote, 'If for a while the imperialists appear to be gaining ground,

---

36 Williams, *White Malice*, p. 491.

37 Kwame Nkrumah, *Neocolonialism: The Last Stage of Imperialism* (London: Thomas Nelson, 1965).

38 Williams, *White Malice*, p. 495.

39 Ludo De Witte, *Moord in Burundi: België en de liquidatie van premier Louis Rwangasore* (Antwerp: EPO, 2021); Bintou Sanankoua, *La chute de Modibo Keïta* (Paris: Editions Chaka, 1990).

40 Ruth First, *The Barrel of the Gun: Political Power in Africa and the Coup d'État*, London: Allen Lane, 1970. In Political Order in Changing Societies, Samuel Huntington made the case for 'military modernisation', namely that in former colonial countries it was only the military that could advance modernisation and, in that case, the US should not oppose military dictatorships. Samuel Huntington, *Political Order in Changing Societies* (New Haven: Yale University Press, 1968).

41 Kwame Nkrumah, *Dark Days in Ghana* (London: Lawrence and Wishart, 1968) p. 50.

we must not be discouraged. For time is on our side. The permanency of the masses is the deciding factor, and no power on earth can prevent its ultimate decisive effect on the revolutionary struggle.'[42] Two phrases are striking here: 'time is on our side' and 'the permanency of the masses is the deciding factor.' Nkrumah, in exile, would not allow his spirit to be held back. His friends called him *Kasapreko*, 'the one who could not be contradicted.' That was not just a personality trait. It was because Nkrumah, like so many other leading national liberation fighters, understood the laws of motion of history and the role to be played by the masses of people, untethered, undaunted, with an irresistible desire for freedom.

In exile in Guinea, Nkrumah began to think seriously about the strategy for national liberation. The path of electoral democracy had worked for a while, but the continent of coups suggested to him that political power had to be attained with mass force; sometimes, this mass force had to be built through armed struggle.[43] This was not illusionary for his time. All around Nkrumah, national liberation had morphed from civic action to armed struggle, not only in the Portuguese colonies, but also in South Africa. Central to Nkrumah's later work is his matured assessment of imperialism and his attempt to find the proper strategy and tactics to undermine the neo-colonial world system.

On 23 September 1960, the Soviet Union put forward a resolution for immediate decolonisation. This resolution was opposed by the entire Western bloc, led by the US. A few months later, 43 countries from Africa and Asia affirmed the Bandung principles and put forward their own resolution. Eventually, on 14 December, the UN General Assembly adopted a resolution, *Declaration on the Granting of Independence to Colonial Countries and Peoples.* This was the resolution originally put forward by the Soviet Union, then re-shaped by African and Asian states. 89 countries – including the Soviet Union – voted for it, no one voted against it, but nine countries abstained: Australia, Belgium, France, Portugal, Spain, the Dominican Republic, Union of South Africa, United Kingdom, and US. The US stood with the old colonial powers and South Africa against a statement that read: 'The process of liberation is irresistible and irreversible.' This statement is key to national liberation thought which was central to Nkrumah. During his time in office, Nkrumah was known as Osagyefo, meaning 'the redeemer' in the Akan language. That was a precise name: he spent his life trying to redeem humanity. Nkrumah died in Bucharest, Romania in April 1972.

The Revolutionary Thoughts of Kwame Nkrumah is not intended to be a comprehensive, academic collection of his work. It is a sample of the range of

---

42 Nkrumah, *Dark Days in Ghana*, p. 159.

43 Kwame Nkrumah, *Handbook of Revolutionary Violence*, New York: International Publishers, 1968.

his commitments and ideas. There are important gaps here; for instance, this volume does not collect his journalistic writings, nor many of his important speeches from his years in power. Nonetheless, the book – which starts in 1949 and closes in 1966 – provides a panorama of the national liberation thought of a mighty leader.

Vijay Prashad,   November 2023
                                        Santiago, Chile

What I Mean by Positive Action

PREAMBLE: PARTY MEMBERS, FRIENDS AND SUPPORTERS

In our present vigorous struggle for self-government, nothing strikes so much terror into the hearts of the imperialists and their agents than the term *Positive Action*. This is especially so because of their fear of the masses responding to the call to apply this final form of resistance in case the British government failed to grant us our freedom consequent on the publication of the Coussey Committee Report.

The term *Positive Action* has been erroneously and maliciously publicised, no doubt, by the imperialists and their concealed agents – provocateurs and stooges. These political renegades, enemies of the Convention People's Party (CPP) and for that matter of Ghana's freedom, have diabolically publicised that the CPP's programme of positive action means riot, looting and disturbances, in a word violence. Accordingly, some citizens of Accra, including myself, were invited to a meeting of the Ga Native Authority and the Ga State Council on Thursday 20 October, at 1 pm 'to discuss', as the invitation stated, 'the unfortunate lawless elements in the country and any possible solution.'

At that meeting, I had the unique opportunity of explaining what *Positive Action* means to the satisfaction of the Ga Native Authority and the Ga State Council, and the meeting concluded with a recommendation by them that I should call a meeting to explain to the members of the CPP as I did to them, what I mean by *Positive Action* in order to disabuse the minds of those who are going about misinterpreting the Positive Action Programme of the CPP.

Before I proceed to my proper topic, I must take this opportunity to dispel the wild rumour, that the Ga Mantse said at the meeting that the CPP should be suppressed and that I should be deported from Accra.[44] Nothing of the sort was ever suggested by the Ga Mantse even though some of the speakers tried to convey such idea, but the Ga Mantse promptly overruled that.

And at this point allow me to protest vehemently against the diabolically false Reuters news which no doubt must have been sent by their correspondent in this country. I read to you the text of the Reuters news:

---

44 *Editor's note:* The Mantse is the title of the king of the Ga-Adangbe people who rules over the southern part of Ghana including Accra.

Local African Chiefs have sent ultimatum to Extremist Home-Rule Leader Kwame Nkrumah demanding undertaking by next Wednesday not to cause trouble when Coussey Report on Constitutional Advancement of Gold Coast is published next week. He has also been told to promise Loyal co-operation of his Convention People's Party. If he refuses African Authority will "Forcibly Eject" him from Accra to his Native Village of Nzima about 250 miles inland. All Political Leaders Promised co-operation in keeping peace except Dr. Nkrumah who said he had "No Guns to Fight" but would resort to Boycott, Strikes and Spiritual Force to carry on struggle. Coussey Commission was set up last January to examine Proposals for Constitutional and Political Reforms in Gold Coast.

Party members, imagine the wicked misrepresentation, chicanery, falsehood, the untruths, the lies and deception, in such news. This is the way our struggle is being misrepresented to the outside world; but the truth shall ultimately prevail.

WHY POSITIVE ACTION?

It is a comforting fact to observe that we have cleared the major obstacle to the realisation of our national goal in that ideologically the people of this country and their chiefs have accepted the idea of self-government even now. With that major ideological victory achieved, what is left now is chiefly a question of strategy and the intensity and earnestness of our demand. The British government and the people of Britain, with the exception of die-hard imperialists, acknowledge the legitimacy of our demand for self-government. However, it is and must be by our own exertion and pressure that the British government can relinquish its authority and hand over the control of affairs, that is, the government, to the people of this country and their chiefs.

THERE ARE TWO WAYS TO ACHIEVE SELF-GOVERNMENT

There are two ways to achieve self-government: either by armed revolution and violent overthrow of the existing regime, or by constitutional and legitimate non-violent methods. In other words, either by armed might or by moral pressure. For instance, Britain prevented the two German attempts to enslave her by armed might, while India liquidated British imperialism there by moral pressure. We believe that we can achieve self-government even now by constitutional means without resort to any violence.

We live by experience and by intelligent adaptation to our environment. From our knowledge of the history of man, from our knowledge of colonial liberation movements, freedom or self-government has never been handed over to any colonial country on a silver platter. The United States, India, Burma, Ceylon and other erstwhile colonial territories have had to wage a bitter and vigorous struggle to attain their freedom. Hence the decision by the CPP to adopt a programme of non-violent Positive Action to attain self-government for the people of this country and their chiefs.

We have talked too much and pined too long over our disabilities – political, social and economic; and it is now time that we embarked on constitutional positive steps to achieve positive results. We must remember that because of the educational backwardness of the colonial countries, the majority of the people of this country cannot read. There is only one thing they can understand and that is action.

WHAT IS POSITIVE ACTION?

By Positive Action we mean the adoption of all legitimate and constitutional means by which we can cripple the forces of imperialism in this country. The weapons of Positive Action are:

1. Legitimate political agitation;

2. Newspaper and educational campaigns and

3. as a last resort, the constitutional application of strikes, boycotts, and non-co-operation based on the principle of absolute non-violence.

HOW IS POSITIVE ACTION TO BE APPLIED?

We have been unduly criticised by our political opponents, that it is wrong for us to tell the imperialists that we shall resort to non-violent strikes and boycotts as a last resort, if need be, to attain our freedom. Their contention is that we should have kept this secret and spring a surprise on the government. As for us, our faith in justice and fair play forbids us to adopt such sneaky methods.

We like to use open methods and to be fair and above board in our dealings. We have nothing to hide from the British government. Secondly, and what is more important, if the CPP is a democratic organisation, then the members must be taken into confidence and their approval secured for such an important policy, and they must be given the opportunity to prepare for any eventuality. Even in the case of declaration of war, notice is first given.

Mr C. V. H. Rao in his book entitled *Civil Disobedience Movement in India* has this to say:

Constitutional agitation without effective sanction behind it of organized national determination to win freedom is generally lost on a country like Britain, which can appreciate only force or its moral equivalent . . . An important contributory factor to the satisfactory settlement of a disputed issue is the extent and the nature of the moral force and public sympathy generated by the righteousness of the cause for which the suffering is undergone and the extent of the moral reaction it has produced on the party against which it is directed.

The passive sympathy of the masses must be converted into active participation in the struggle for freedom; there must also be created a widespread political consciousness and a sense of national self-respect. These can only be achieved when the mass of the people understands the issue. These are not the days when people follow leaders blindly.

WHEN TO CALL POSITIVE ACTION INTO PLAY

As already explained, Positive Action has already begun by our political education, by our newspaper agitation and platform speeches and also by the establishment of the Ghana Schools and Colleges as well as the fearless and legitimate activities of the CPP.

But as regards the final stage of Positive Action, namely nationwide non-violent sit-down-at-home strikes, boycotts and non-co-operation, we shall not call them into play until all the avenues of our political endeavours of attaining self-government have been closed. They will constitute the last resort. Accordingly, we shall first carefully study the report of the Coussey Committee. If we find it favourable, we shall accept it and sing alleluia. But if we find it otherwise, we shall first put forward our own suggestions and proposals and upon refusal to comply with them, we shall invoke Positive Action straight away on the lines indicated above.

What we all want is self-government so that we can govern ourselves in our own country. We have the natural, legitimate and inalienable right to decide for ourselves the sort of government we want and we cannot be forced against our will into accepting or perpetuating anything that will be detrimental to the true interests of the people of this country and their chiefs.

Therefore, whilst we are anxiously awaiting the report of the Coussey Constitution Committee, I implore you all in the name of the party to be calm but resolute. Let us advance fearlessly and courageously armed with the Party's programme of Positive Action based on the principle of absolute non-violence. Long live the CPP.

Long live the Convention People's Party. Long live the forward march of the people of this country. Long live the new Ghana that is to be.

The Motion of Destiny, 1953

Suffering and sacrifice are inevitable in revolutionary struggle since no reactionary regime makes a voluntary surrender of its power. It may, in the initial stages of a revolutionary struggle, try by velvet glove treatment, to block revolutionary progress. But when direct confrontation occurs, and vital pillars of the reactionary power structure are threatened by revolutionary forces, it resorts to the most brutal and repressive action to suppress them. It is at this stage that the heaviest casualties of revolution occur. Sometimes there is open armed conflict; in which case there are casualties in the physical sense, and loss of life. Other times, the confrontation is non-violent and the casualties of the revolution are those who suffer arrest and imprisonment, victimisation, persecution, and all the many other forms of repression employed by reactionaries when their backs are against a wall.

With the call for Positive Action in the Gold Coast in 1950, a point of open and direct confrontation between the CPP and the colonial administration had been reached. The response of the government was immediate. A state of emergency was declared, a curfew imposed, public meetings banned, and progressive newspapers closed down. Most of the CPP leadership was arrested and thrown into prison.

During my imprisonment in James Fort, I was able to keep in touch with the party by writing messages on sheets of toilet paper. These were smuggled out to party headquarters by a friendly warder, who also brought me in news of the political situation. I used to write the messages at night in the small patches of light made on the floor and wall by a streetlamp which shone into our cell. On one night, having scrounged as much toilet paper as possible from other prisoners, I remember writing over 50 sheets.

Conditions in the prison were very bad. There were 11 of us crowded into one small cell, and for sanitation a single bucket in the comer. The food was scanty and poor. But our morale was high. Before long, we had organised committees of party members in the prison; and unknown to the prison authorities, we met regularly. There were plans to be made and policies to be decided upon so that the party could participate in the general election due to take place on 8 February 1951. The CPP had to win a majority in the new legislative assembly, and it was vital that every seat should be contested. I insisted that my name be registered on the electoral roll for Accra Central and arranged for party members to pay my deposit and sign the necessary papers on my behalf. I then set to work to write the party manifesto. This was soon completed and smuggled out to party headquarters.

It was in the early hours of the morning of 9 February that I was told that I had been elected for Accra Central, and that I had received the largest individual poll ever recorded in the country – 22,780 votes out of a possible 23,122. The following day, the executive committee of the CPP were permitted by the governor of the prison to discuss with him the question of my release, since it was likely that as leader of the CPP I would be asked to form a government.

On the morning of the 12 February 1951, after having served 14 months of my three-year sentence, I was released from prison and driven through immense, cheering crowds first to the Arena for an expiation ceremony, and then to party headquarters. The next day the governor invited me to form a government, for the CPP had won 34 out of a possible 38 elected seats in the municipal and rural areas, and the party had also a majority in the assembly over the nominated candidates. A meeting of the central committee was convened, and a government was formed. As leader of the majority party in the assembly, I became Leader of Government Business.

It was going to be difficult to work under the conditions of the Coussey Constitution, but I at once made it clear that we intended to go ahead with our campaign for full self-government. Our sweeping victory at the polls was our mandate; and nothing would stand in our way. We did not rule out the possibility of further Positive Action if colonial officialdom obstructed our purpose. 'The die is cast,' I said in an address to CPP members of the assembly, 'the exploited and oppressed people of colonial Africa and elsewhere are looking up to us for hope and inspiration. Progressive people in Britain and elsewhere are also solidly behind us. The torch of the Liberation Movement has been lifted up in Ghana for the whole of West Africa, and it will blaze a trail of freedom for other oppressed territories.'

The decision to continue the struggle for national liberation by constitutional means was taken simply because it was considered to be the method most likely to succeed in the circumstances of the time. For the sole criterion in deciding what form a revolutionary struggle should take at a particular time is the revolutionary objective, and how best to achieve it. If the CPP had contracted out of the procedure of parliamentary government which the colonial power had foisted upon us, the progress towards national liberation could not have gone ahead at that time, and the political revolution would have been immeasurably delayed. By participating in the general election of 1951, and winning it, the party was able to demand my release from prison before even half my sentence had been served, and the CPP was able to form a government and proceed with the practical business of carrying out its revolutionary objectives. We therefore decided for as long as it suited our purpose, to make use of the parliamentary procedures which the colonial administration had always practised and which it could not therefore condemn or refuse to recognise.

On 5 March 1952, the governor told the assembly that the colonial secretary of state had announced in the British House of Commons a change in the Coussey Constitution, removing the office of Leader of Government Business, and providing for the establishment of the office of Prime Minister. Henceforth, the governor was to consult the Prime Minister before submitting to the assembly the names of persons he proposed for appointment as representative members of the executive council and before allocating them portfolios. Some two weeks later, on 21 March the assembly approved my appointment as Prime Minister.

Clearly further constitutional changes were necessary, and I began to initiate steps for the replacement of the three ex-officio ministers by representative ministers, and to plan the reform of the legislative assembly, the latter contained three ex-officio members, six special members, and 75 other members. Of the 56 members representing the colony, Ashanti and Southern Togoland, 18, or one third, represented the chiefs and traditional authorities, and were elected not by universal adult suffrage, but by the Joint Provincial Council, the Asanteman Council, and the Trans Volta Southern Togoland Electoral College. Obviously, this state of affairs could be tolerated no longer.

After exhaustive discussions and consultations throughout the country, a Government White Paper on constitutional reform was published. Shortly afterwards, I called an emergency delegates' conference of the CPP, and told them that the party's national executive had decided to call on the delegates' conference to recommend that the government of the Gold Coast make representations to the Queen in Council, through the secretary of state for the colonies, that the chiefs and people of the Gold Coast demanded immediate self-government, and that an Act of Independence be simultaneously passed by the United Kingdom parliament and the Gold Coast Legislative Assembly declaring the Gold Coast to be, under the new name of Ghana, a sovereign and independent state. A motion on constitutional reform was moved in the legislative assembly on 10 July 1953. It is this motion which has become popularly known as the Motion of Destiny. The motion was passed unanimously. The Coussey Constitution had been amended, but it was still necessary to call a general election to give effect to the changes, and by a further CPP victory at the polls to bring the final pressure to bear on the British government to force the ending of colonial rule in the Gold Coast. Our employment of the colonial power's own parliamentary procedures was bringing results and justifying the party's constitutional tactics at that stage of the revolutionary struggle.

THE MOTION OF DESTINY

Mr. Speaker, I beg to move that this assembly in adopting the government's White Paper on constitutional reform do authorise the government to request that Her Majesty's Government as soon as the necessary constitutional and administrative arrangements for independence are made, should introduce an Act of Independence into the UK parliament declaring the Gold Coast a sovereign and independent state within the Commonwealth; and further, that this assembly do authorise the government to ask Her Majesty's Government, without prejudice to the above request, to amend as a matter of urgency the Gold Coast (Constitution) Order in Council 1950, in such a way as to provide *inter alia* that the legislative assembly shall be composed of members directly elected by secret ballot, and that all members of the cabinet shall be members of the assembly and directly responsible to it.

Mr. Speaker, it is with great humility that I stand before my countrymen and before the representatives of Britain, to ask this House to give assent to this motion. In this solemn hour, I am deeply conscious of the grave implications of what we are about to consider and, as the great honour of proposing this motion has fallen to my lot, I pray God to grant me the wisdom, strength and endurance to do my duty as it should be done.

We are called upon to exercise statesmanship of a high order, and I would repeat, if I may, my warning of October, that 'every idle or ill-considered word – will militate against the cause which we all have at heart. It is, as Edmund Burke said (and I am quoting him here):

> our business carefully to cultivate our minds, to rear to the most perfect vigour and maturity, every sort of generous and honest feeling that belongs to our nature. To bring the dispositions that are lovely in private life into the service and conduct of the commonwealth, so to be patriots as not to forget we are gentlemen.

At the outset, I would like to remind Honourable Members of a passage in the White Paper, that only after the legislative assembly debate will the proposals of this government take their final shape and be communicated to the UK government. Therefore, let your arguments be cogent and constructive. The range of this debate must be national, not regional; patriotic, not partisan; and I now ask that a spirit of co-operation and goodwill pervade this debate. It was Aristotle, the master who knows, who said:

> In practical matters the end is not mere speculative knowledge of what is to be done, but rather the doing of it. It is not enough to know about virtue, then, but we must endeavour to possess it, and to use it...

As with virtue, so with self-government: we must endeavour to possess it, and to use it. And the motion which I have prepared is the means to possess it.

In seeking your mandate, I am asking you to give my government the power to bring to fruition the longing hopes, the ardent dreams, the fervent aspirations of the chiefs and people of our country. Throughout a century of alien rule our people have, with ever increasing tendency, looked forward to that bright and glorious day when they shall regain their ancient heritage, and once more take their place rightly as free men in the world.

Mr Speaker, we have frequent examples to show that there comes a time in the history of all colonial peoples when they must, because of their will to throw off the hampering shackles of colonialism, boldly assert their God-given right to be free of a foreign ruler. Today we are here to claim this right to our independence.

Mr Speaker, the motion is in two parts. The first part not merely states our aim, but poses the question to Her Majesty's Government which is more fully set out in the White Paper. There is a general demand in the Gold Coast for self-government within the Commonwealth, and the UK government should be informed and be requested to make a declaration recognising the existence of this demand and expressing Her Majesty's Government's readiness to introduce an Act of Independence. This is the question which we are asking Her Majesty's Government in terms which clearly require an answer. That is the first thing we want: a declaration. But, even more important, we want to possess our self-government; we want an Act of Independence.

The second half of the motion sets out in a straightforward manner to obtain the authority of the House for the presentation to Her Majesty's Government of the detailed proposals which we have made for immediate constitutional reform. We ask that these proposals may be considered on their merits and without prejudice to the request which has been made in the first half of the motion. We request that the composition of our assembly may be so amended that all its members shall be directly elected by secret ballot. Similarly, we have gone forward to request that the whole Cabinet may be composed of representative ministers. We have also made other proposals of immediate and striking importance, and I am confident that this assembly will give the motion before it its unanimous endorsement and support.

Last year, I brought this House changes in the constitution which were, at the time, regarded as of minor importance. I was accused, indeed, of personal ambition in seeking the title of Prime Minister. We can now, Mr Speaker, see the result for ourselves. Certainly, nobody outside the Gold Coast has regarded my position as anything but what the name implies. The prestige of the Gold Coast government overseas has, in fact, been enhanced by this change. Even the co-ordination of the functions of my own colleagues has been made more successful by the increase in status. I believe that there is more decision in our activities as a Cabinet than there was before, and that we are better equipped to get things done. The freedom we demand is for our children, for the generations yet unborn, that they may see the light of day and live as men and women with the right to work out the destiny of their own country.

Mr Speaker, our demand for self-government is a just demand. It is a demand admitting of no compromise. The right of a people to govern themselves is a fundamental principle, and to compromise on this principle is to betray it. To quote you a great social and political scientist:

> To negotiate with forces that are hostile on matters of principle means to sacrifice principle itself. Principle is indivisible. It is either wholly kept or wholly sacrificed. The slightest concession on matters of principle implies the abandonment of principle.

The right of a people to decide their own destiny, to make their way in freedom, is not to be measured by the yardstick of colour or degree of social development. It is an inalienable right of peoples which they are powerless to exercise when forces, stronger than they themselves, by whatever means, for whatever reasons, take this right away from them. If there is to be a criterion of a people's preparedness for self-government, then I say it is their readiness to assume the responsibilities of ruling themselves. For who but a people themselves can say when they are prepared? How can others judge when that moment has arrived in the destiny of a subject people? What other gauge can there be?

Mr Speaker, never in the history of the world has an alien ruler granted self-rule to a people on a silver platter. Therefore, Mr Speaker, I say that a people's readiness and willingness to assume the responsibilities of self-rule is the single criterion of their preparedness to undertake those responsibilities.

I have described on a previous occasion in this House what were the considerations which led me to agree to the participation of my party in the General Election of 1951, and hence in the government of the Gold Coast under the terms of the 1950 Constitution Order in Council. In making that decision, I took on the task of proving to the world that we were prepared to perform our duties with responsibility, to set in motion the many reforms which our people needed, and to work from within the government and within the assembly, that is, by constitutional means, for the immediate aim of self-government. We have only been in office, Mr Speaker, for two and a half years, and we have kept these objectives constantly in mind.

Let there be no doubt that we are equally determined not to rest until we have gained them. We are encouraged in our efforts by the thought that in so acting we are showing that we are able to govern ourselves and thereby we are putting an end to the myth that Africans are unable to manage their own affairs, even when given the opportunity. We can never rest satisfied with what we have so far achieved. The government certainly is not of that mind. Our country has proved that it is more than ready. For despite the legacies of a century of colonial rule, in the short space of time since your representative ministers assumed the responsibilities of office, we have addressed ourselves boldly to the task of laying sound economic and social foundations on which this beloved country of ours can raise a solid democratic society. The spirit of responsibility and enterprise which has animated our actions in the past two years will continue to guide us in the future, for we shall always act in the spirit of our party's motto: 'Forward ever, backward never'. For we know notwithstanding that the essence of politics is the realisation of what is possible.

Mr Speaker, we have now come to the most important stage of our constitutional development; we can look back on these stages through which we have passed during these last few years: first, our discussions with the secretary of state leading to the changes of last year; then the questions posed in the October statement, which were to be answered by all parties, groups and councils interested in this great issue; the consultations with the Territorial Councils, with the political parties, with the Trades Union Congress (TUC). We have proceeded logically and carefully, and as I view it, the country has responded fully to my call. Every representation which we received – and there were many – has received my careful consideration. The talks which I had with the political parties and the TUC and the committees of the Asanteman and Joint Provincial Councils, were frank and cordial.

I had also received a special invitation to attend a meeting in Tamale with the Territorial Council, the traditional rulers and the members of the legislative assembly. Naturally I accepted the invitation, because it was clear that if I had not held discussions with the Northern Territories, the unity of the Gold Coast might have been endangered and our progress towards self-government might have been delayed. The reverse has been the case. We have adapted some of our proposals to meet Northern Territories' wishes and have been able to set their minds at rest on several issues of the greatest importance to them and to the Gold Coast as a whole. Mr Speaker, sir, the days of forgetting about our brothers in the North, and in the Trust Territory, are over.

Criticisms have been levelled against the government for the secrecy with which these talks were surrounded, and I should like to tell the country why this was necessary. When we went to the talks, of course, the government members had some idea of the way their collective views on the representations were being formulated. We carefully explained, however, that our views were not finally decided and they would not be until we had had an opportunity of hearing any further views which these bodies might care to express in addition to their memoranda submitted. Having heard these views, we also sought an expression of opinion on specific problems which had occurred to us. But in order that our discussions could be of true value, frank and unreserved, I stated at an early stage that I should be grateful if the conversations could be regarded as strictly confidential. I am glad to place on record the value of the discussions which we held and the extent to which the undertaking which I was given was honoured. I hope that the bodies which were consulted also feel that the discussions were worthwhile.

Mr Speaker, knowing full well, therefore, the will of the chiefs and people whom we represent, I am confident that with the support of this House,

Her Majesty's government will freely accede to our legitimate and righteous demand to become a self-governing unit within the Commonwealth.

I put my confidence in the willing acceptance of this demand by Her Majesty's government, because it is consistent with the declared policy of successive UK governments. Indeed, the final transition from the stage of responsible government as a colony to the independence of a sovereign state guiding its own policies, is the apotheosis of this same British policy in relation to its dependencies.

Mr Speaker, pray allow me to quote from Britain's own ministers. Mr Creech Jones, as colonial secretary in the first post-war Labour government, stated that, 'The central purpose of British Colonial policy is simple. It is to guide the Colonial Territories to responsible self-government within the Commonwealth in conditions that ensure to the people concerned both a fair standard of living and freedom from oppression from any quarter.'

Again, on 12 July 1950, in the House of Commons, Mr James Griffiths, Mr Creech Jones' successor, reiterated this principle: 'The aim and purpose,' he said 'is to guide the Colonial Territories to responsible self-government within the Commonwealth and, to that end, to assist them to the utmost of our capacity and resources to establish those economic and social conditions upon which alone self-government can be soundly based.' Last, I give you the words of Mr Oliver Lyttleton, colonial secretary in Her Majesty's Conservative government of today: 'We all aim at helping the Colonial Territories to attain self-government within the Commonwealth.'

Nor is this policy anything new in British colonial history. The right to self-government of colonial dependencies has its origin in the British North American Act of 1867, which conceded to the provinces of Canada, complete self-rule. The independence of the other white dominions of Australia and New Zealand was followed by freedom for South Africa. And since the end of the Second World War (WWII), our coloured brothers in Asia have achieved independence, and we are now proud to be able to acknowledge the sovereign states of India, Pakistan, Ceylon and Burma.

There is no conflict that I can see between our claim and the professed policy of all parties and governments of the UK. We have here in our country a stable society. Our economy is healthy, as good as any for a country of our size. In many respects, we are very much better off than many sovereign states. And our potentialities are large. Our people are fundamentally homogeneous, nor are we plagued with religious and tribal problems. And, above all, we have hardly any colour bar. In fact, the whole democratic tradition of our society precludes the *herrenvolk* doctrine. The remnants of this doctrine are now an anachronism in our midst, and their days are numbered.

Mr Speaker, we have travelled long distances from the days when our fathers came under alien subjugation to the present time. We stand now at the threshold of self-government and do not waver. The paths have been tortuous, and fraught with peril, but the positive and tactical action we have adopted is leading us to the New Jerusalem, the golden city of our hearts' desire! I am confident, therefore, that I express the wishes and feelings of the chiefs and people of this country in hoping that the final transfer of power to your representative ministers may be done in a spirit of amity and friendship, so that, having peacefully achieved our freedom, the peoples of both countries – Britain and the Gold Coast – may form a new relationship based on mutual respect, trust and friendship. Thus, may the new partnership implicit in the Statute of Westminster be clothed in a new meaning. For then shall we be one of the 'autonomous communities within the British Empire, equal in status, in no way subordinate one to another in any aspect of their domestic or external affairs, though united by a common allegiance to the Crown, freely associated as members of the British Commonwealth of Nations', in accordance with the Balfour Declaration of 1926 which was embodied in the Statute of Westminster in 1931.

Today, more than ever before, Britain needs more 'autonomous communities freely associated.' For freely associated communities make better friends than those associated by subjection. We see today, Mr Speaker, how much easier and friendlier are the bonds between Great Britain and her former dependencies of India, Pakistan and Ceylon. So much of the bitterness that poisoned the relations between these former colonies and the UK has been absolved by the healing power of a better feeling that a new friendship has been cemented in the free association of autonomous communities.

These, and other weighty reasons, allied with the avowed aim of British colonial policy, will, I am confident, inspire Britain to make manifest once more to a side and weary world her duty to stand by her professed aim. A free and independent Gold Coast, taking its rightful place in peace and amity by the side of the other dominions, will provide a valid and effective sign that freedom can be achieved in a climate of good will and thereby accrue to the intrinsic strength of the Commonwealth. The old concepts of Empire, of conquest, domination and exploitation are fast dying in an awakening world. Among the colonial peoples, there is a vast, untapped reservoir of peace and goodwill towards Britain, would she but divest herself of the outmoded, moth-eaten trappings of two centuries ago, and present herself to her colonial peoples in a new and shining vestment and hand us the olive branch of peace and love, and give us a guiding hand in working out our own destinies.

In the very early days of the Christian era, long before England had assumed any importance, long even before her people had united into a nation, our ancestors had attained a great empire, which lasted until the 11th century, when it fell before the attacks of the Moors of the north. At its height that empire stretched from Timbuktu to Bamako, and even as far as the Atlantic. It is said that lawyers and scholars were much respected in that empire and that the inhabitants of Ghana wore garments of wool, cotton, silk and velvet.

There was trade in copper, gold and textile fabrics, and jewels and weapons of gold and silver were carried.

Thus, may we take pride in the name of Ghana, not out of romanticism, but as an inspiration for the future. It is right and proper that we should know about our past. For just as the future moves from the present so the present has emerged from the past. Nor need we be ashamed of our past. There was much in it of glory. What our ancestors achieved in the context of their contemporary society gives us confidence that we can create, out of that past, a glorious future, not in terms of war and military pomp, but in terms of social progress and of peace. For we repudiate war and violence. Our battles shall be against the old ideas that keep men trammelled in their own greed; against the crass stupidities that breed hatred, fear and inhumanity. The heroes of our future will be those who can lead our people out of the stifling fog of disintegration through serfdom, into the valley of light where purpose, endeavour and determination will create that brotherhood which Christ proclaimed 2 000 years ago, and about which so much is said, but so little done.

Mr Speaker, in calling up our past, it is meet, on an historic occasion such as this, to pay tribute to those ancestors of ours who laid our national traditions, and those others who opened the path which made it possible to reach today the great moment at which we stand. As with our enslaved brothers dragged from these shores to the United States and to the West Indies, throughout our tortuous history, we have not been docile under the heel of the conqueror. Having known by our own traditions and experience the essentiality of unity and of government, we constantly formed ourselves into cohesive blocs as a means of resistance against the alien forces within our borders. And so today we recall the birth of the Ashanti nation through Okomfo Anokye and Osei Tutu and the symbolism entrenched in the Golden Stool; the valiant wars against the British, the banishment of Nana Prempeh the First to the Seychelle Islands; the temporary disintegration of the nation and its subsequent reunification. And so we come to the Bond of 1884. Following trade with the early merchant adventurers who came to the Gold Coast, the first formal association of Britain with our country was effected by the famous Bond of 1844, which accorded Britain trading rights in the country. But from these humble beginnings of trade and friendship, Britain assumed political control of this country. But our inalienable right still remains, as my friend, George Padmore, puts it in his recent book, *The Gold Coast Revolution*, and I quote – 'When the Gold Coast Africans demand self-government today they are, in consequence, merely asserting their birthright which they never really surrendered to the British who, disregarding their treaty obligations of 1844, gradually usurped full sovereignty over the country.'

Then the Fanti Confederation – the earliest manifestation of Gold Coast nationalism occurred in 1868 when Fanti Chiefs attempted to form the Fanti Confederation in order to defend themselves against the might of Ashanti and the incipient political encroachments of British merchants. It was also a union of the coastal states for mutual economic and social development. This was declared a dangerous conspiracy with the consequent arrest of its leaders.

Then the Aborigines Rights Protection Society was the next nationalist movement to be formed with its excellent aims and objects, and by putting up their titanic fight for which we cannot be sufficiently grateful, they formed an unforgettable bastion for the defence of our God-given land and thus preserved our inherent right to freedom. Such men as Mensah-Sarbah, Atta Ahuma, Sey and Wood have played their role in this great fight.

Next came the National Congress of British West Africa. The end of the first Great War brought its strain sand stresses and the echoes of the allied slogan, 'We fight for freedom' did not pass unheeded in the ears of Casely-Hayford, Hutton-Mills and other national stalwarts who were some of the moving spirits of the National Congress of British West Africa. The machinations of imperialism did not take long to smother the dreams of the people concerned, but today their aims and objects are being more than gratified with the appointment of African judges and other improvements in our national life.

As with the case of the National Congress of British West Africa, the United Gold Coast Convention (UGCC) was organised at the end of WWII to give expression to the people's desire for better conditions. The British government, seeing the threat to its security here, arrested six members of the convention and detained them for several weeks until the Watson Commission came. The stand taken by the TUC, the fanners, students and women of the country, provides one of the most epic stories in our national struggle.

In June 1949, the CPP with its uncompromising principles led the awakened masses to effectively demand their long lost heritage. And today, the country moves steadily forward to its proud goal. Going back over the years to the establishment of constitutional development, we find that the first legislative council to govern the country was established in 1850; 38 years later the first African, in the person of John Sarbah, was admitted to that council. It was not until 1916 that the Clifford Constitution increased the number of Africans, which was four in 1910, to six. But these were mainly councils of officials.

The Guggisberg Constitution of 1925 increased the unofficial representation in the council almost to par with the officials. This position was reversed by the Bums Constitution of 1946 which created an unofficial majority. The abortive Colony-Ashanti Collaboration of 1944 was the prelude to this change.

The Coussey Constitution of 1951 further democratised the basis of representation; and now, for the first time in our history, this government is proposing the establishment of a freely elected assembly with ministers directly responsible to it.

We have experienced Indirect Rule, we have had to labour under the yoke of our own disunity, caused by the puffed-up pride of those who were lucky to enjoy better opportunities in life than their less fortunate brothers; we have experienced the slow and painful progress of constitutional changes by which, from councils on which Africans were either absent or merely nominated, this august House has evolved through the exercise by the enfranchised people of their democratic right to a voice in their own affairs and in so doing they have shown their confidence in their own countrymen by placing on us the responsibility for our country's affairs.

And so through the years, many have been laid to final rest from the stresses and dangers of the national struggle and many, like our illustrious friends of the opposition, notwithstanding the fact that we may differ on many points, have also contributed a share to the totality of our struggle. And we hope that whatever our differences, we shall today become united in the demand for our country's freedom.

As I said earlier, what we ask is not for ourselves on this side of the House, but for all the chiefs and people of this country – the right to live as free men in the comity of nations. Were not our ancestors ruling themselves before the white man came to these our shores? I have earlier made reference to the ancient history of our more distant forebears in Ghana. To assert that certain people are capable of ruling themselves while others are not 'ready,' as the saying goes, smacks to me more of imperialism than of reason. Biologists of repute maintain that there is no such thing as a 'superior' race. Men and women are as much products of their environment – geographic, climatic, ethnic, cultural, social – as of instincts and physical heredity. We are determined to change our environment, and we shall advance in like manner.

According to the motto of the valiant *Accra Evening News* – 'We prefer self-government with danger to servitude in tranquility.' Doubtless we shall make mistakes as have all other nations. We are human beings and hence fallible. But we can try also to learn from the mistakes of others so that we may avoid the deepest pitfalls into which they have fallen. Moreover, the mistakes we may make will be our own mistakes, and it will be our responsibility to put them right. As long as we are ruled by others we shall lay our mistakes at their door, and our sense of responsibility will remain dulled. Freedom brings responsibilities and our experience can be enriched only by the acceptance of these responsibilities.

In the two years of our representative government, we have become most deeply conscious of the tasks which will devolve upon us with self-rule. But we do not shrink from them; rather are we more than ever anxious to take on the reins of full self-government. And this, Mr Speaker, is the mood of the chiefs and people of this country at this time. On the fundamental choice between colonial status and self-government, we are unanimous. And the vote that will be taken on the motion before this assembly will proclaim this to the world.

Honourable Members, you are called, here and now, as a result of the relentless tide of history, by Nemesis as it were, to a sacred charge, for you hold the destiny of our country in your hands.[45] The eyes and ears of the world are upon you; ye, our oppressed brothers throughout this vast continent of Africa and the New World are looking to you with desperate hope, as an inspiration to continue their grim fight against cruelties which we in this corner of Africa have never known – cruelties which are a disgrace to humanity, and to the civilisation which the white man has set himself to teach us. At this time, history is being made; a colonial people in Africa has put forward the first definite claim for independence. An African colonial people proclaim that they are ready to assume the stature of free men and to prove to the world that they are worthy of the trust.

I know that you will not fail those who are listening for the mandate that you will give to your representative ministers. For we are ripe for freedom, and our people will not be denied. They are conscious that the right is theirs, and they know that freedom is not something that one people can bestow on another as a gift. They claim it as their own and none can keep it from them.

And yet, while we are making our claim for self-government I want to emphasise, Mr Speaker, that self-government is not an end in itself. It is a means to an end, to the building of the good life to the benefit of all, regardless of tribe, creed, colour or station in life. Our aim is to make this country a worthy place for all its citizens, a country that will be a shining fight throughout the whole continent of Africa, giving inspiration far beyond its frontiers. And this we can do by dedicating ourselves to unselfish service to humanity. We must learn from the mistakes of others so that we may, in so far as we can, avoid a repetition of those tragedies which have overtaken other human societies.

We must not follow blindly but must endeavour to create. We must aspire to lead in the arts of peace. The foreign policy of our country must be dedicated to the service of peace and fellowship. We repudiate the evil doctrines of tribal chauvinism, racial prejudice and national hatred. We repudiate these evil ideas because in creating that brotherhood to which we aspire, we hope to make a reality, within the bounds of our small country, of all the grandiose ideologies which are supposed to form the intangible bonds holding together the British Commonwealth of Nations in which we hope to remain. We repudiate racial prejudice and national hatred because we do not wish to be a disgrace to these high ideals.

Her Majesty, Queen Elizabeth the Second has just been crowned – barely one month ago – the memory is still fresh in our minds; the Queen herself has not forgotten the emotions called forth as she first felt the weight of the Crown upon her head; the decorations in London streets are hardly down; the millions of words written about the coronation and its meaning will endure

---

45 *Editor's note*: Nemesis was the ancient Greek god of retribution. The name Nemesis was derived from the Greek word νέμειν, *némein*, meaning 'to give what is due.'

for centuries; the prayers from millions of lips are still fresh; the vows of dedication to duty which the Queen made are a symbol of the duties devolving on the Commonwealth. And so, we repudiate the evil doctrines which we know are promulgated and accepted elsewhere as the truth.

To Britain this is the supreme testing moment in her African relations. When we turn our eyes to the sorry events in South, Central and East Africa, when we hear the dismal news about Kenya and Central African Federation, we are cheered by the more cordial relationship that exists between us and Britain. We are now asking her to allow that relationship to ripen into golden bonds of freedom, equality and fraternity, by complying without delay to our request for self-government. We are sure that the British government will demonstrate its goodwill towards the people of the Gold Coast by granting us the self-government which we now so earnestly desire. We enjoin the people of Britain and all political parties to give our request their ardent support.

The self-government which we demand, therefore, is the means by which we shall create the climate in which our people can develop their attributes and express their potentialities to the full. As long as we remain subject to an alien power, too much of our energy is diverted from constructive enterprise. Oppressive forces breed frustration. Imperialism and colonialism are two-fold evil. This theme is expressed in the truism that 'no nation which oppresses another can itself be free.' Thus, we see that this evil not only wounds the people which is subject, but the dominant nation pays the price in a warping of their finer sensibilities through arrogance and greed. Imperialism and colonialism are a barrier to true friendship.

For the short time since we Africans have had a bigger say in our affairs, the improved relations between us and the British have been most remarkable. Today there exists the basis of real friendship between us and His Excellency the Governor, Sir Charles Arden-Clarke, and the ex-officio ministers of defence and external affairs, of finance and of justice. I want to pay tribute to these men for their valuable co-operation in helping us to make a success of our political advance. I feel that they have done this, firstly because as officers in the British Colonial Service, it is their duty to guide the subject territory in the attainment of self-government in accordance with the expressed aim of British colonial policy and, secondly, because we have, by our efforts in managing our own affairs, gained their respect, and they are conscious of the justice of our aspirations.

Let me recall the words of the great Casely-Hayford which he spoke in 1925:

It must be recognised that co-operation is the greatest word of the century. With co-operation we can command peace, goodwill and concord. Without: chaos, confusion and ruin. But there can really be no co-operation between inferiors and superiors. Try as they may, there must come a time when the elements of superiority will seek to dictate, and the inferior ones will resent such dictation. It logically follows, therefore, that unless an honest effort is made to raise the inferior up to the prestige of the superior, and the latter can suffer it, all our talk of co-operation is so much empty gas. . .

Unless, therefore, our claim to independence is met now, the amicable relations which at present exist between us and the British may become strained. Our chiefs and people will brook no delay. But I feel confident that our claim, because of the reasons I have already given, will be accepted and our amity towards Britain will be deepened by our new association.

The strands of history have brought our two countries together. We have provided much material benefit to the British people, and they in turn have taught us many good things. We want to continue to learn from them the best they can give us and we hope that they will find in us qualities worthy of emulation. In our daily lives, we may lack those material comforts regarded as essential by the standards of the modern world, because so much of our wealth is still locked up in our land; but we have the gifts of laughter and joy, a love of music, a lack of malice, an absence of the desire for vengeance for our wrongs, all things of intrinsic worth in a world sick of injustice, revenge, fear and want.

We feel that there is much the world can learn from those of us who belong to what we might term pretechnological societies. These are values which we must not sacrifice unheedingly in pursuit of material progress. That is why we say that self-government is not an end in itself.

We have to work hard to evolve new patterns, new social customs, new attitudes to life, so that while we seek the material, cultural and economic advancement of our country, while we raise their standards of life, we shall not sacrifice their fundamental happiness. That, I should say, Mr Speaker, has been the greatest tragedy of Western society since the industrial revolution.

In harnessing the forces of nature, man has become the slave of the machine, and of his own greed. If we repeat these mistakes and suffer the consequences which have overtaken those that made them, we shall have no excuse. This is a field of exploration for the young men and women now in our schools and colleges, for our sociologists and economists, for our doctors and our social welfare workers, for our engineers and town planners, for our scientists and our philosophers.

Mr Speaker, when we politicians have long passed away and been forgotten, it is upon their shoulders that will fall the responsibility of evolving new forms of social institutions, new economic instruments to help build in our rich and fertile country a society where men and women may live in peace, where hate, strife, envy and greed, shall have no place.

Mr Speaker, we can only meet the challenge of our age as a free people. Hence our demand for our freedom, for only free men can shape the destinies of their future.

Mr Speaker, Honourable Members, we have great tasks before us. I say, with all seriousness, that it is rarely that human beings have such an opportunity for service to their fellows.

Mr Speaker, for my part, I can only re-echo the words of a great man: 'Man's dearest possession is life, and since it is given him to live but once, he must so live as not to be besmeared with the shame of a cowardly existence and trivial past, so live that dying he might say: all my life and all my strength were given to the finest cause in the world – the liberation of mankind.'

Mr Speaker, 'Now God be thank'd, Who has match'd us with His hour!'

Midnight Speech on Ghana's Independence, 6 March 1957

At long last, the battle has ended! And thus, Ghana, your beloved country is free forever!

And yet again, I want to take the opportunity to thank the people of this country; the youth, the farmers, the women who have so nobly fought and won the battle.

Also, I want to thank the valiant ex-service men who have so co-operated with me in this mighty task of freeing our country from foreign rule and imperialism.

And, as I pointed out ... from now on, today, we must change our attitudes and our minds. We must realise that from now on we are no longer a colony but free and independent people.

But also, as I pointed out, that also entails hard work. That new Africa is ready to fight his own battles and show that, after all, the black man is capable of managing his own affairs.

We are going to demonstrate to the world, to the other nations, that we are prepared to lay our foundation – our own African personality.

As I said to the Assembly a few minutes ago, I made a point that we are going to create our own African personality and identity. It is the only way we can show the world that we are ready for our own battles.

But today, may I call upon you all, on this great day let us all remember that nothing can be done unless it has the purport and support of God.

We have won the battle and again rededicate ourselves ... OUR INDEPENDENCE IS MEANINGLESS UNLESS IT IS LINKED UP WITH THE TOTAL LIBERATION OF AFRICA.

Let us now, fellow Ghanaians, ask for God's blessing for only two seconds, and in your thousands and millions.

I want to ask you to pause for only one minute and give thanks to Almighty God for having led us through our difficulties, imprisonments, hardships, and sufferings, to have brought us to our end of troubles today. One minute silence.

Ghana is free forever! And here I will ask the band to play the Ghana National Anthem.

Reshaping Ghana's destiny, I am depending on the millions of the country, and the chiefs and the people, to help me to reshape the destiny of this country.

We are prepared to pick it up and make it a nation that will be respected by every nation in the world.

We know we are going to have difficult beginnings, but again, I am relying on your support ... I am relying upon your hard work.

Seeing you in this ... It doesn't matter how far my eyes go I can see that you are here in your millions. And my last warning to you is that you are to stand firm behind us so that we can prove to the world that when the African is given a chance, he can show the world that he is somebody!

We have awakened. We will not sleep anymore. Today, from now on, there is a new African in the world!

Dawn Broadcast to the Nation: Osagyefo Calls a Halt to Self-seeking

Good morning, friends and countrymen.

In accordance with the cherished customs of our fathers, whereby advice is sought or given at early dawn, I have come to the microphone this early morning to share some thoughts with you in a homely chat.

Four years ago, we achieved independence and set out on a new road to nationhood. On 1 July 1960, we consolidated this political achievement by setting up the republic as an expression of our sovereign will. That day marked the real beginning of the life of our nation and settled upon us responsibility not only for the development and reconstruction of Ghana, but also for the faithful duty of assisting other African territories to achieve their freedom and independence.

This responsibility casts upon all Ghanaians an obligation to protect the national stability we have so ably created and to guard ever jealously the solidarity of our nation. For this reason, I have been rather unhappy about reports which I have received since my return from the United Kingdom; and this has led me to you this morning, to examine the matters forming the subject of these reports, and to discuss them openly and sincerely.

When I was away, certain matters arose concerning the Trades Union Congress (TUC), the National Assembly, the Co-operative Movement, and the United Ghana Farmers Council. These matters created misunderstandings and led to some regrettable demonstrations. I do not think that at this stage of our national life, when all our efforts should be concentrated upon building a first-class nation, we should allow petty misunderstandings and squabbles to divert our attention from our great and worthy aims and objectives.

What was the cause of these unfortunate circumstances? Some parliamentarians criticised the TUC and the other wing organisations of the Convention People's Party (CPP). The officials of these organisations objected to the criticism and made countercriticisms against certain parliamentarians and this started a vicious circle of criminations and recriminations. This is clearly unfortunate. I have taken certain steps, and I hope that no occasion will arise to cause a recurrence of a similar situation.

The CPP is a great brotherhood. Its strength is embedded in the unity of its membership and since both sides of this unfortunate dispute are members of the CPP, I wish to examine the situation and look deeper for the causes of this incident.

I have stated over and over again that members of the CPP must not use their party membership or official position for personal gain or for the amassing of wealth. Such tendencies directly contradict our party Constitution, which makes it clear that the aims and objects of the party, among other things, are the building of a socialist pattern of society in which the free development of each is the condition for the free development of all – a pattern or society consonant with African situations, circumstances, and conditions.

I have explained very clearly this socialist structure and have on many occasions elaborated the five sectors into which our economy may be divided. These sectors are: first, the state sector, in which all enterprises are entirely state-owned; second, the joint state-private sector, which will incorporate enterprises owned jointly by government and foreign private capital; third, the co-operative sector, in which all enterprises will be undertaken by co-operative organisations affiliated with the National Co-operative Council; fourth, the private enterprise sector, which will incorporate those industries which are open freely to foreign private enterprise; and fifth, the workers' enterprise sector.

I have had occasions to emphasise the part which private enterprise will continue to play in our economic and industrial life. A different situation arises with Ghanaian businessmen who attempt to combine business with political life. Being a party member of the assembly – and much more, being a ministerial secretary or a minister – means that the persons who take up these positions owe a duty to those who have elected them or who have given them their positions with confidence. To be able to maintain this confidence, therefore, they should not enter into any type of industrial or commercial undertaking. Any party member of parliament who wants to be a businessman can do so, but he should give up his seat in parliament. In other words, no minister, ministerial secretary or party member of parliament should own a business or be involved in anyone else's business, Ghanaian or foreign.

In spite of my constant clarifications and explanations of our aims and objectives, some party members in parliament pursue a course of conduct in direct contradiction of our party aims. They are tending, by virtue of their functions and positions, to become a separate social group aiming to become a new ruling class of self-seekers and careerists. This tendency is working to alienate the support of the masses and to bring the national assembly into isolation.

Members of parliament must remember at all times that they are representatives of their constituencies only by reason of their party membership, and that on no account should they regard constituency representation as belonging to them in their own right. In other words, constituencies are not the property of members of parliament. It is the party that sends them there and fights for them to become members of parliament. I am sure that from now on all parliamentarians will be guided accordingly in their conduct of representing the party in parliament.

When I look at the other side of the picture, I must say that some trade union officials have now and again indulged in loose talk and reprehensible statements which do no good either, to the party, to the government or to the nation. This is not the time for unbridled militant trade unionism in our country. Trade union officials must shed their colonial character and their colonial thinking. The approach of the TUC to our national issues should be reasoned and constructive in accordance with our present circumstances.

Let me now turn to some other causes which I consider plague Ghanaian society generally and militate against undisturbed progress. A great deal of rumour-mongering goes on all over the country.

'Berko said that the Odikro informed Asamani that the Ohene said he paid a sum of money to a party official to become a paramount chief.'

'Kojo said that Mensah told him that Kweku took a bribe.'

'Abina stated that Ekua said that Esi uses her relations with Kweku to get contracts through the District Commissioner with the support of the Regional Commissioner and the blessing of a minister in Accra.'

So, day after day, night after night, all types and manner of wild allegations and rumours are circulated and they are always well sprinkled with: *They say, they say, wo see, wo see, akee, akee!*

Many members of the party and the public are guilty of this conduct. I have directed that in future, any allegations or rumours so made or circulated against any person must immediately be brought before the central committee of the party for investigation.

One of the most degrading aspects of party conduct is the tendency on the part of some comrades to go around using the names of persons in prominent positions to collect money for themselves. Equally degrading is the tendency on the part of some persons in prominent positions to create agents for collecting money. This is a shameful and highly criminal tendency which must be crushed in the most ruthless manner.

May I take this opportunity to stress an essential point? Statements which may be regarded as government policy statements are those which I make myself, personally, and those which are clearly stated in the text to be the official policy of the government.

In recent months, people in Ghana and abroad have frequently been confused and the government's policies made uncertain as a result of unauthorised statements which have been made by persons employed by the government, or quasi-government bodies. Often these statements have conflicted with the government's policies, and although they have been corrected subsequently by the government, much harm has been done, and confusion and suspicion have resulted.

In spite of freedom of speech which can reasonably be allowed in such cases, I consider that firm action should, in the national interest, be taken. From now on, therefore, no public statement affecting government policy will be made by any minister, ministerial secretary, member of a government corporation or institution, government official or any other person employed by the government, unless that statement has first had presidential or Cabinet approval. It is my intention to take strong disciplinary action against any individual who infringes this procedure.

I am aware that the evil of patronage finds a good deal of place in our society. I consider that it is entirely wrong for persons placed in positions of eminence or authority to use the influence of office in patronising others, in many cases, wrong persons for immoral favours. I am seeing to it that this evil shall be uprooted, no matter whose ox is gored. The same thing goes for nepotism, which is, so to speak, a twin brother of the evil of patronage.

At this point, I would like to make a little divergence and touch upon civil service red tape. It amazes me that up to the present many civil servants do not realise that we are living in a revolutionary era. This Ghana, which has lost so much time serving colonial masters, cannot afford to be tied down to archaic snail-pace methods of work which obstruct expeditious progress. We have lost so much time that we need to do in ten years what has taken others a 100 years to accomplish. Civil servants, therefore, must develop a new orientation, a sense of mission and urgency to enable them to eliminate all tendencies towards red tape-ism, bureaucracy, and waste. Civil servants must use their initiative to make the civil service an effective instrument in the rapid development of Ghana.

In order to promote greater efficacy in the machinery of the government, I have decided to re-organise slightly the existing ministerial set-up. In view of the increasingly important part being played by Ghana at the present time in the African liberation movement, I have decided to create a Ministry of African Affairs, as distinct from the present Ministry of Foreign Affairs. This new ministry will be responsible for all African matters, including the present duties undertaken by the Bureau of African Affairs and the African Affairs Centre. It will also liaise with the AU-African People's Secretariat and the All-African Trade Union Federation.

The Ministry of Labour and Co-operatives and the Ministry of Social Welfare will be abolished. Ministerial responsibility for labour, social welfare and community development matters will be undertaken by the Ministry of Education, which will therefore be known as the Ministry of Education, Labour, and Social Welfare. The staff of the Co-operative Department will be seconded to the National Co-operative Council to assist the council in the supervision and co-ordination of co-operative activities throughout the country.

Responsibility for consumer co-operatives, agricultural co-operatives and industrial co-operatives will be undertaken by the Ministry of Trade, the Ministry of Agriculture and the Developmental Secretariat, respectively.

Let me say a few words about the purchase of cocoa. The reports I have received so far indicate that the statement made in parliament some time ago by the Minister of Labour and Co-operatives that a state buying agency would be established by the government and would control the purchase of cocoa throughout the country, has not been favourably received by the farmers. After careful consideration, I have come to the conclusion that this proposal, which was announced to parliament, is perhaps not the best way we can handle this important matter of the purchase of cocoa. It is of the utmost importance that the arrangements for the purchase of our cocoa, which is not only the source of livelihood for the majority of people in this country, but also of such utmost importance to our economy, should be as simple and sufficient as possible. I have therefore instructed that the United Ghana Farmers' Council (UGFC), which embraces all the farmers of Ghana, should be given the sole responsibility for organising the purchase of all cocoa produced in Ghana on behalf of the Cocoa Marketing Board.

I am assured by the UGFC that they have made all the necessary arrangements and are prepared to undertake the purchase of cocoa as from the main crop this year. A satisfactory safeguard in respect of this matter has been provided in an arrangement which I have directed for the auditing of the accounts of the UGFC by the auditor-general. By this arrangement the accounts of the UGFC, all public corporations, the TUC and all other bodies concerned, shall be audited by the auditor-general who shall have the same powers in relation to them as are conferred upon him by the Constitution in relation to government accounts.

As I said at the recent civic luncheon arranged in my honour at the Ambassador Hotel by the Accra City Council, I am very anxious that the city of Accra should be developed as quickly as possible in view of its increasing international importance. In order to speed up the process, I have appointed a Special Commissioner for Accra Development, who will be responsible to me, through the Minister of Works and Housing, for the rapid development of all public works in respect of the city of Accra and the development of the city.

In particular, he will be concerned with the development within the city of Accra of parks, children's playgrounds, public swimming pools and other such amenities, and also with the construction of streets and slum clearance schemes and of a sewerage system. I trust that the special commissioner will receive the full co-operation of the Accra City Council and the people of Accra in this most important assignment.

I have recently been alarmed at the amount of travelling abroad which is undertaken by ministers, ambassadors, ministerial secretaries and civil servants of all ranks. In many cases, it is clear that approval is sought from no one before the journeys concerned are made. In future, travelling abroad, unless approved by Cabinet, will not be paid for by the government. The cost of any journeys which are undertaken without this approval will be surcharged to the persons concerned. I have also directed that instructions should be given to the heads of all public boards and corporations, to ensure that no officers of these boards and corporations travel outside Ghana at government expense without my specific approval or that of Cabinet.

Ghanaian ambassadors take their children with them when they proceed to their stations, at the expense of the government. I am taking steps to discourage this practice, for it seems to me that on psychological and other grounds, it is better for these young children to begin their education at home. At any rate this practice cannot be justified on financial grounds. In future, ambassadors and foreign service officers will not be allowed to take their children abroad unless such children are below the age of five years. The procedure will apply equally to civil servants and other Ghanaian public functionaries serving abroad. Let me now come back to the party.

It is most important to remember that the strength of the CPP derives from the masses of the people. These men and women include those whom I have constantly referred to as the unknown warriors – dedicated men and women who serve the party loyally and selflessly without hoping for reward. It is therefore natural for the masses to feel some resentment when they see comrades whom they have put into power and given the mandate to serve the country on their behalf, begin to forget themselves and indulge in ostentatious living. High party officials, ministers, ministerial secretaries, chairmen of statutory boards and corporations must forever bear this in mind. Some of us very easily forget that we ourselves have risen from amongst the masses. We must avoid any conduct that will breed antagonism and uneasy relations. Let us always keep in mind the fact that constant examination and correction are necessary for maintaining the solidarity of the party. The aim of all correction, however, must be to build and not to destroy. The central committee proposes to issue instructions shortly on the duties and rights of party members.

Coming to the integral organisations of the party, I consider it essential to emphasise once more that the TUC, the UGFC, the National Co-operative Council (NCC) and the National Council of Ghana Women (NCGW), are integral parts of the CPP, and in order to correct certain existing anomalies, the central committee has decided that separate membership cards of integral organisations shall be abolished forthwith. The membership card of the party will be the only qualification for membership within these organisations, namely, the TUC, the UGFC, the NCC and the NCGW, and no other membership card other than that of the CPP shall be recognised by these bodies. In all regional headquarters, provision will be made for the central party and these integral organisations to be housed in one building. It is necessary for effective co-ordination and control. Also, the separate flags used by these organisations will be abolished and replaced by the flag of the CPP.

At this stage, I wish to take the opportunity to refer to an internal matter of the TUC. It has come to my notice that dues of four shillings per month are being paid by some unions, whereas others pay two shillings monthly as membership dues. I understand that this position is causing some irritation. I have therefore instructed, after consultation with the TUC officials, that union dues shall remain at two shillings per month.

Finally, I wish to state that in considering remedial measures, I have found it necessary to direct that a limit be imposed on property acquisition by ministers, party officials and ministerial secretaries in order to enable them to conform to the modest and simple way of life demanded by the ideals and principles of the CPP.

Countrymen: our mission to Ghana and to Africa and the unique personality of our party as a vanguard of the African liberation movement impose upon us increasing responsibility, not only to set our own house in order, but also to set very high standards from which all who seek to emulate us shall draw devotion and inspiration in their own struggles.

I wish you all good luck and a good weekend.

Towards our Goal

**SESSIONAL REVIEW OF THE SECOND SESSION OF THE FIRST PARLIAMENT
OF THE REPUBLIC OF GHANA**

Mr. Speaker, Members of the National Assembly,

I am commanded by Osagyefo, the president, to deliver the following message which contains a report of the Second Session of the First Parliament of the Republic of Ghana.[46]

It is a little over a year ago when I addressed you. Once again, the time has come for me to present to you a review of the significant events that have taken place during the past session. Many important developments have occurred both in Africa and the world which have proved to us the soundness of the basic conceptions of our policy.

The two fundamental objectives which govern our foreign policy are African independence and African unity. Our primary aim is to see that all the peoples of Africa are free from colonial domination. It is also our desire that all the peoples of Africa should come together and unite as one people of one continent. It is our view that it is only when Africa is united that they can withstand and foil the various subtle manoeuvres of neo-colonialism.

Another aim of our foreign policy is World Peace. I have said time and again that we in Africa have a vested interest in world peace, because we hope to achieve the reconstruction of our new nations and the consolidation of our newly won independence. It is for these reasons that we have striven and are still striving to persuade the nuclear powers to avoid making the mistake of resorting to the use of the lethal weapons at their disposal as a means of settling their disputes and by so doing endanger the lives of innocent people throughout the world. We have laboured for too long under colonial rule and suppression; now that we have won our independence and nationhood, we desire to be left in peace in order to reconstruct and build our nation and society with the ultimate aim of contributing in our own way towards the betterment of the life of our people. We therefore appeal to our friends in non-aligned countries to rise up as one force and bring reason to bear on the great powers to stop nuclear testing and all preparations for world destruction.

In pursuit of our foreign policy of African independence we have expressed our views and have condemned vehemently in international organisations, actions which have been taken by colonial powers to perpetuate colonialism,

---

46 *Editor's note*: The speech in this chapter was read out by the leader of the house.

imperialism and racial discrimination against African peoples. Ghana played an active role at the United Nations in exposing the evils of apartheid by her persistent and unreserved condemnation of the practice, Ghana was chiefly instrumental in getting the International Labour Organisation (ILO) to conduct an investigation into conditions of forced labour in Angola and other Portuguese territories; we also actively advocated the expulsion of South Africa from the ILO.

We have given eloquent expression to the other facet of our foreign policy, which is positive neutralism and non-alignment. We have done this by participating in international conferences held either in the East or the West. Members of this honourable house will recall that in July, last year, I personally led a Ghana delegation on a visit to the USSR., a number of Eastern European countries and China. During the visits to these countries, discussions were held on important matters of mutual interest in regard to trade and cultural exchanges between us and the host countries. As a result of these friendly discussions, we have been able to sign a number of useful trade and payments and cultural exchange agreements which will benefit Ghana. We have also established diplomatic missions in the socialist countries of Bulgaria, Poland, Romania, Albania, Hungary and Czechoslovakia. In addition to these missions in Eastern European countries, new embassies have been established in the Latin American countries of Brazil, Cuba and New Mexico. Ghana is thus effectively represented in both the East, and the West, in Asia, South America and in Africa.

During the session under review Ghana played host to foreign dignitaries representing the East, the West and Africa, I refer to the memorable visit of Her Majesty Queen Elizabeth II of England, head of the Commonwealth, the friendly visit of Mr Anastas Ivanovich Mikoyan, First Deputy Chairman of the USSR. Council of Ministers, the brotherly visits of His Excellencies Hamani Diori, president of the Republic of Niger, Moktar Ould Daddah, president of the Islamic Republic of Somalia, and finally the exciting visit of the first Soviet spaceman, Major Yuri Gagarin.

Members of the Commonwealth are now discussing the terms of Britain's application to enter the European Economic Community. Ghana has made her position and attitude clear towards Britain's move in this direction. We are not opposed to Britain's entry into the European Common Market, but we will not allow ourselves to be pressed into an association which will stem our economic development and reduce our political sovereignty to impotent verbiage. Contacts have been made with other member countries of the Commonwealth on this subject. All that need be said is that we will put our views across and with all the force at our command to the other members of the Commonwealth at the Prime Ministers' meeting now being held in London.

We have proposed that an African Common Market should be established as an alternative to the European Common Market; action has been initiated to consult other African states on this matter.

Now to the subject of world peace, the third pre-occupation of our foreign policy. In our general relations with other countries of the world whether in the East or the West, we have consistently applied our policy regarding the maintenance and preservation of world peace. We have appealed to the major powers to refrain from nuclear testing in the atmosphere, underground and underwater. We have urged that a spirit of compromise should be maintained on the disarmament negotiation so that mankind may be spared the horrors of another worldwide holocaust. Throughout the world there is deep but inarticulate desire for peace. It is therefore the duty of countries which follow a policy of positive neutralism like ourselves to help to stir up this world desire and assert its full weight.

You as members of parliament, realised the extreme urgency of the question of disarmament and therefore when an appeal was made to you, you made available the generous sum of £G50,000 to cover the expenses of the Accra Assembly on the World Without the Bomb. I am sure you all recall the meeting of the Accra Assembly which was a tremendous success. The assembly met for eight days here in Accra. There were 150 participants, made up of experts and observers who attended the assembly not as representatives of their countries but as individuals whose convictions on the subject of peace have earned them world acclamation.

They spoke and acted with an independent mind. They were free to consider objectively a number of problems including the reduction in international tension, and the methods of effective inspection and control of disarmament. This unique gathering of individuals held many useful discussions and offered concrete proposals which, though may not offer an immediate solution to the problems of peace, nevertheless have indicated at least a line of approach which may lead to fruitful discussions and negotiations. A skeleton Secretariat has been established under the direct supervision of the Council of the Accra Assembly. It has been proposed that the Accra Assembly should hold another meeting in Accra in September next year. Thereafter, regular meetings will be held in other non-aligned countries until the problem of disarmament is fully resolved and international peace firmly guaranteed.

Ghana sent a strong delegation under my leadership to the Belgrade Conference of Non-aligned States. At this conference we emphasised once again the vested interests that Ghana has in world peace.

And now to come nearer home to our own Africa, I have stated earlier on that the foremost aim of our foreign policy is our desire for African independence and African unity. To this end we have continued to take effective measures to foster independence for African peoples still under colonial rule. We participated in a number of conferences designed to achieve political, cultural and economic co-operation not only among the member states of the Union of African States – Ghana. Guinea and Mali – and the Casablanca Group but also among other African countries. We have organised various conferences for the youth of Africa to come together here in Accra in order to bring home to them more forcefully their role in the new Africa that is emerging.

We also convened a conference of African Women representing various women's organisations in Africa to inspire and to develop the new womanhood Africa needs today. And more recently we called together African farmers for a conference in Accra to discuss among themselves their common problems and to generate in them the new type of African farmer required to produce abundant crops to feed the growing populations of Africa. At a meeting held in Accra in January this year by members of our brothers of the Casablanca Group, it was decided that we should not participate in the Lagos Conference of African Heads of State. Our decision was based on the grounds that the sponsors of the conference failed to invite our heroic Algerian brothers who were then on the verge of winning their long and courageous battle against the French imperialists. We declined the invitation to attend this conference because we also felt that our individual states were not property consulted in regard to the preliminary arrangements made for the conference.

To quicken the pace of African independence we sponsored in Ghana, this year, one of the most important conferences of freedom fighters. Delegates from almost all African countries still dependent who are actively engaged in the struggle to liberate themselves from colonial domination attended this conference. Observers from independent African states also attended the conference. The meeting together of all freedom fighters and their supporters gave us an opportunity to re-examine critically the trend of events in regard to our common struggle against imperialism, colonialism and neo-colonialism. We reviewed our strength and strategy as well as that of the common enemy, and we re-organised our plans and moves and reinforced our energy to carry the struggle forward to a successful end.

In my statement to parliament on 20 January 1962, I informed members that the main contract for the construction of the Volta Dam and the power plant in connection with our gigantic Volta River Project had been awarded to Impregilo, an Italian consortium. Since then, arrangements have been concluded for the signing of the master agreement with the Volta Aluminium Company. We have also concluded agreements for loans from the International Monetary Fund, the United Kingdom government and the government of the United States of America. We have also awarded the contracts for the supply of equipment and the construction of transmission lines. All the contracts for the Volta River Project have been awarded and we are now looking forward confidently to the successful completion of this project.

The construction activity of the project to date has been concentrated on those items pertaining to the diversion of the Volta River and the preparation of watering the power dam foundation. The diversion tunnel which is capable of carrying the entire river flow except during flood periods was completed in June of this year. The up-stream coffer dam will be completed by December this year. By the end of June this year over 10 per cent of the overall construction programme at Akosombo had been completed. The whole of the Akosombo area has been planned for development as a modern township.

Whilst the dam construction is going on, preparations have been made for resettling the 67,000 people living in the areas to be inundated by the lake. Various ministries, departments and agencies are doing detailed field work required to demarcate the lake boundary, assess value of properties, study the social structure of the population in the areas to be inundated, plan towns and settlements in the lake basin, secure land, organise agriculture, provide water and roads and assist the people to construct their own houses. Government is taking necessary measures to ensure that no one suffers any hardship as a result of the implementation of this project. Already the project employs in all over 3,000 Ghanaians and some 300 overseas personnel. Construction of the dam at Akosombo has so far attracted about 40,000 visitors including local and foreign dignitaries. Relations between workers and employment organisations have been excellent and most of the trade disputes were settled peaceably through the established machinery provided under the Industrial Relations Act.

A national system of vocational guidance and vocational training has been set up. Public employment centres throughout the country increased from 19 to 40 and these placed 55,924 persons in employment during the period. Leaflets have been prepared as a guidance for school leavers. To increase the level of skills attained by many tradesmen, the government has set up an Apprenticeship Board to co-ordinate and standardise training in all trades throughout the country.

One hundred and sixty day nurseries have been established to cater for more than 11,000 children. The training of the staff of these day nurseries has also been accelerated.

The Young Pioneer Movement continues to grow rapidly in membership and organisational strength. The movement has been established in every region and has offices in all districts of the country. A contingent of 100 Gambian youth is receiving training at the Kwame Nkrumah Youth Training Centre at Teshie.

In furtherance of our avowed aim of providing adequate facilities for education to the vast masses of the people, 2,493 new primary and 374 new middle schools were opened during the year under review. The provision of secondary education is also proceeding at a fast rate. The target of 6,000 Form I intakes proposed for 1964 was almost reached in 1961 when the number of intake of new pupils rose to 5,500. As a result of the increased output of our universities and the operation of technical agreement programmes it has been possible during the year to allot many more graduate teachers to secondary schools and training colleges. This year has seen the first output of technical teachers. These teachers have been employed in the technical institutes. Far-reaching fundamental changes in education have been made, for example a shortened primary school course is now followed by vocational training.

An inspectorate has been established for the inspection and supervision of the work of secondary schools and training colleges. The teaching of science has received new impetus at all levels of the educational system, thus a firm foundation is being laid for the production of future scientists for Ghana. In the field of scientific research Ghana has made a notable start with the creation of the National Research Council and the Ghana Academy of Sciences both under my chairmanship. These organisations, which will soon merge as the Ghana Academy of Sciences, now conducts research into agriculture, building, road construction, utilisation of forest products, mining, metallurgy and geology. Their activities are being co-ordinated with those of the University of Ghana and the Kwame Nkrumah University (Kumasi). The University of Ghana and the Kwame Nkrumah University, now independent, have maintained their high academic standards.

In October last year, two permanent commissions were set up by the government, the National Planning Commission and the State Control Commission. The State Control Commission has been charged with the responsibility of ensuring that expenditure in all directions is properly controlled. The Planning Commission has the vital task of drawing up a new comprehensive Seven Year Plan for the social and economic development of the country.

I am glad to say that the first comprehensive Seven Year Plan which will completely transform the economy of Ghana and accelerate industrialisation has now been drawn up and will be implemented as from January 1963. The preparation of the new plan based on modern scientific techniques reveals the importance and value of economic and social statistics, and the Central Bureau of Statistics has made considerable progress in its attempt to develop an efficient statistical service for the nation.

The analysis of the 1960 Population Census has resulted in the publication of the first two volumes of the Census Report. The First Phase of a National Census of Industrial Production and Distribution has been completed. A National Census of Agriculture is scheduled to start soon. This is expected to provide statistics on the structure and organisation of the agricultural sector of the national economy. The government attaches great importance to the work connected with these censuses without which it would be almost impossible to carry through our policy of development planning and provide targets for the various sectors of our economy.

The ministry of agriculture has been re-organised to undertake large-scale mechanised farming. The State Farms Division formed a few months ago has already achieved spectacular progress, with over 3,000 acres planted in annuals such as groundnuts, maize and guinea corn. Besides, large plantations of tree crops such as citrus, kola nut, oil palm as well as tobacco have been established. Cattle ranches in Pong-Tamale and Damongo alone hold between them some 1,400 cattle; in Damongo alone about 200 sheep are reared. The Workers' Brigade increased its acreage under cultivation from 3,600 in 1961 to over 6,000 acres in the first season in 1962. Storage centres have been established by the Agriculture Produce Marketing Board in both production and distribution centres. Many of you have no doubt read of the reported survey by the Food and Agriculture Organisation of UN which records 30 per cent to 120 per cent increased crop yield in Ghana due to the introduction of fertilisers.

A firm basis for Inter-African Trade was bid by our trade and payments agreements with Mali, Dahomey and Upper Volta on the basis of most favoured nation treatment. As a result of the customs union treaty of the Casablanca States, the African Common Market has been virtually created and will become fully operative when the treaty is ratified. As a result of the government's new Import/Export Control Policy, the deterioration in Ghana's balance of payments position has been arrested and the inflationary pressure on our economy counteracted.

The Ghana National Trading Corporation has been set up in an effort to reduce the price of goods. The corporation has absorbed the trading interests of Commonwealth Trust Limited, Laco Stores and A. G. Leventis. A number of industries have been established throughout the country. Early in June, I cut the sod to mark the beginning of the first steel works at Tema, which will doubtless make a worthy contribution to the reconstruction of Ghana. In addition to this, a paper conversion factory has been established at Takoradi, a jute bag factory capable of producing all our requirements of cocoa bags is being constructed at Kumasi, and work is in progress on the construction of a plastic shoe factory at Tema. Industrial Development will be accelerated when power from the Volta and other sources of power become available.

In the field of small industries, factories have been built at Demi, Asesewa, Atebubu, Tamale and Bawku for the milling of edible oils and a number of motor car repair depots are being established at Accra, Kumasi, Takoradi, Sunyani and Swedru. Contracts have also been signed for the supply of plant and machinery for the setting up of a number of other industries including factories for the manufacture of pharmaceutical products, aluminium cutlery, aluminium cables and electrical appliances. Tema Harbour was officially opened in February 1962, and nine out of its ten quays are now in use.

Detailed surveys for complete electrification of the country have been undertaken and already 55 towns have been selected for this purpose. It is expected that when the Bui and Volta River projects are completed there will be enough supply of electricity for distribution to all the important towns and villages in the country.

The supply of adequate drinking water was undertaken for a number of towns throughout the country.

The scheme for modernising our hospitals which was mentioned in my last review has been carried out with great success in many parts of the country. Those of you who have visited Korle Bu recently will find adequate testimony of this. Almost on all sides new constructions are still in progress. Major extensions have also been started on hospitals at Sekondi, Mpraeso, Oda, and Axim. Dental clinics have been opened at the Accra Ridge Hospital, Ho, Koforidua and Sunyani and it is expected to establish another one at Wa soon. To reduce congestion in the large towns while at the same time bringing medical facilities closer to the people, urban health centres are being built. One of these health centres was opened recently in Tema and seven more are under construction at Accra, Kumasi, and Sekondi. Rural health centres and doctors' bungalows have been constructed at Agona Nkwanta, New Tafo, Anyinase. Anyinam and Juaso while work on 18 more is continuing.

The problem of shortage of nurses and midwives has also been seriously tackled. In addition to providing increased training institutions for these, the conditions of service for nurses and midwives have been radically improved, and 39 scholarships have been awarded to doctors to do courses leading to specialist qualifications.

Expansion, modernisation and re-equipment of the armed forces have continued apace and I am glad to say that except for a few medical and engineering specialists, the Africanisation of the armed forces is now virtually complete. As a result of the government's firm policy, the internal security of the state has been maintained intact and calm and orderly progress of Ghana continues without disruption. In this the masses of our people have co-operated whole-heartedly.

And now, members of the national assembly, you all remember too well what took place at Kulungugu. I and a Ghana delegation, having successfully negotiated on behalf of the government a free trade and payments agreement with the government of Upper Volta, were returning home. In the border village of Kulungugu we were brutally attacked with bomb explosion. As you know, four persons died and 77 were wounded, many very seriously. That I am here with you today can only be attributed to a miracle. Members of the national assembly of Ghana, these attacks show only too clearly how desperate the enemy now is. But let me remind all believers in violence that the government has a clear mandate from the people of Ghana to lead this country and has no intention of shirking its responsibilities. Ever since the Kulungugu incident the people of Ghana have deplored the incident in no uncertain terms and in various ways demonstrated their loyalty to me personally and to the Government.

The very big strides we are making in industry and agriculture are proof of our economic and political stability and we are determined to maintain this stability under which our second revolution will be carried out to a successful and final conclusion.

Members of the national assembly, I thank you for the funds which you voted for the public services during the period under review.

Freedom First

It is my deep conviction that all peoples wish to be free, and that the desire for freedom is rooted in the soul of every one of us. A people long subjected to foreign domination, however, does not always find it easy to translate that wish into action. Under arbitrary rule, people are apt to become lethargic; their senses are dulled. Fear becomes the dominant force in their lives; fear of breaking the law, fear of the punitive measures which might result from an unsuccessful attempt to break loose from their shackles. Those who lead the struggle for freedom must break through this apathy and fear. They must give active expression to the universal longing to be free. They must strengthen the peoples' faith in themselves, and encourage them to take part in the freedom struggle. Above all, they must declare their aims openly and unmistakably, and organise the people towards the achievement of their goal of self-government.

The essential forger of the political revolution is a strong, well-organised, broadly based political party, knit together by a programme that is accepted by all the members, who also submit themselves to the party's discipline. Its programme should aim for 'Freedom first.' 'Seek ye first the political kingdom,' became the principal slogan of the Convention People's Party, for without political independence none of our plans for social and economic development could be put into effect.

There has been a good deal of talk about dependent territories making themselves viable before attempting to take upon themselves the responsibilities of self-government. That is precisely what they cannot do. As long as the government of less developed countries remains in the hands of colonial administrators, their economies are set to a pattern determined by the interests, not of the indigenous inhabitants, but of the national beneficiaries of the ruling country. Improvement in living conditions for the bulk of the people will not come until political power passes into their hands. Thus, every movement for independence in a colonial situation contains two elements: the demand for political freedom and the revolt against poverty and exploitation. Resolute leadership is required to subordinate the understandable desire of the people for better living conditions to the achievement of the primary aim of the abolition of colonial rule.

Before the Second World War (WWII), a number of political demonstrations and strikes took place in various parts of colonial Africa. The most common demands were for reforms; few people envisaged at that time the emergence of national political parties demanding independence.

During the 1940s, however, many African national organisations were formed. For example, in 1944, the National Council of Nigeria and the Cameroons was founded, and, in the same year, the Nyasaland National Congress.[47] Two years later, the Kenya African Union was formed; and the Rassemblement Démocratique Africain (RDA), a federation of the various organisations which had developed throughout the French colonies in West and Equatorial Africa. There followed, in 1947, the formation of the Northern Rhodesian African National Congress, and in our country the United Gold Coast Convention (UGCC), with its aim: self-government in the shortest possible time.[48] On 12 June 1949, came the split with the UGCC when I founded the CPP with the declared aim of achieving 'Self-Government Now.'

The 1950s saw the emergence of the Uganda National Congress (1952), the Tanganyika African National Union (1953) and the African National Congress in Southern Rhodesia.[49] There were also national organisations formed in the Congo. In Portuguese Africa, the Uniao dos Populacaos de Angola (UPA) and the Movimento Popular de Libertação de Angola (MPLA) were formed. Eventually, in 1959, they merged to form the African Revolutionary Front Against Portuguese Colonialism. This organisation includes supporters in Mozambique and Portuguese Guinea. I have mentioned only a few of the many African political organisations formed during and after WWII. There are many others. Their structure, organisation, and the quality of their leadership have varied, but all have had in common the determination to struggle for the abolition of colonial rule and the improvement of economic and social conditions.

On the eve of WWII, only Liberia, Ethiopia and Egypt were independent. But by the end of 1959, that is, 20 years later, there were nine independent African States: Egypt, Sudan, Morocco, Tunisia, Libya, Liberia, Ethiopia, Ghana and Guinea. In 1960, Nigeria, the Congo, French Togoland, the French Cameroons and Somalia achieved independence. They were followed, in 1961, by Sierra Leone, Tanganyika, Uganda and Nyasaland. The independence of Kenya, Northern Rhodesia and Zanzibar cannot long be delayed.

This fundamental change in the African situation has been brought about by the struggles and sacrifices of the African peoples themselves, and nothing can now stop the rushing tide of nationalism. As long as a single foot of African soil remains under foreign domination, the battle must continue.

---

47 This was banned in 1958 and the Malawi Congress Party set up in its place.

48 When the Central African Federation was formed in 1953, this party split up, and others emerged, e.g. the United National Independence Party under Kenneth Kaunda in 1958.

49 This was originally founded in 1920. It was banned in 1959, and the National Democratic Party was formed.

It may be that the time has come to have a common political party with a common aim and programme. For instance, instead of the CPP in Ghana, there might be the Ghana People's Party. In Kenya, the progressive party could be the Kenya People's Party; in Guinea, the Guinea People's Party, and so on; each party having one common aim and objective, the freedom and unity of Africa.

The various people's parties, with their common aim, would co-operate with each other. A central organisation would undoubtedly be necessary, and also a highly trained headquarters staff. If this kind of solidarity on the political party level could be achieved, it would surely strengthen African continental freedom and unity.

Party leaders in countries which are still not free would be able to derive strength and inspiration from close association with their opposite numbers in independent countries. Though beset by difficulties, they would gain confidence from being part of a strong continental organisation with immense resources, which they could draw upon in time of need. From its inception, the CPP declared in its Constitution that it would 'seek to establish fraternal relations with, and offer guidance and support to all nationalist, democratic and socialist movements, in Africa and elsewhere, which are fighting for national independence and self-determination!'

Among independent countries the common party would act as a unifying force. Also, if a common domestic policy could be worked out it would help immeasurably in the planning and development of the African continent, as a whole, in the economic and social spheres.

The unevenness of development in Africa, both political and economic, is a major problem. Some countries are poor in natural resources; others rich. Some achieved independence comparatively easily, and peacefully; others are still struggling. The obvious solution is unity, so that development can be properly and cohesively planned.

Countries under alien rule achieve independence in different ways. India was promised freedom by 'steady evolution towards self-government in ordered constitutional stages.' In fact, it took 27 years of civil commotion and passive disobedience for India to achieve her aim. Libya was granted independence by the United Nations Organisation (UN) as a direct result of Italy's defeat in the WWII. The Portuguese colony of Goa was liberated by India. Several countries in the Middle East owe their existence as separate states to the Western powers, when they carved up the Ottoman Empire after the First World War (WWI). In Africa, the nature of the freedom struggle has varied according to the background conditions against which it has had to operate and the position of the international scene at a given time.

Generally, in territories where there is a settler problem, the struggle has been more prolonged and sometimes violent, as in Kenya during the Mau Mau period. Where there is no settler problem, as in West Africa, the struggle has been hard, though on the whole peaceful and constitutional. I have already told how independence was achieved in *Ghana*.[50]

Looking back and trying to determine the reasons for the successful outcome of our struggle for freedom, one factor stands out above all others, namely, the strength of a well-organised political party, representative of the broad mass of the people. The CPP represented the ordinary, common folk who wanted social justice and a higher standard of living. It kept in daily, living touch with the ordinary mass of people it represented, unlike the opposition, which was supported by a galaxy of lawyers and members of other conservative professions, the self-styled 'aristocracy' of the Gold Coast. They did not understand the new mood of the people, the growing nationalism, and the revolt against economic hardship. Thinking that their lofty assertions were enough to win adherents to their ranks, they made little effort to come into close contact with the masses in the way that I had done in my early days as secretary of the UGCC, and continued through my years of leadership of the CPP.

As a matter of fact, when the leaders of the UGCC discovered that I had spearheaded a mass movement, they recoiled in fright. That was something they had not bargained for. They had wanted me to build up a movement whose ranks would not question their self-assumed right to political leadership, but would nevertheless provide a solid enough base for them to pose as the national champions in pressing for constitutional change. It was when the leaders of the UGCC demanded I get rid of the mass following I had built up, that I withdrew from their secretariat, and formed the CPP. Unwilling to come down to the masses, whom they scorned as 'flotsam and jetsam', it was not surprising that those leaders failed to make headway with the ordinary people and were constantly rejected by them.

In the early years of the CPP, and frequently since, I urged members to follow the advice of the Chinese:

Go to the people
Live among them
Learn from them
Love them
Serve them
Plan with them
Start with what they know
Build on what they have.

This would be my advice to members of any nationalist and progressive party.

The campaign of the CPP was helped by the press. On the very day I left the UGCC the first issue of my paper *The Accra Evening News* was published, with

---

50 In my autobiography, *Ghana* (Thomas Nelson & Sons, 1957).

its challenging motto: 'We prefer self-government with danger to servitude in tranquillity.' I reached a wide circle of readers through the columns of this paper, and hammered home the message of full self-government and the need to organise for victory: 'The strength of the organised masses is invincible ... We must organise as never before, for organisation decides everything.'[51]

The whole question of publicity, the spreading of information about the aims and achievements of any political party, is of supreme importance. In the struggle for independence, where the colonial government controls the major avenues of information and gives its blessing to the reactionary press, the mechanics of propaganda employed by the freedom movement are vital. The reach of the press is, of course, narrower in areas where there is a high degree of illiteracy; but even in those areas the people can always be reached by the spoken word. And frequently the written word becomes the spoken word.

A popular anti-colonial press developed in Africa during the 1930s. In 1932, Habib Bourguiba founded the *Action Tunisienne*. In Morocco, the *Action du Peuple* edited by Mohamed Hassan Ouazzani appeared in August 1938; the editorial committee contained the nucleus of the leadership of Morocco's Comite d'Action Marocaine. In the Ivory Coast, *L'Eclaireur de la Côte d'Ivoire* began in 1935. Three years later, in 1938, Dr Nnamdi Azikiwe's *African Pilot* prepared the ground for the independence movement in Nigeria.

These, and other newspapers, have undoubtedly helped in the spread of African nationalism. They have emphasised the need for 'freedom first' and then development. If we are to banish colonialism utterly from our continent, every African must be made aware of his part in the struggle. Freedom involves the untiring efforts of everyone engaged in the struggle for it. The vast African majority must be accepted as the basis of government in Africa.

---

51 *The Accra Evening News*, 14 January 1949.

Towards African Unity

There are those who maintain that Africa cannot unite because we lack the three necessary ingredients for unity: a common race, culture, and language. It is true that we have for centuries been divided. The territorial boundaries dividing us were fixed long ago, often quite arbitrarily, by the colonial powers. Some of us are Moslems, some Christians; many believe in traditional, tribal gods. Some of us speak French, some English, some Portuguese, not to mention the millions who speak only one of the hundreds of different African languages. We have acquired cultural differences which affect our outlook and condition our political development.

All this is inevitable, due to our historical background. Yet, in spite of this, I am convinced that the forces for making unity far outweigh those which divide us. In meeting fellow Africans from all parts of the continent I am constantly impressed by how much we have in common. It is not just our colonial past, or the fact that we have aims in common, it is something which goes far deeper. I can best describe it as a sense of one-ness in that we are Africans.

In practical terms, this deep-rooted unity has shown itself in the development of Pan-Africanism, and, more recently, in the projection of what has been called the African Personality in world affairs. The expression 'Pan-Africanism' did not come into use until the beginning of the 20th century when Henry Sylvester-Williams of Trinidad, and William Edward Burghardt Du Bois of the USA, both of African descent, used it at several Pan-African Congresses which were mainly attended by scholars of African descent of the New World. A notable contribution to African nationalism and Pan-Africanism was the 'Back to Africa' movement of Marcus Garvey.

The First Pan-African Congress was held in Paris in 1919 while the peace conference was in session. The French Prime Minister [Georges] Clemenceau, when asked what he thought of the holding of a Pan-African Congress, remarked: 'Don't advertise it, but go ahead.' His reaction was fairly typical among Europeans at the time. The very idea of Pan-Africanism was so strange that it seemed unreal and yet at the same time perhaps potentially dangerous. Fifty-seven representatives from various African colonies and from the USA and the West Indies attended. They drafted various proposals, though nothing much came of them. For example, they proposed that the allied and associated powers should establish a code of law 'for international protection of the natives of Africa.'

The Second Pan-African Congress was held in London in 1921. The British government, if not sympathetic, was tolerant, and 113 delegates attended. This congress, though far from being truly representative of African opinion, nevertheless went some way towards putting the African case to the world.

In a declaration called 'To the World', drafted at the closing session, it was stated that 'the absolute equality of races, physical, political and social, is the founding stone of world and human advancement.' They were more concerned in those days with social than with political improvement, not yet recognising the pre-emption of the latter in order to engage the former.

Two years later, in 1923, a Third Pan-African Congress was held in London. Among the resolutions passed was one which asked for a voice for Africans in their own governments; and another which asked for the right of access to land and its resources. The political aspect of social justice was beginning to be understood. But in spite of the work of Du Bois and others, progress was slow. The movement lacked funds and membership was limited. The delegates were idealists rather than men of action. However, a certain amount of publicity was achieved, and Africans and men of African descent for the first time gained valuable experience in working together.

A Fourth Pan-African Congress was held in New York in 1927, which 208 delegates attended, but after that the movement seemed to fade out for a time. A non-party organisation, the International African Service Bureau (IASB), was set up in 1937, and this was the forerunner of the Pan-African Federation, the British section of the Pan-African Congress movement. Its aim was 'to promote the well-being and unity of African peoples and peoples of African descent through-out the world', and also 'to strive to co-operate between African peoples and others who share our aspirations.'

Pan-Africanism and African nationalism really took concrete expression when the Fifth Pan-African Congress met in Manchester in 1945. For the first time the necessity for well-organised, firmly knit movements as a primary condition for the success of the national liberation struggle in Africa was stressed.

The congress was attended by more than 200 delegates from all over the world. George Padmore and I had been joint secretaries of the organisational committee which planned the congress and we were delighted with the results of our work. Among the declarations addressed to the imperialist powers asserting the determination of the colonial people to be free was the following:

The Fifth Pan-African Congress calls on intellectuals and professional classes of the Colonies to awaken to their responsibilities. The long, long night is over. By fighting for trade union rights, the right to form co-operatives, freedom of the press, assembly, demonstration and strike, freedom to print and read the literature which is necessary for the education of the masses, you will be using the only means by which your liberties will be won and maintained. Today there is only one road to effective action – the organisation of the masses.[52]

---

52 *Declaration to the Colonial Peoples of the World* by Kwame Nkrumah, approved and adopted by the Pan-African Congress held in Manchester, England, 15–21 October 1945.

A definite programme of action was agreed upon. Basically, the programme centred around the demand for constitutional change, providing for universal suffrage. The methods to be employed were based on the Gandhist technique of non-violent non-co-operation, in other words, the withholding of labour, civil disobedience, and economic boycott. There were to be variations of emphasis from territory to territory according to the differing circumstances. The fundamental purpose was identical: national independence leading to African unity. The limited objective was combined with the wider perspective.

Instead of a rather nebulous movement, concerned vaguely with black nationalism, the Pan-African movement had become an expression of African nationalism. Unlike the first four congresses, which had been supported mainly by middle-class intellectuals and bourgeois reformists, the Fifth Pan-African Congress was attended by workers, trade unionists, farmers, and students, most of whom came from Africa.

When the Congress ended, having agreed on the programme for Pan-African nationalism, a working committee was set up with Du Bois as chairman and myself as general secretary. The congress headquarters were moved to London, where shortly afterwards the West African National Secretariat was also established. Its purpose was to put into action, in West Africa, the policies agreed upon in Manchester. I was offered, and accepted, the secretaryship.

We published a monthly paper called *The New African* and called two West African Conferences in London. By this time the political conscience of African students was thoroughly aroused, and they talked of little else but the colonial liberation movement. The more enthusiastic among us formed a kind of inner group which we called 'The Circle.' Only those working genuinely for West African freedom and unity were admitted, and we began to prepare ourselves actively for revolutionary work in any part of the African continent.

It was at this point that I was asked to return to the Gold Coast to become general secretary of the UGCC. I accepted with some hesitation. There was my work for the West African National Secretariat to consider, and also the preparations which were being made for the calling of a West African National Conference in Lagos in October 1948.

I called at Freetown and Monrovia on the way home, and spoke with African nationalists there, telling them of the conference plans and urging them to attend. The political contacts I made in both Sierra Leone and Liberia were to prove significant later, though the conference in Lagos never, in fact, took place.

When I returned to West Africa in 1947, it was with the intention of using the Gold Coast as a starting-off point for African independence and unity. With the mass movement I was able to build up in the CPP, the Gold Coast secured its freedom and emerged as the sovereign state of Ghana in 1957. I at once made it clear that there would be no meaning to the national independence of Ghana unless it was linked with the total liberation of the African continent. While our independence celebrations were actually taking place, I called for a conference of all the sovereign states of Africa, to discuss plans for the future of our continent.

The first Conference of Independent African States met in Accra in April 1958. There were then only eight, namely, Egypt, Ghana, Sudan, Libya, Tunisia, Liberia, Morocco, and Ethiopia. Our purpose was to exchange views on matters of common interest; to explore ways and means of consolidating and safeguarding our independence; to strengthen the economic and cultural ties between our countries; to decide on workable arrangements for helping fellow Africans still subject to colonial rule; and to examine the central world problem of how to secure peace.

When, on 15 April 1958, I welcomed the representatives to the conference, I felt that at last Pan-Africanism had moved to the African continent where it really belonged. It was a historic occasion. Free Africans were actually meeting together, *in Africa* to examine and consider African affairs. Here was a signal departure from established custom, a jar to the arrogant assumption of non-African nations that African affairs were solely the concern of states outside our continent. The African personality was making itself known.

Because many of the speeches made at the conference were similar in content, it was alleged in some quarters that there had been previous collaboration. I am able to state categorically that all of us who spoke had prepared our speeches independently. If they showed identity of thought and belief, it was because our attitudes in Africa were assuming an identity of vision and purpose.

The Accra Conference resulted, as indeed I hoped it would, in a great upsurge of interest in the cause of African freedom and unity. But matters did not rest there. Some weeks after the conference ended some of my colleagues and I set out on a tour of the countries which took part in the conference. Our purpose was to convey to the heads of states and governments, many of whom were unable to attend the conference personally, the good wishes of the government and people of Ghana.

Everywhere we went we were enthusiastically received and were able to discuss ways and means of strengthening further the ties of friendship between our respective countries. Plans to improve cultural and economic relations were the subject of a series of communiques. Our common background and basic common interests drew us together.

The year 1958 was memorable not only for the first conference of independent African states, but also for the opening of the All-African People's Conference in Accra in December 1958. Delegates from 62 African nationalist organisations attended the conference.

The will to unity which the conference expressed was at least equal to the determination to carry forward the process of independence throughout Africa. The enthusiasm generated among the delegates returning to their own countries profoundly influenced subsequent developments. The Belgian Congo, Uganda, Tanganyika, Nyasaland, Kenya, the Rhodesias, South Africa, all were affected by the coming together in Accra of representatives of the various freedom movements of the continent. The total liberation and the unity of the continent at which we aimed were evolving and gaining reality in the experience of our international gatherings.

In November 1959, representatives of trade unions all over Africa met in Accra to organise an All-African Trade Union Federation (AATUF). The African labour movement has always been closely associated with the struggle for political freedom, as well as with economic and social development.

A further step forward in the direction of all-African co-operation took place a few months later when the conference to discuss Positive Action and Security in Africa opened in Accra in April 1960. It was called by the government of Ghana, in consultation with other independent African states, to consider the situation in Algeria and in South Africa, and also to discuss and plan future action to prevent Africa being used as a testing ground for nuclear weapons. Equally important matters to be considered were the total liberation of Africa, and the necessity to guard against neo-colonialism and balkanisation, both of which would impede unity.

In mid-1960 a further conference of independent African states, twelve in number, was held in Addis Ababa, and yet another all-African conference met in Accra. The latter, a conference of African women to discuss common problems, opened on 18 July. The delegates spoke of freedom and unity, and of the urgent need for social and economic progress. While their conference was taking place, events in the newly independent Congo were causing one international crisis after another. The province of Katanga was attempting to secede from the Republic of Congo, and Patrice Lumumba, the Congolese prime minister, had asked for UN aid.

Some of the dangers of neo-colonialism and balkanisation, which we had foreseen, now became realities. Foreign business interests, as well as policies connected with the Cold War, began to dominate the Congo political scene and prevented early action by the UN which, if it had been used to effect the purpose for which it had been called in, could well have been decisive in maintaining the sovereignty of Lumumba's government.

If at that time, July 1960, the independent states of Africa had been united, or had at least a joint military high command and a common foreign policy, an African solution might have been found for the Congo; and the Congo might have been able to work out its own destiny, unhindered by any non-African interference.

As it was, the position in the Congo steadily worsened, and all the unrest and dangers of disunity became fully apparent. The only people to score from the situation were the neo-colonialists and their allies in South Africa and the Rhodesias, who used the struggle in the Congo as an argument to demonstrate the inability of Africans to manage their own affairs.

In a last-minute attempt to save the situation, and to show some kind of African solidarity, a conference of independent African states met in Leopoldville from 25–30 August, at the invitation of Patrice Lumumba. At the conference, which was at foreign ministers' level, delegates aired their views on the Congo crisis. Although the conference did not achieve its purpose, it was significant in that it enabled the delegates to see for themselves what was really going on in the Congo and to report on this personally to their governments. A valuable object lesson, however, on the imperative need for unity in defence of the independence of Africa had been demonstrated.

Against a background of continuing struggle in the Congo, and of trouble in South Africa, Algeria, and other parts of the continent, an All-African People's Conference met in Cairo early in 1961. About two hundred delegates attended. The conference warned independent African states to beware of neo-colonialism, which was associated with the UK, the USA, France, Western Germany, Israel, Belgium, the Netherlands, and South Africa. It also warned states to be on their guard against imperialist agents in the guise of religious or philanthropic organisations. Resolutions included a call to the 'anti-imperialist' bloc to help the development of African economies by granting long-term loans at low interest rates to be paid in local currencies. They demanded the expulsion of South Africa from the UN; the dismissal of UN Secretary-General Dag Hammarskjold; the immediate release of Jomo Kenyatta; the immediate independence of the Rhodesias and the dissolution of the Central African Federation. The conference also called for a trade boycott of the Rhodesias; criticised policies in Angola, Cameroon and the Congo; and affirmed that [Antoine] Gizenga's regime in Stanleyville was the legitimate Congo government.

As the years go by, further All-African People's Conferences will take place, and their resolutions and declarations will become increasingly significant as they gain more power. Other all-African gatherings will continue to make their impression, whether they are held to discuss political, social or economic problems. Hardly a week goes by without news of some gathering together of Africans from different parts of the continent. As the whole of Africa becomes free, these gatherings will gain in membership, strength and effectiveness. But it is only when full political unity has been achieved that we will be able to declare the triumphant end of the Pan-African struggle and the African liberation movements.

Continental Government for Africa

We have seen, in the example of the United States, how the dynamic elements within society understood the need for unity and fought their bitter civil war to maintain the political union that was threatened by the reactionary forces. We have also seen, in the example of the Soviet Union, how the forging of continental unity along with the retention of national sovereignty by the federal states, has achieved a dynamism that has lifted a most backward society into a most powerful unit within a remarkably short space of time. From the examples before us, in Europe and the USA, it is therefore patent that we in Africa have the resources, present and potential, for creating the kind of society that we are anxious to build. It is calculated that by the end of this century the population of Africa will probably exceed 500 million.

Our continent gives us the second largest land stretch in the world. The natural wealth of Africa is estimated to be greater than that of almost any other continent in the world. To draw the most from our existing and potential means for the achievement of abundance and a fine social order, we need to unify our efforts, our resources, our skills, and intentions.

Europe, by way of contrast, must be a lesson to us all. Too busy hugging its exclusive nationalisms, it has descended, after centuries of wars interspersed with intervals of uneasy peace, into a state of confusion, simply because it failed to build a sound basis of political association and understanding. Only now, under the necessities of economic stringency and the threat of the new German industrial and military rehabilitation, is Europe trying – unsuccessfully – to find a modus operandi for containing the threat. It is deceptively hoped that the European Community will perform this miracle. It has taken two world wars and the break-up of empires to press home the lesson, still only partly digested, that strength lies in unity.

While we in Africa, for whom the goal of unity is paramount, are striving to concert our efforts in this direction the neo-colonialists are straining every nerve to upset them by encouraging the formation of communities based on the languages of their former colonisers. We cannot allow ourselves to be so disorganised and divided. The fact that I speak English does not make me an Englishman. Similarly, the fact that some of us speak French or Portuguese does not make us Frenchmen or Portuguese. We are Africans first and last, and as Africans our best interests can only be served by uniting within an African Community. Neither the Commonwealth nor a Franco-African Community can be a substitute.

To us, Africa with its islands is just one Africa. We reject the idea of any kind of partition. From Tangier or Cairo in the north to Cape Town in the south, from Cape Guardafui in the east to Cape Verde Islands in the west, Africa is one and indivisible.

I know that when we speak of political union, our critics are quick to observe an attempt to impose leadership and to abrogate sovereignty. But we have seen from the many examples of union put forward, that equality of the states is jealously guarded in every single Constitution and that sovereignty is maintained. There are differences in the powers allotted to the central government and those retained by the states, as well as in the functions of the executive, legislature, and judiciary. All of them have a common trade and economic policy. All of them are secular, in order that religion might not be dragged across the many problems involved in maintaining unity and securing the greatest possible development.

We in Africa who are pressing now for unity are deeply conscious of the validity of our purpose. We need the strength of our combined numbers and resources to protect ourselves from the very positive dangers of returning colonialism in disguised forms. We need it to combat the entrenched forces dividing our continent and still holding back millions of our brothers. We need it to secure total African liberation. We need it to carry forward our construction of a socio-economic system that will support the great mass of our steadily rising population at levels of life which will compare with those in the most advanced countries.

But we cannot mobilise our present and potential resources without concerted effort. If we developed our potentialities in men and natural resources in separate isolated groups, our energies would soon be dissipated in the struggle to outbid one another. Economic friction among us would certainly lead to bitter political rivalry, which for many years hampered the pace of growth and development in Europe.

At present most of the independent African states are moving in directions which expose us to the dangers of imperialism and neo-colonialism. We therefore need a common political basis for the integration of our policies in economic planning, defence, foreign, and diplomatic relations. That basis for political action need not infringe the essential sovereignty of the separate African states. These states would continue to exercise independent authority, except in the fields defined and reserved for common action in the interests of the security and orderly development of the whole continent.

In my view, therefore, a united Africa – that is, the political and economic unification of the African continent – should seek three objectives:

Firstly, we should have overall economic planning on a continental basis. This would increase the industrial and economic power of Africa. So long as we remain balkanised, regionally or territorially, we shall be at the mercy of colonialism and imperialism. The lesson of the South American republics vis-à-vis the strength and solidarity of the USA is there for all to see.

The resources of Africa can be used to the best advantage and the maximum benefit to all only if they are set within an overall framework of a continentally planned development. An overall economic plan, covering an Africa united on a continental basis, would increase our total industrial and economic power. We should therefore be thinking seriously now of ways and means of building up a Common Market of a United Africa and not allow ourselves to be lured by the dubious advantages of association with the so-called European Common Market.

We in Africa have looked outward too long for the development of our economy and transportation. Let us begin to look inwards into the African continent for all aspects of its development. Our communications were devised under colonial rule to stretch outwards towards Europe and elsewhere, instead of developing internally between our cities and states. Political unity should give us the power and will to change all this. We in Africa have untold agricultural, mineral, and water-power resources. These almost fabulous resources can be fully exploited and utilised in the interest of Africa and the African people, only if we develop them within a union government of African states. Such a government will need to maintain a common currency, a monetary zone and a central bank of issue. The advantages of these financial and monetary arrangements would be inestimable since monetary transactions between our several states would be facilitated and the pace of financial activity generally quickened. A central bank of issue is an inescapable necessity, in view of the need to re-orientate the economy of Africa and place it beyond the reach of foreign control.

Secondly, we should aim at the establishment of a unified military and defence strategy. I do not see much virtue or wisdom in our separate efforts to build up or maintain vast military forces for self-defence which, in any case, would be ineffective in any major attack upon our separate states. If we examine this problem realistically, we should be able to ask ourselves this pertinent question: which single state in Africa today can protect its sovereignty against an imperialist aggressor? In this connection, it should be mentioned that anti-apartheid leaders have alleged that South Africa is building a great military force with all the latest weapons of destruction, in order to crush nationalism in Africa. Nor is this all. There are grave indications that certain settler governments in Africa have already been caught in the dangerous arms race and are now arming themselves to the teeth. Their military activities constitute a serious threat not only to the security of Africa, but also to the peace of the world. If these reports are true, only the unity of Africa can prevent South Africa and these other governments from achieving their diabolical aims.

If we do not unite and combine our military resources for common defence, the individual states, out of a sense of insecurity, may be drawn into making defence pacts with foreign powers which may endanger the security of us all.

There is also the expenditure aspect of this problem. The maintenance of large military forces imposes a heavy financial burden on even the most wealthy states. For young African states, who are in great need of capital for internal development, it is ridiculous – indeed suicidal – for each state separately and individually to assume such a heavy burden of self-defence, when the weight of this burden could be easily lightened by sharing it among themselves. Some attempt has already been made by the Casablanca Powers and the Afro-Malagasy Union in the matter of common defence, but how much better and stronger it would be if, instead of two such ventures, there was one overall (Land, Sea, and Air) Defence Command for Africa.

The third objective which we should have in Africa stems from the first two which I have just described. If we in Africa set up a unified economic planning organisation and a unified military and defence strategy, it will be necessary for us to adopt a unified foreign policy and diplomacy to give political direction to our joint efforts for the protection and economic development of our continent. Moreover, there are some 60 odd states in Africa, about 32 of which are at present independent. The burden of separate diplomatic representation by each state on the continent of Africa alone would be crushing, not to mention representation outside Africa. The desirability of a common foreign policy which will enable us to speak with one voice in the councils of the world, is so obvious, vital, and imperative that comment is hardly necessary.

I am confident that it should be possible to devise a constitutional structure applicable to our special conditions in Africa and not necessarily framed in terms of the existing Constitutions of Europe, America, or elsewhere, which will enable us to secure the objectives I have defined and yet preserve to some extent the sovereignty of each state within a Union of African States.

We might erect for the time being a constitutional form that could start with those states willing to create a nucleus, and leave the door open for the attachment of others as they desire to join or reach the freedom which would allow them to do so. The form could be made amenable to adjustment and amendment at any time the consensus of opinion is for it. It may be that concrete expression can be given to our present ideas within a continental parliament that would provide a lower and an upper house, one to permit the discussion of the many problems facing Africa by a representation based on population; the other, ensuring the equality of the associated states, regardless of size and population, by a similar, limited representation from each of them, to formulate a common policy in all matters affecting the security, defence, and development of Africa. It might, through a committee selected for the purpose, examine likely solutions to the problems of union and draft a more conclusive form of constitution that will be acceptable to all the independent states.

The survival of free Africa, the extending independence of this continent, and the development towards that bright future on which our hopes and endeavours are pinned, depend upon political unity.

Under a major political union of Africa there could emerge a United Africa, great and powerful, in which the territorial boundaries which are the relics of colonialism will become obsolete and superfluous, working for the complete and total mobilisation of the economic planning organisation under a unified political direction. The forces that unite us are far greater than the difficulties that divide us at present, and our goal must be the establishment of Africa's dignity, progress, and prosperity.

Proof is therefore positive that the continental union of Africa is an inescapable desideratum if we are determined to move forward to a realisation of our hopes and plans for creating a modern society which will give our peoples the opportunity to enjoy a full and satisfying life. The forces that unite us are intrinsic and greater than the superimposed influences that keep us apart. These are the forces that we must enlist and cement for the sake of the trusting millions who look to us, their leaders, to take them out of the poverty, ignorance and disorder left by colonialism into an ordered unity in which freedom and amity can flourish amidst plenty.

Here is a challenge which destiny has thrown out to the leaders of Africa. It is for us to grasp what is a golden opportunity to prove that the genius of the African people can surmount the separatist tendencies in sovereign nationhood by coming together speedily, for the sake of Africa's greater glory and infinite well-being, into a Union of African States.

Charter of the Organisation of African Unity (OAU), Addis Ababa, 25 May 1963, and Address to the Conference of African Heads of State and Government, 24 May 1963

In January 1963, six months before the Conference of Independent African States met in Addis Ababa, I sent proposals for the setting up of a unified political organisation to the heads of state and governments of all independent African states. The purpose was to provide a basis of discussion from which a positive programme of African unification could be formulated. The text, dated 1 January 1963, was as follows:

Your Excellency,

For some time now it has been the burning desire of the leaders and people of Africa to find a way of bringing about the unity of the African continent. Various attempts have been made recently to give expression to this great impulse. Thus, a Conference of Independent African States was held at Accra in April 1958, and the All-African People's Conference in December of the same year. In 1958, Guinea and Ghana came together and formed a union which was regarded as a nucleus for the achievement of African unity. In an attempt to expand the basis of this nucleus, Guinea, Ghana, and Liberia, met at Sanniquellie in 1959, where further advances were made in the concept of African unity. Later, after the break-up of the Mali Federation, the Republic of Mali joined Guinea and Ghana to form a union, which was reconstituted into the Union of African States. A further step towards the consolidation of African unity was taken when Guinea, the United Arab Republic, Libya, Mali, Morocco, Algeria and Ghana met at Casablanca in January 1961, to consider joint measures for dealing with the Congo problem and other dangers which threatened the freedom and independence of Africa. These efforts were calculated to stress the importance of political unity for dealing with the problems that confront the independent African states.

Shortly afterwards, the Monrovia and Brazzaville Conferences also took place. All these conferences, as indicated in their respective charters, were clear manifestations of the desire to achieve African unity, which is the goal to which all of us greatly aspire. Indeed, there is a general feeling throughout Africa today that development into separate political or economic groupings is unfortunate, since it tends, among other things, to a dispersal of energy, resources and general inter-state or inter-territorial co-operative effort. We must therefore express concern not only about territorial balkanisation but also regional balkanisation of Africa. If we are to fulfil our purpose of achieving continental unity and averting foreign oppression, interference, and intimidation, we must all work together and devise a common political framework within which the existing independent African states and others soon to become independent can find free scope for development. For this reason, I am convinced that we the leaders and people of Africa have a duty, at this serious and critical moment in the history of our continent, to adopt concrete measures that can unite us all – states and territories of our continent – without necessarily involving changes in the territorial boundaries of the independent African states or in their national sovereignty.

I hope that by this proposal we shall be able to steer clear of the superficial differences among us, which those who seek to dominate us in their interests have successfully emphasised and exaggerated in the past. I accordingly venture to put forward the following views for earnest and serious consideration.

I am convinced that under such a proposal frontier disputes, economic difficulties, political disagreements among African states and neo-colonialism, still hanging like the sword of Damocles over the independent African states, can all be resolved within the framework of a Union Government of African States. In a united Africa there would be no frontier claims between Ethiopia and Somalia, Zanzibar and Kenya, Guinea and Liberia, Mauritania and Mali, or between Togo and Ghana, because we would regard ourselves as one great continental family within a Union of African States. There is no time to waste, for we must unite now or perish, since no single African state is large or powerful enough to stand on its own against the unbridled imperialist exploitation of her men and resources and the growing complexities of the modern world.

1. A Common Foreign Policy and Diplomacy

There are some 60 odd states in Africa, about 32 of which are at present independent. The burden of separate diplomatic representation by each state on the continent of Africa alone would be crushing, not to mention representation outside Africa. The desirability of a common foreign policy which will enable us to speak with one voice in the councils of the world is so obvious, vital and imperative that comment is hardly necessary.

2. Common Continental Planning for Economic and Industrial Development of Africa

The resources of Africa can be used to the best advantage and the maximum benefit to all only if they are set within an overall framework of a continental planned development. An overall economic plan, covering an Africa united on a continental basis would increase our total industrial and economic power. We should therefore be thinking seriously now of ways and means of building up a Common Market of a United Africa and not allow ourselves to be lured by the dubious advantages of association with the so-called European Common Market.

We in Africa have looked outward too long for development of our economy and transportation. Let us begin to look inwards into the African continent for all aspects of its development. Our communications were devised under colonial rule to stretch outwards towards Europe and elsewhere, instead of developing internally between our cities and states. Political unity should give us the power and will to change all this. We in Africa have untold agricultural, mineral and water-power resources. These almost fabulous resources can be fully exploited and utilised in the interest of Africa and the African people, only if we develop them within a Union Government of African States.

3. A Common Currency, a Monetary Zone and a Central Bank of Issue

The advantages of this would be inestimable since monetary transactions between our several states would be facilitated and the pace of financial activity generally quickened. A central bank of issue is an inescapable necessity, in view of the need to orientate the economy of Africa and place it beyond the reach of foreign control.

4. A Common Defence System

Because we do not yet have a common system of defence, some African countries feel insecure and have therefore naturally entered into defence pacts with foreign governments. This endangers the security of all Africa.

The present practice whereby each state tries to establish its own individual defence system is intolerably expensive at a time when money is most urgently needed for the compelling task of education and other social welfare activities. Some attempt has already been made by the Casablanca Powers and the Afro-Malagasy Union in the matter of common defence, but how much better and stronger would it be, if instead of two such ventures there were one overall (Land, Sea and Air) Defence Command for Africa?

To implement the above proposal, a Central Political Organisation with its own constitution would have to be drawn up as a matter of urgency. It is suggested that this Union of African States should consist of an upper house and a lower house. Each state would have the right to send two representatives to the upper house, irrespective of the size and population of the state; while admission to the lower house would be secured on the basis of proportional representation in accordance with the population of each state. This proposal does not in any way interfere with the internal constitutional arrangements of any state. The overriding concern of the Union of African States would be to give political direction in regard to the implementations of the proposals mentioned above. From the standpoint of accessibility, the Central African Republic could provide the most central site for the Union Government, if the right approach is made.

This message has been addressed to all heads of state and governments of the independent African states. I trust therefore that when the foreign ministers of the independent African states meet, this could form the basis of discussion from which a positive programme of African unity could be formulated. Such understanding among the leaders of Africa will fling wide open the gates of continental unity, and Africa will be able to speak with one voice and some authority to the world. I am sure that we can achieve political unity without sacrificing our sovereignties.

Representatives of 31 independent African states attended the conference in Addis Ababa in May 1963, and signed the Charter of the Organisation of African Unity (OAU) on 25 May. It seemed that at last the foundation had been laid for the freedom and political unification of Africa, and that the existing blocs and political groupings were at an end. It was with these high hopes that I addressed the conference on the 24 May 1963.

ADDRESS TO THE CONFERENCE OF AFRICAN HEADS OF STATE AND GOVERNMENT, 24 MAY 1963

Your Excellencies, Colleagues, Brothers and Friends,

I am happy to be here in Addis Ababa on this most historic occasion. I bring with me the hopes and fraternal greetings of the government and people of Ghana to His Imperial Majesty Haile Selassie and to all heads of African states gathered here in this ancient capital in this momentous period in our history. Our objective is African Union now. There is no time to waste. We must unite now or perish. I am confident that by our concerted effort and determination we shall lay here the foundations for a continental Union of African States.

At the first gathering of African heads of state, to which I had the honour of playing host, there were representatives of eight independent states, only. Today, five years later, here at Addis Ababa, we meet as the representatives of no less than 32 states, the guests of His Imperial Majesty, Haile Selassie the First, and the government and people of Ethiopia. To his Imperial Majesty, I wish to express, on behalf of the government and people of Ghana my deep appreciation for a most cordial welcome and generous hospitality.

The increase in our number in this short space of time is open testimony to the indomitable and irresistible surge of our peoples for independence. It is also a token of the revolutionary speed of world events in the latter half of this century. In the task which is before us of unifying our continent, we must fall in with that pace or be left behind. The task cannot be attacked in the tempo of any other age than our own. To fall behind the unprecedented momentum of actions and events in our time will be to court failure and our own undoing.

A whole continent has imposed a mandate upon us to lay the foundation of our union at this conference. It is our responsibility to execute this mandate by creating here and now the formula upon which the requisite superstructure may be erected.

On this continent it has not taken us long to discover that the struggle against colonialism does not end with the attainment of national independence. Independence is only the prelude to a new and more involved struggle for the right to conduct our own economic and social affairs; to construct our society according to our aspirations, unhampered by crushing and humiliating neo-colonialist controls and interference.

From the start, we have been threatened with frustration where rapid change is imperative and with instability where sustained effort and ordered rule are indispensable.

No sporadic act nor pious resolution can resolve our present problems. Nothing will be of avail, except the united act of a united Africa. We have already reached the stage where we must unite or sink into that condition which has made Latin America the unwilling and distressed prey of imperialism after one and a half centuries of political independence.

As a continent we have emerged into independence in a different age, with imperialism grown stronger, more ruthless and experienced, and more dangerous in its international associations. Our economic advancement demands the end of colonialist and neo-colonialist domination in Africa.

But just as we understood that the shaping of our national destinies required of each of us our political independence and bent all our strength to this attainment, so we must recognise that our economic independence resides in our African Union and requires the same concentration upon the political achievement.

The unity of our continent, no less than our separate independence, will be delayed, if indeed, we do not lose it, by hobnobbing with colonialism. African unity is, above all, a political kingdom which can only be gained by political means. The social and economic development of Africa will come only within the political kingdom, not the other way round. The USA, the USSR, were the political decisions of revolutionary peoples before they became mighty realities of social power and material wealth.

How, except by our united efforts, will the richest and still enslaved parts of our continent be freed from colonial occupation and become available to us for the total development of our continent? Every step in the decolonisation of our continent has brought greater resistance in those areas where colonial garrisons are available to colonialism, and you all here know that.

This is the great design of the imperialist interests that buttress colonialism and neo-colonialism, and we would be deceiving ourselves in the most cruel way were we to regard their individual actions as separate and unrelated. When Portugal violates Senegal's border, when [Hendrik] Verwoerd allocates one-seventh of South Africa's budget to military and police, when France builds as part of her defence policy an interventionist force that can intervene, especially in French-speaking Africa, when [Roy] Welensky talks of Southern Rhodesia joining South Africa, when Britain sends arms to South Africa, it is all part of a carefully calculated pattern working towards a single end: the continued enslavement of our still dependent brothers and an onslaught upon the independence of our sovereign African states.[53]

Do we have any other weapon against this design but our unity? Is not our unity essential to guard our own freedom as well as to win freedom for our oppressed brothers, the freedom fighters? Is it not unity alone that can weld us into an effective force, capable of creating our own progress and making our valuable contribution to world peace? Which independent African state, which of you here will claim that its financial structure and banking institutions are fully harnessed to its national development? Which will claim that its material resources and human energies are available for its own national aspirations? Which will disclaim a substantial measure of disappointment and disillusionment in its agricultural and urban development?

In independent Africa we are already re-experiencing the instability and frustration which existed under colonial rule. We are fast learning that political independence is not enough to rid us of the consequences of colonial rule.

The movement of the masses of the people of Africa for freedom from that kind of rule was not only a revolt against the conditions which it imposed. Our people supported us in our fight for independence because they believed that African governments could cure the ills of the past in a way which could never be accomplished under colonial rule. If, therefore, now that we are independent we allow the same conditions to exist that existed in colonial days, all the resentment which overthrew colonialism will be mobilised against us.

---

53 *Editor's note*: Hendrik Verwoerd was prime minister of South Africa from 1958–1966 and is considered by many to have been the architect of apartheid. Roy Welensky was the prime minister of the Federation of Rhodesia and Nyasaland (which is modern-day Malawi, Zambia and Zimbabwe) from 1956–1963.

The resources are there. It is for us to marshal them in the active service of our people. Unless we do this by our concerted efforts, within the framework of our combined planning, we shall not progress at the tempo demanded by today's events and the mood of our people. The symptoms of our troubles will grow, and the troubles themselves become chronic. It will then be too late even for Pan-African unity to secure for us stability and tranquility in our labours for a continent of social justice and material well-being. Unless we establish African unity now, we who are sitting here today shall tomorrow be the victims and martyrs of neo-colonialism.

There is evidence on every side that the imperialists have not withdrawn from our affairs. There are times, as in the Congo, when their interference is manifest. But generally, it is covered up under the clothing of many agencies, which meddle in our domestic affairs, to foment dissension within our borders and create an atmosphere of tension and political instability. As long as we do not do away with the root causes of discontent, we lend aid to these neocolonialist forces, and shall become our own executioners. We cannot ignore the teachings of history.

Our continent is probably the richest in the world for minerals and industrial and agricultural primary materials. From the Congo alone, Western firms exported copper, rubber, cotton, and other goods to the value of $2,773 million in the ten years between 1945 and 1955, and from South Africa, Western gold mining companies have drawn a profit, in the six years between 1947 and 1951, of $814 million. Our continent certainly exceeds all the others in potential hydroelectric power, which some experts assess as 42 per cent of the world's total. What need is there for us to remain hewers of wood and drawers of water for the industrialised areas of the world?

It is said, of course, that we have no capital, no industrial skill, no communications and no internal markets, and that we cannot even agree among ourselves how best to utilise our resources for our own social needs. Yet all the stock exchanges in the world are pre-occupied with Africa's gold, diamonds, uranium, platinum, copper and iron ores. Our capital flows out in streams to irrigate the whole system of Western economy. Fifty-two per cent of the gold in Fort Knox at this moment, where the USA stores its bullion, is believed to have originated from our shores. Africa provides more than 60 per cent of the world's gold. A great deal of the uranium for nuclear power, of copper for electronics, of titanium for supersonic projectiles, of iron and steel for heavy industries, of other minerals and raw materials for lighter industries – the basic economic might of the foreign powers – come from our continent.

Experts have estimated that the Congo Basin alone can produce enough food crops to satisfy the requirements of nearly half the population of the whole world and here we sit talking about regionalism, talking about gradualism, talking about step by step. Are you afraid to tackle the bull by the horn?

For centuries Africa has been the milch cow of the Western world. Was it not our continent that helped the Western world to build up its accumulated wealth?

It is true that we are now throwing off the yoke of colonialism as fast as we can, but our success in this direction is equally matched by an intense effort on the part of imperialism to continue the exploitation of our resources by creating divisions among us.

When the colonies of the American continent sought to free themselves from imperialism in the 18th century there was no threat of neo-colonialism in the sense in which we know it today in Africa. The American states were therefore free to form and fashion the unity which was best suited to their needs and to frame a Constitution to hold their unity together without any form of interference from external sources. We, however, are having to grapple with outside interventions. How much more, then do we need to come together in the African unity that alone can save us from the clutches of neo-colonialism and imperialism.

We have the resources. It was colonialism in the first place that prevented us from accumulating the effective capital; but we ourselves have failed to make full use of our power in independence to mobilise our resources for the most effective take-off into thoroughgoing economic and social development. We have been too busy nursing our separate states to understand fully the basic need of our union, rooted in common purpose, common planning and common endeavour. A union that ignores these fundamental necessities will be but a sham. It is only by uniting our productive capacity and the resultant production that we can amass capital.

And once we start, the momentum will increase. With capital controlled by our own banks, harnessed to our own true industrial and agricultural development, we shall make our advance. We shall accumulate machinery and establish steel works, iron foundries and factories; we shall link the various states of our continent with communications by land, sea and air. We shall cable from one place to another, phone from one place to the other and around the world with our hydro-electric power; we shall drain marshes and swamps, clear infested areas, feed the under-nourished, and rid our people of parasites and disease. It is within the possibility of science and technology to make even the Sahara bloom into a vast field with verdant vegetation for agricultural and industrial developments. We shall harness the radio, television, giant printing presses to lift our people from the dark recesses of illiteracy.

A decade ago, these would have been visionary words, the fantasies of an idle dreamer. But this is the age in which science has transcended the limits of the material world, and technology has invaded the silences of nature. Time and space have been reduced to unimportant abstractions. Giant machines make roads, clear forests, dig dams, lay out aerodromes; monster trucks and planes distribute goods; huge laboratories manufacture drugs; complicated geological surveys are made; mighty power stations are built; colossal factories erected – all at an incredible speed. The world is no longer moving through bush paths or on camels and donkeys.

We cannot afford to pace our needs, our development, our security, to the gait of camels and donkeys. We cannot afford not to cut down the overgrown bush of outmoded attitudes that obstruct our path to the modern open road of the widest and earliest achievement of economic independence and the raising up of the lives of our people to the highest level.

Even for other continents lacking the resources of Africa, this is the age that sees the end of human want. For us it is a simple matter of grasping with certainty our heritage by using the political might of unity: All we need to do is to develop with our united strength the enormous resources of our continent. A united Africa will provide a stable field of foreign investment, which will be encouraged as long as it does not behave inimically to our African interests. For such investment would add by its enterprises to the development of the continental national economy, employment and training of our people, and will be welcome to Africa. In dealing with a united Africa, investors will no longer have to weigh with concern the risks of negotiating with governments in one period which may not exist in the very next period. Instead of dealing or negotiating with so many separate states at a time they will be dealing with one united government pursuing a harmonised continental policy.

What is the alternative to this? If we falter at this stage, and let time pass for neo-colonialism to consolidate its position on this continent, what will be the fate of our people who have put their trust in us? What will be the fate of our freedom fighters? What will be the fate of other African territories that are not yet free?

Unless we can establish great industrial complexes in Africa – which we can only do in a united Africa – we must leave our peasantry to the mercy of foreign cash crop markets, and face the same unrest which overthrew the colonialists. What use to the farmer is education and mechanisation, what use is even capital for development, unless we can ensure for him a fair price and a ready market? What has the peasant, worker and farmer gained from political independence, unless we can ensure for him a fair return for his labour and a higher standard of living?

Unless we can establish great industrial complexes in Africa, what have the urban worker, and those peasants on overcrowded land, gained from political independence? If they are to remain unemployed or in unskilled occupation, what will avail them the better facilities for education, technical training, energy and ambition which independence enables us to provide?

There is hardly any African state without a frontier problem with its adjacent neighbours. It would be futile for me to enumerate them because they are already so familiar to us all. But let me suggest to Your Excellencies that this fatal relic of colonialism will drive us to war against one another as our unplanned and uncoordinated industrial development expands, just as happened in Europe. Unless we succeed in arresting the danger through mutual understanding on fundamental issues and through African unity, which will render existing boundaries obsolete and superfluous, we shall have fought in vain for independence. Only African unity can heal this festering sore of boundary disputes between our various states.

Your Excellencies, the remedy for these ills is ready in our hands. It stares us in the face at every customs barrier, it shouts to us from every African heart. By creating a true political union of all the independent states of Africa, with executive powers for political direction we can tackle hopefully every emergency, every enemy, and every complexity. This is not because we are a race of supermen, but because we have emerged in the age of science and technology in which poverty, ignorance and disease are no longer the masters, but the retreating foes of mankind. We have emerged in the age of socialised planning, where production and distribution are not governed by chaos, greed and self-interest, but by social needs. Together with the rest of mankind, we have awakened from utopian dreams to pursue practical blueprints for progress and social justice.

Above all, we have emerged at a time when a continental land mass like Africa with its population approaching 300 million are necessary to the economic capitalisation and profitability of modern productive methods and techniques. Not one of us working singly and individually can successfully attain the fullest development. Certainly, in the circumstances, it will not be possible to give adequate assistance to sister states trying, against the most difficult conditions, to improve their economic and social structures. Only a united Africa functioning under a union government can forcefully mobilise the material and moral resources of our separate countries and apply them efficiently and energetically to bring a rapid change in the conditions of our people.

If we do not approach the problems in Africa with a common front and a common purpose, we shall be haggling and wrangling among ourselves until we are colonised again and become the tools of a far greater colonialism than we suffered hitherto.

Unite we must. Without necessarily sacrificing our sovereignties, big or small, we can here and now forge a political union based on defence, foreign affairs and diplomacy, and a common citizenship, an African currency, an African Monetary Zone and an African Central Bank. We must unite in order to achieve the full liberation of our continent. We need a common defence system with an African High Command to ensure the stability and security of Africa.

We have been charged with this sacred task by our own people, and we cannot betray their trust by failing them. We will be mocking the hopes of our people if we show the slightest hesitation or delay in tackling realistically this question of African unity.

The supply of arms or other military aid to the colonial oppressors in Africa must be regarded not only as aid in the vanquishment of the freedom fighters battling for their African independence, but as an act of aggression against the whole of Africa. How can we meet this aggression except by the full weight of our united strength?

Many of us have made non-alignment an article of faith on this continent. We have no wish, and no intention of being drawn into the Cold War. But with the present weakness and insecurity of our states in the context of world politics, the search for bases and spheres of influence brings the Cold War into Africa with its danger of nuclear warfare. Africa should be declared a nuclear-free zone and freed from Cold War exigencies. But we cannot make this demand mandatory unless we support it from a position of strength to be found only in our unity.

Instead, many independent African states are involved by military pacts with the former colonial powers. The stability and security which such devices seek to establish are illusory, for the metropolitan powers seize the opportunity to support their neo-colonialist controls by direct military involvement. We have seen how the neo-colonialists use their bases to entrench themselves and even to attack neighbouring independent states. Such bases are centres of tension and potential danger spots of military conflict. They threaten the security not only of the country in which they are situated but of neighbouring countries as well.

How can we hope to make Africa a nuclear-free zone and independent of Cold War pressure with such military involvement on our continent? Only by counter-balancing a common defence force with a common desire for an Africa untrammelled by foreign dictation or military and nuclear presence. This will require an all-embracing African High Command, especially if the military pacts with the imperialists are to be renounced. It is the only way we can break these direct links between the colonialism of the past and the neo-colonialism which disrupts us today.

We do not want nor do we visualise an African High Command in the terms of the power politics that now rule a great part of the world, but as an essential and indispensable instrument for ensuring stability and security in Africa.

We need unified economic planning for Africa. Until the economic power of Africa is in our hands, the masses can have no real concern and no real interest for safeguarding our security, for ensuring the stability of our regimes, and for bending their strength to the fulfilment of our ends. With our united resources, energies and talents we have the means, as soon as we show the will, to transform the economic structures of our individual states from poverty to that of wealth, from inequality to the satisfaction of popular needs. Only on a continental basis shall we be able to plan the proper utilisation of all our resources for the full development of our continent.

How else will we retain our own capital for our development? How else will we establish an internal market for our own industries? By belonging to different economic zones, how will we break down the currency and trading barriers between African states, and how will the economically stronger amongst us be able to assist the weaker and less developed states?

It is important to remember that independent financing and independent development cannot take place without an independent currency. A currency system that is backed by the resources of a foreign state is ipso facto subject to the trade and financial arrangements of that foreign country.

Because we have so many customs and currency barriers as a result of being subject to the different currency systems of foreign powers, this has served to widen the gap between us in Africa. How, for example, can related communities and families trade with, and support one another successfully, if they find themselves divided by national boundaries and currency restrictions? The only alternative open to them in these circumstances is to use smuggled currency and enrich national and international racketeers and crooks who prey upon our financial and economic difficulties.

No independent African state today, by itself, has a chance to follow an independent course of economic development, and many of us who have tried to do this have been almost ruined or have had to return to the fold of the former colonial rulers. This position will not change unless we have a unified policy working at the continental level. The first step towards our cohesive economy would be a unified monetary zone, with, initially, an agreed common parity for our currencies. To facilitate this arrangement, Ghana would change to a decimal system. When we find that the arrangement of a fixed common parity is working successfully, there would seem to be no reason for not instituting one common currency and a single bank of issue. With a common currency from one common bank of issue, we should be able to stand erect on our own feet because such an arrangement would be fully backed by the combined national products of the states composing the union. After all, the purchasing power of money depends on productivity and the productive exploitation of the natural, human and physical resources of the nation.

While we are assuring our stability by a common defence system, and our economy is being orientated beyond foreign control by a common currency, monetary zone and central bank of issue, we can investigate the resources of our continent. We can begin to ascertain whether in reality we are the richest, and not, as we have been taught to believe, the poorest among the continents. We can determine whether we possess the largest potential in hydroelectric power, and whether we can harness it and other sources of energy to our own industries. We can proceed to plan our industrialisation on a continental scale, and to build up a common market for nearly 300 million people.

Common continental planning for the industrial and agricultural development of Africa is a vital necessity. So many blessings flow from our unity; so many disasters must follow on our continued disunity, that our failure to unite today will not be attributed by posterity only to faulty reasoning and lack of courage, but to our capitulation before the forces of neo-colonialism and imperialism.

The hour of history which has brought us to this assembly is a revolutionary hour. It is the hour of decision. For the first time, the economic imperialism which menaces us is itself challenged by the irresistible will of our people.

The masses of the people of Africa are crying for unity. The people of Africa call for the breaking down of the boundaries that keep them apart. They demand an end to the border disputes between sister African states – disputes that arise out of the artificial barriers raised by colonialism. It was colonialism's purpose that divided us. It was colonialism's purpose that left us with our border irredentism, that rejected our ethnic and cultural fusion.

Our people call for unity so that they may not lose their patrimony in the perpetual service of neo-colonialism. In their fervent push for unity, they understand that only its realisation will give full meaning to their freedom and our African independence.

It is this popular determination that must move us on to a Union of independent African states. In delay lies danger to our well-being, to our very existence as free states. It has been suggested that our approach to unity should be gradual, that it should go piecemeal. This point of view conceives of Africa as a static entity with 'frozen' problems which can be eliminated one by one and when all have been cleared then we can come together and say: 'Now all is well. Let us now unite.' This view takes no account of the impact of external pressures. Nor does it take cognisance of the danger that delay can deepen our isolations and exclusiveness; that it can enlarge our differences and set us drifting further and further apart into the net of neo-colonialism, so that our union will become nothing but a fading hope, and the great design of Africa's full redemption will be lost, perhaps, forever.

The view is also expressed that our difficulties can be resolved simply by a greater collaboration through co-operative association in our inter-territorial relationships. This way of looking at our problems denies a proper conception of their inter-relationship and mutuality. It denies faith in a future for African advancement in African independence. It betrays a sense of solution only in continued reliance upon external sources through bilateral agreements for economic and other forms of aid.

The fact is that although we have been co-operating and associating with one another in various fields of common endeavour even before colonial times, this has not given us the continental identity and the political and economic force which would help us to deal effectively with the complicated problems confronting us in Africa today. As far as foreign aid is concerned, a united Africa would be in a more favourable position to attract assistance from foreign sources. There is the far more compelling advantage which this arrangement offers, in that aid will come from anywhere to a united Africa because our bargaining power would become infinitely greater. We shall no longer be dependent upon aid from restricted sources. We shall have the world to choose from.

What are we looking for in Africa? Are we looking for charters, conceived in the light of the UN example? A type of UN organisation whose decisions are framed on the basis of resolutions that in our experience have sometimes been ignored by member states? Where groupings are formed and pressures develop in accordance with the interest of the groups concerned? Or is it intended that Africa should be turned into a loose organisation of states on the model of the Organisation of American States, in which the weaker states within it can be at the mercy of the stronger or more powerful ones politically or economically and all at the mercy of some powerful outside nation or group of nations? Is this the kind of association we want for ourselves in the united Africa we all speak of with such feeling and emotion?

Your Excellencies, permit me to ask: Is this the kind of framework we desire for our united Africa? An arrangement which in future could permit Ghana or Nigeria or the Sudan, or Liberia, or Egypt or Ethiopia for example, to use pressure, which either superior economic or political influence gives, to dictate the flow and direction of trade from, say, Burundi or Togo or Nyasaland to Mozambique or Madagascar? We all want a united Africa, united not only in our concept of what unity connotes, but united in our common desire to move forward together in dealing with all the problems that can best be solved only on a continental basis.

When the first Congress of the USA met many years ago at Philadelphia one of the delegates sounded the first chord of unity by declaring that they had met in 'a state of nature.' In other words, they were not in Philadelphia as Virginians, or Pennsylvanians, but simply as Americans. This reference to themselves as Americans was in those days a new and strange experience. May I dare to assert equally on this occasion. Your Excellencies, that we meet here today not as Ghanaians, Guineans, Egyptians, Algerians, Moroccans, Malians, Liberians, Congolese or Nigerians but as Africans. Africans united in our resolve to remain here until we have agreed on the basic principles of a new compact of unity among ourselves which guarantees for us and our future a new arrangement of continental government.

If we succeed in establishing a new set of principles as the basis of a new charter or statute for the establishment of continental unity for Africa and the creation of social and political progress for our people, then, in my view, this conference should mark the end of our various groupings and regional blocs. But if we fail and let this grand and historic opportunity slip by then we shall give way to greater dissension and division among us for which the people of Africa will never forgive us. And the popular and progressive forces and movements within Africa will condemn us. I am sure therefore that we shall not fail them.

I have spoken at some length, Your Excellencies, because it is necessary for us all to explain not only to one another present here but also to our people who have entrusted to us the fate and destiny of Africa. We must therefore not leave this place until we have set up effective machinery for achieving African unity. To this end, I propose for your consideration the following:

As a first step, Your Excellencies, a declaration of principles uniting and binding us together and to which we must all faithfully and loyally adhere, and laying the foundations of unity should be set down. And there should also be a formal declaration that all the independent African states here and now agree to the establishment of a Union of African States.

As a second and urgent step for the realisation of the unification of Africa, an All-Africa Committee of Foreign Ministers must be set up now, and that before we rise from this conference a date should be fixed for them to meet.

This committee should establish on behalf of the heads of our governments, a permanent body of officials and experts to work out a machinery for the Union Government of Africa. This body of officials and experts should be made up of two of the best brains from each independent African state. The various charters of the existing groupings and other relevant documents could also be submitted to the officials and experts. A praesidium consisting of the heads of governments of the independent African states should be called upon to meet and adopt a Constitution and other recommendations which will launch the Union Government of Africa.

We must also decide on a location where this body of officials and experts will work as the new headquarters or capital of our Union Government. Some central place in Africa might be the fairest suggestion, either at Bangui in the Central African Republic or Leopoldville in Congo. My colleagues may have other proposals. The Committee of Foreign Ministers, officials and experts should be empowered to establish:

1. a commission to frame a Constitution for a Union Government of African States;

2. a commission to work out a continent-wide plan for a unified or common economic and industrial programme for Africa; this plan should include proposals for setting up:
   a. A Common Market for Africa;
   b. An African Currency;
   c. An African Monetary Zone;
   d. An African Central Bank, and
   e. A continental communication system.

3. a commission to draw up details for a Common Foreign Policy and Diplomacy.

4. a commission to produce plans for a Common System of Defence.

5. a commission to make proposals for a Common African Citizenship.

These commissions will report to the Committee of Foreign Ministers who should in turn submit within six months of this conference their recommendations to the praesidium. The praesidium meeting in conference at the union headquarters will consider and approve the recommendations of the Committee of Foreign Ministers.

In order to provide funds immediately for the work of the permanent officials and experts of the headquarters of the union, I suggest that a special committee be set up to work out a budget for this.

Your Excellencies, with these steps, I submit, we shall be irrevocably committed to the road which will bring us to a Union Government for Africa. Only a united Africa with central political direction can successfully give effective material and moral support to our freedom fighters, in Southern Rhodesia, Angola, Mozambique, South-West Africa, Bechuanaland, Swaziland, Basutoland, Portuguese Guinea, etc., and of course South Africa. All Africa must be liberated now. It is therefore imperative for us here and now to establish a liberation bureau for African freedom fighters. The main object of this bureau, to which all governments should subscribe, should be to accelerate the emancipation of the rest of Africa still under colonial and racialist domination and oppression. It should be our joint responsibility to finance and support this bureau. On their successful attainment of Independence these territories will automatically join our Union of African States, and thus strengthen the fabric of Mother Africa. We shall leave here, having laid the foundation for our unity. Your Excellencies, nothing could be more fitting than that the unification of Africa should be born on the soil of the state which stood for centuries as the symbol of African independence.

Let us return to our people of Africa not with empty hands and with high-sounding resolutions, but with the firm hope and assurance that at long last African unity has become a reality. We shall thus begin the triumphant march to the kingdom of the African Personality, and to a continent of prosperity, and progress, of equality and justice and of work and happiness. This shall be our victory – victory within a continental government of a Union of African States. This victory will give our voice greater force in world affairs and enable us to throw our weight more forcibly on the side of peace. The world needs peace in which the greatest advantage can be taken of the benefits of science and technology. Many of the world's present ills are to be found in the insecurity and fear engendered by the threat of nuclear war. Especially do the new nations need peace in order to make their way into a life of economic and social well-being amid an atmosphere of security and stability that will promote moral, cultural and spiritual fulfilment.

If we in Africa can achieve the example of a continent knit together in common policy and common purpose, we shall have made the finest possible contribution to that peace for which all men and women thirst today, and which will lift once and forever the deepening shadow of global destruction from mankind, Ethiopia shall stretch forth her hands unto God.

AFRICA MUST UNITE.

Speech Delivered at the Summit Conference of the Organisation of African Unity, Cairo 19th July 1964

The second Summit Conference of the OAU took place in Cairo from the 17–21 July 1964. The OAU, just over a year old, was already in difficulties. There was deep dissatisfaction among freedom fighters at the ineffectiveness of the OAU Liberation Committee. They complained of lack of supplies and of training facilities. Serious disputes had broken out between Ethiopia and Somalia; between Morocco and Algeria; and between Somalia and Kenya. There had been army mutinies in Tanzania, Uganda, and Kenya, which were suppressed not with the assistance of troops from a sister African state, but with the help of British troops. Foreign interference in the Congo's internal affairs was continuing to cause untold misery and suffering to the Congolese people. Mozambique, Angola, Guinea-Bissau, Bechuanaland, Basutoland, Swaziland, and other territories in Africa were still suffering under colonialism. In Southern Rhodesia, a white settler minority regime was still refusing to allow even the most elementary of human rights to the vast majority of the population. And while African disunity and balkanisation continued, virtually no improvement was being made in the living conditions of the African masses. Only foreign interests, and with them, the interests of the African bourgeoisie, flourished.

In the light of all that had taken place since the foundation of the OAU, I was more than ever convinced that the creation of a Union Government for Africa provided the only solution for Africa's continued political instability and underdevelopment. The OAU as established in Addis Ababa in 1963 had been shown to be unable to deal effectively with the problems facing it, and was by its very ineffectiveness blocking the advance of the African Revolution, and thereby aiding the forces of reaction. The whole purpose of my address to the conference on 19 July 1964 was, therefore, to stress the urgent need for the immediate setting up of a union government for Africa. The specific areas of unified action which I had in mind were: defence, foreign policy and economic development, the last implying a common currency for Africa.

To my great disappointment, it was clear from the speeches of some of the conference members that there were some who were still not ready for such a radical step to be taken. There was general agreement on the need for a union government, but it was decided that the whole matter should be examined by specialised commissions of the OAU, and that the question should be discussed again at the next summit conference which it was agreed should be held in Accra in 1965.

PROPOSALS FOR A UNION GOVERNMENT OF AFRICA

Mr Chairman,

In the year that has passed since we met at Addis Ababa and established the OAU, I have had no reason to change my mind about the concrete proposals which I made to you then, or about the reasons I gave for my conviction that only a union government can guarantee our survival. On the contrary, every hour since then, both in the world at large and on our own continent, has brought events to prove that our problems as individual states are insoluble except in the context of African unity, that our security as individual states is indivisible from the security of the whole continent, that the freedom of our compatriots still in foreign chains and under colonial rule awaits the redeeming might of an African continental government.

We took a monumental decision at the summit meeting in Addis Ababa last year. No amount of disappointment or impatience with the pace at which our charter has been implemented, can detract from the epoch-making and irrevocable nature of our decision to affirm the unity of our continent.

It was an act of faith, a recognition of reality. We forged the OAU fully conscious of all the difficulties facing our various states in committing themselves to common obligations. We have passed through the first year victorious over trials on our loyalty, and over hostile forces seeking to disrupt our unity.

Wherever and whenever the subsidiary bodies set up by the Addis Ababa Charter have met, the spirit of unity, of co-operation and goodwill have prevailed. On that score, none of us can complain; none of us have cause to doubt the strength and permanence of the spirit of unity which found its expression in our charter.

Yet, even more than last year, I must urge that the historical conditions in which African independence has emerged and the concrete manifestations of our weaknesses and difficulties, call for immense radical and urgent measures which the Addis Ababa conference did not fulfil. Measures which would have been accounted adequate for dealing with our problems a few years ago, cannot now meet the exigencies of the African revolution.

It is not single states or single continents which are undergoing de-colonialisation, but the greater portion of the world. It is not one empire which is expiring, but the whole system of imperialism which is at bay. It is not individual communities, but the whole of humanity which is demanding a different and better way of life for the world's growing millions.

Great positive and social revolutions have created mighty nations and empires, and the waves of those revolutions lap our shores no less than they do those of other continents. Great technological and industrial revolutions have transformed the economies of large portions of the world, and the waves of those revolutions will not stop short on the continent of Africa. A revolution in communications brings knowledge of every change in the world to the remotest corners of our continent. The world will not wait – nor will it move step by step, however much we may wish this.

It is against this background of great political, social, cultural, scientific, and technological revolutions that the emergence of African independence and the development of Africa must be viewed. None of us imagines that we can keep our own pace, immune from interference, isolated from the world's upsurges and revolutions. What differences there are between us arise from a difference in appreciation of the sense of urgency, not in the understanding we have of our tasks and responsibilities.

Time, indeed, is the crucial factor, for time acts for those who use it with purpose, and not for those who let it slip by. Those who do not use time as their agent, give the advantage to those who do.

When we met last year, we were at the beginning of an era of peaceful co-existence. The risk of a world war was abating, and the prospect of peaceful co-operation between the Great Powers appeared to bring to an end the struggle of foreign influences in Africa. We embraced non-alignment in order to escape involving ourselves in the prevailing Cold War politics. Instead, we have witnessed the menacing upsurge of imperialism and a revival of colonialism itself in Africa, and foreign interference and subversion in the internal affairs of our African states.

The one essential factor which united us at Addis Ababa – the overriding factor which made all differences and difficulties seem trivial and irrelevant – was the need to free that part of our continent which is still in the grip of imperialism. In spite of our charter, in spite of our common front at the United Nations and in other international gatherings, what have we witnessed?

Far from deterring the imperialists and neo-colonialists from giving support to the apartheid regime in South Africa and to the fascist regime in Portugal, the NATO (North Atlantic Treaty Organisation) powers, on the contrary, have poured and are pouring vast sums of money and vast armaments into the apartheid regime of South Africa and Portugal. Not only is South Africa being assisted to grow stronger economically and militarily, but the cruelty, repression and exploitation of our African brothers have reached new heights.

At this point I must comment on the activities of the Liberation Committee set up under the OAU at Addis Ababa last year, on which both we and the freedom fighters pinned so much hope. It is with great regret that I raise the matter at all, but I would be failing in my duty to the freedom fighters and to the cause of African liberation if I remain silent about the general dissatisfaction which exists regarding the functioning of this committee.

The frequent and persistent reports from freedom fighters about the shortcomings of the aid and facilities for training offered to them, make it impossible for the government of Ghana to turn over its contribution to this committee until a reorganisation has taken place for more effective and positive action.

This is not a situation in which individuals or individual governments can be held to blame. It is our first essay in a task of stupendous magnitude and with stupendous difficulties. But some of the failures of the committee are inexcusable because they were so unnecessary. It failed, for instance, to make the best use of our resources since some military specialists have been excluded on ideological grounds.

If the Liberation Committee had made effective use of the military experience of Egypt and of Algeria, where neo-colonialist interference and espionage have been frustrated and held at bay, we would have given freedom fighters the necessary help in their liberation struggle.

The choice of the Congo (Leopoldville) as a training base for freedom fighters was a logical one, and there was every reason to accept the offer of the Congolese government to provide offices and accommodation for the representatives of the liberation movements. Africa's freedom fighters should not, however, have been exposed to the espionage, intrigues, frustrations, and disappointments which they have experienced in the last eight months.

What could be the result of entrusting the training of freedom fighters against imperialism into the hands of an imperialist agent? Under the Liberation Committee set up at Addis Ababa, the freedom fighters had no real security, and were not provided with instruments for their struggle, nor were food, clothing and medicine given for the men in training. Thus, their training scheme collapsed within two months under the eyes of the Liberation Committee, and the freedom fighters became disappointed, disgruntled and frustrated.

I am giving you no more than the bare bones of the complaints of the freedom fighters. It will not avail us to have a lengthy postmortem over past failures. But these failures must be understood and acknowledged. The disappointment and frustration of the freedom fighters must not be dismissed as unreal or unreasonable. Not only the Liberation Committee, but all of us are to blame, for the way in which we allowed the Liberation Committee to let down the freedom fighters.

We dare not say that they could have done their work better until we have all done better. The enormous task of liberating our continent cannot be undertaken in a spirit of compromise and surrender.

By raising a threat at Addis Ababa and not being able to take effective action against apartheid and colonialism, we have worsened the plight of our kinsmen in Angola, Mozambique, Southern Rhodesia and South Africa. We have frightened the imperialists sufficiently to strengthen their defences and repression in Southern Africa, but we have not frightened them enough to abandon apartheid supremacy to its ill-fated doom.

It must be said that by merely making resolutions on African unity, and not achieving our goal of a Union Government of Africa, we have made our task of freeing the rest of the African continent harder and not easier.

The NATO powers have not been deterred one whit from sending all the arms needed by the [António de Oliveira] Salazar regime to keep down our kinsmen in its colonies. The Portuguese fascist regime has not made a single move to negotiate with the UN or with the nationalist forces. It has become more insolent, more mendacious, and more repressive since our conference in Addis Ababa.

What has gone wrong?

The imperialists regard our Charter of Unity as token unity; they will not respect it until it assumes the form of a union government. It is incredible that they will defy a united continent. But it is easy to understand that they do not believe that we will be able to accomplish the next stage – to organise and centralise our economic and military and political forces to wage a real struggle against apartheid, Portuguese fascism and those who support these evils with trade, investments, and arms.

We have not yet made the imperialists to believe that we can set our continent in order as a mighty economic force, capable of standing together as a united and progressive people.

Serious border disputes have broken out and disturbed our continent, since our last meeting. Fortunately, good sense and African solidarity have prevailed in all those instances. But the disputes have been smothered, not settled. The artificial divisions of African states are too numerous and irrational for real permanent and harmonious settlements to be reached, except within the framework of a continental union.

How, for example, can we prevent the people of Western Somalia, whose whole livelihood is cattle-grazing, from continuing to look for fresh fields for grazing by travelling beyond traditional barriers without bringing them into clashes with their compatriots in Ethiopia?

And yet, in a united Africa, Ethiopian land and Somalian land, even though they may be separately sovereign within the framework of a Union Government of Africa, will belong to a common pool which would assist the general development of cattle-rearing in that part of our continent, because there would be no artificial barriers to such development. The benefit of the development will be for the benefit of both Ethiopia and Somalia.

I said a little while ago, and I repeat, that the real border disputes will grow with the economic development and national strengthening of the African states as separate balkanised governmental units. That was the historical process of independent states in other continents. We cannot expect Africa, with its legacy of artificial borders, to follow any other course, unless we make a positive effort to arrest that danger now; and we can do so only under a union government. In other words, the careers, and ambitions of political leaders, on the one hand, and balkanised nationalism on the other, if allowed to grow and become entrenched, could constitute a brake on the unification of African states. The Balkan states of Europe are a lesson for us.

History has shown that where the Great Powers cannot colonise, they balkanise. This is what they did to the Austro-Hungarian Empire and this is what they have done and are doing in Africa. If we allow ourselves to be balkanised, we shall be re-colonised and be picked off one after the other.

Now is the time for Africa's political and economic unification.

By far the greatest wrong which the departing colonialists inflicted on us, and which we now continue to inflict on ourselves in our present state of disunity, was to leave us divided into economically unviable states which bear no possibility of real development. As long as the chief consideration of the industrial nations was our raw materials at their own prices, this policy made sense for them, if not for us.

Now that their technological impetus is such that they need Africa even more as a market for their manufactured goods than as a source of raw materials, our economic backwardness no longer makes sense for them any more than for us. The output of their great industrial complexes is no longer the primitive and simple implements like hoes and shovels. They now need vaster and more prosperous markets for heavy agricultural tractors and electronic machines. They wish to sell to us, not Ford motors propelled by magnetos or turbo-prop transport aircraft, but the latest in supersonic jets and atomic-powered merchant vessels. Which of us, trading separately in these highly developed market areas, can survive more than a year or two without remaining either economically backward, indebted, bankrupt or re-colonised?

There is much re-thinking on this score among the industrially advanced countries, although their outlook is obscured because their economies are still geared to monopolistic devices for getting hold of our oil and gas deposits, uranium, gold, diamonds and other raw materials, cheap, and selling their manufactured goods back to us at exorbitant prices.

The poverty of the developing world has become a blot on the ethics and common sense of the industrial nations. The recent United Nations Conference on Trade and Development (UNCTAD) was not organised by accident or solely by pressure from the developing nations. The growing economic gap between the two worlds spells misery for the developing countries, but it also threatens the industrialised nations with unemployment and with dangerous recessions and economic explosion.

We have reason to think that the imperialists themselves are in divided councils about the unity of Africa. They must remain ambivalent, however, as long as they retain direct control over Southern Africa and neo-colonialist control of the Congo. The vast mineral wealth of those territories represents profits which they cannot willingly give up, even for greater markets in the rest of Africa.

But a union government of Africa would end the dilemma of the industrialised nations, because inevitably that wealth will be converted into capital for the development of Africa. The fact that imperialism and neo-colonialism are in that dilemma should be for us the clearest indication of the course we must follow. We must unite for economic viability, first of all, and then to recover our mineral wealth in Southern Africa, so that our vast resources and capacity for development will bring prosperity for us and additional benefits for the rest of the world. That is why I have written elsewhere that the emancipation of Africa could be the emancipation of mankind.

Is there any need to point out again that we are potentially the world's richest continent, not only in mineral wealth, but also in hydro-electric power? The wealth of the Sahara is yet untapped; the waters and rivers of Tanganyika and Ethiopia are yet unharnessed. All the capital we need for the development of these regions flows out of Africa today in gold, diamonds, copper, uranium and other minerals from Southern Africa, Northern Rhodesia, the Congo and other parts of the continent. Every year in the Sahara and in other parts of Africa, new stores of mineral, chemical and petroleum wealth are discovered.

What is lacking for us in Africa, but the will and the courage to unite a divided but compact continent?

Today, in countless ways, our people learn that their poverty is not a curse from the gods or a burden imposed by the imperialists, but a political defect of our independence. The general realisation grows that independence is not enough without the unity of Africa, for that is the only road towards the economic emancipation and development of our continent.

We in Africa are living in the most momentous era of our history. In a little less than one decade, the majority of the territories in our continent have emerged from colonialism into sovereignty and independence. In a few years from now, we can envisage that all Africa will be free from colonial rule. Nothing can stem our onward march to independence and freedom.

While we have cause to rejoice in this achievement, our central problem as independent states is the fragmentation of our territories into little independent states and of our policies and programmes into a patchwork of conflicting objectives and unco-ordinated development and plans.

While the post-war years have seen a phenomenal rise in the prices of manufactured goods which we need to sustain progress and development in our states, the prices of the raw materials which we export to these countries have shown an alarmingly steady decline. So the disparity between the 'haves' or the highly developed nations and the 'have-nots' or developing nations, becomes inevitably wider and wider as our needs grow greater and greater. How can we resolve this tragic paradox, except by uniting our forces and working together in Africa as a team?

Let us look further back on the year that has just passed since we first met at Addis Ababa last year. Think of the unfortunate clashes between Algeria and Morocco, between Somalia and Ethiopia and between Somalia and Kenya which nearly damaged and disrupted our new spirit of understanding and unity. If we had lived within a continental federal government in which the fortunes and fate of one were the fortunes and fate of all, could we have been drawn into such bloodshed with needless loss of precious African lives?

What shall I say of the military upheavals and mutinies in our sister states of Tanganyika, Uganda, and Kenya? While no one among us here can tolerate indiscipline and mutiny in our armies, which of us was happy to learn that in their hour of need, our brothers were compelled to resort to the use of foreign troops – the troops of a former colonial power, at that – to bring these disturbances under control. Before the damage was completely done, our brothers were able to send away these foreign troops and, in one case, called for the assistance of troops from a sister African state.

Surely, these events have a dear lesson for us all! How can we maintain the safety and security of our respective states as our responsibilities increase and our problems become more complex, except through a united defence arrangement which will invest us with the effective and powerful means for joint action at short notice?

Last year at Addis Ababa, I gave the warning that if we did not come together as speedily as possible under a union government, there would be border clashes and our people, in their desperation to get the good things of life, would revolt against authority. Subsequent events have fully endorsed that warning.

Look at events in the Congo. Why did they remain so confused, so frustrating and even so tragic for so long? If we had all been jointly responsible for bringing our brothers in the Congo the assistance they needed in their hour of travail, who would have dared to interfere from outside Africa in Congolese affairs? Instead of this, what did we see in the Congo?

On the one hand, internal disagreements and discord, endless manoeuvring for positions among the political leaders, and even the tragedy of fratricidal strife. On the other hand, foreign intervention and pressures, intrigues and coercion, subversion, and cajolery.

In all this confusion, the power of imperialism has a fertile ground. It even dares to use openly certain African states to promote its selfish plans for the exploitation and degradation of the Congo. We are unable to hold back foreign intrigues because we are divided among ourselves. None of us is free and none of us can be safe, while there is frustration and instability in any part of this continent.

I do not need to go on citing specific instances of our common problems and difficulties to prove the urgency and the need for united action on a continental basis in Africa today. There is not one of us here now who does not suffer from the handicaps of our colonial past. Let us therefore move forward together in unity and in strength, confident in the knowledge that with such immense national and human resources as we possess in our continent, we cannot fail to make Africa one of the happiest, most prosperous and progressive areas of the world.

Two years ago, we were exposed to the ridicule of the world because they saw us as a divided Africa. They called us names which helped to widen the apparent breach among us: the 'radical' Casablanca Powers, the 'moderate' Monrovia Group, and the 'pro-French' Brazzaville states. There was no justification for these labels, but to the imperialists they were a very convenient means of giving the dog a bad name and hanging him!

It is to our eternal credit that last year at Addis Ababa we put our enemies to shame by forging a common charter from these groupings and emerging as the OAU. Let it be said that at Cairo we put them to greater shame by agreeing to the establishment of a union government of Africa. Have you noticed, brother presidents and prime ministers, that so soon as we achieved this measure of agreement at Addis Ababa, the neo-colonialists and their agents proceeded to sow new seeds of disruption and dissension among us?

They became particularly active and vocal in preaching the new and dangerous doctrine of the 'step by step' course towards unity. If we take one step at a time, when they are in a position to take six steps for every single one of ours, our weakness will, of course, be emphasised and exaggerated for their benefit. One step now, two steps later, then all will be fine in Africa for imperialism and neocolonialism. To say that a union government for Africa is premature is to sacrifice Africa on the altar of neo-colonialism. Let us move forward together to the wider fields of our heritage, strong in our unity, where our common aspirations and hopes find abundant expression in the power of our united endeavours.

All over Africa the essential economic pattern developed under colonialism remains. Not one of us, despite our political independence, has yet succeeded in breaking, in any substantial measure, our economic subservience to economic systems external to Africa. It is the purpose of neo-colonialism to maintain this economic relationship.

The developed countries need the raw materials of Africa to maintain their own industries and they are anxious to find markets in Africa for their manufactured goods. But there can be no market for these manufactured goods unless the people of Africa have the money with which to buy them. Therefore, I say that the developed countries have a vested interest in Africa's prosperity.

In many cases our most valuable raw materials – such as minerals – are owned and exploited by foreign companies. Large parts of the wealth of Africa, which could be used for the economic development of Africa, are drained out of the continent in this way to bolster the economies of the developed nations.

It is true that the whole world is poised at a delicate economic balance and that economic collapse in any one part of the world would have grave repercussions on us. Our situation in Africa is so weak that we are bound to be the first and the worst sufferers if economic difficulties should set in, in Europe or America, and the effect upon us would be absolute and catastrophic. We have nothing to fall back on. We have become so utterly dependent upon these outside economic systems that we have no means of resistance to external economic fluctuations. We have no economic resilience whatsoever within our own continent.

We are so cut off from one another that in many cases the road systems in each of our countries peter out into bush as they approach the frontier of our neighbour. How can we trade amongst ourselves when we do not even have proper means of physical communication? It is now possible to travel by air from Accra to London in six hours. I can fly from Accra to Nairobi or from Accra to Cairo in half a day. It is easy for us to get together to talk. But on the ground over which we fly with such ease and nonchalance, it is frequently impossible to engage in the most elementary trade simply because there are no proper roads, and because we are artificially divided and balkanised.

Our few and negligible roads and railways always lead, ultimately, to some port. In a sense they have become symbols of our economic subservience and our dependence on trade outside the African continent. We have inherited from colonialism an economic pattern from which it is difficult to escape. Great forces are arrayed to block our escape. When individually we try to find some economic independence, pressures are brought against us that are often irresistible owing to our disunity.

I am not arguing that we should cut off all economic relationships with countries outside Africa. I am not saying that we should spurn foreign trade and reject foreign investment. What I am saying is that we should get together, think together, plan together and organise our African economy as a unit, and negotiate our overseas economic relations as part of our general continental economic planning. Only in this way can we negotiate economic arrangements on terms fair to ourselves.

The OAU was a declaration of intention to unite. It was an optimistic beginning. But we need more than this. We must unite NOW under a union government if this intention is to have any meaning and relevance.

Talk is worthless if it does not lead to action. And so far as Africa is concerned, action will be impossible if it is any further delayed. Those forces which endanger our continent do not stand still. They are not moving step by step. They are marching in double step against us.

Every day we delay the establishment of a union government of Africa, we subject ourselves to outside economic domination. And our political independence as separate states becomes more and more meaningless.

Brother presidents and prime ministers: as I said a few minutes ago, this decade is Africa's finest hour. Great things are in store for us if we would but take our courage in our hands and reach out towards them. How would South

Africa dare to sentence Nelson Mandela and his seven brave colleagues against protests of a united Africa? How could Portugal dare think of continuing the violation of the sovereignty of Angola and Mozambique or so-called 'Portuguese Guinea', if these formed part of a united government of Africa? How could a white settler minority government in Southern Rhodesia dare to lock up [Joshua] Nkomo and [Ndabaningi] Sithole?

We have gone to Geneva to seek a major victory in our quest for fair play and justice in international trade. There were no less than 75 of us in one group set against the few of the great industrialised communities of Europe and the US. And yet how weak was our bargaining power because of our political and economic disunity and divisions.

How much more effective would our efforts have been if we had spoken with the one voice of Africa's millions. With all our minerals and waterpower and fertile lands, is it not a cause for shame that we remain poor and content to plead for aid from the very people who have robbed us of our riches in the past? How can Egypt, strategically situated as it is, combat the imperialism and neo-colonialism and solve the pressing and urgent problems of the Middle East unless it has the backing of a union government of Africa? Only a union government can assist effectively in the solution of the problems of the Middle East, including the Palestinian question.

Mr Chairman,

Let us remember, brother presidents and prime ministers, the Sahara no longer divides us. We do not see ourselves merely as Arab Africa, Black Africa, English Africa, or French Africa. We are one people, one continent with one destiny.

I see no way out of our present predicament except through the force and power of a union government of Africa. By this I do not mean the abrogation of any sovereignty. I seek no regional unions as a basis for unity. Indeed, the more independent states there are within our union government, the stronger will be our unity, and the freer will be each sovereign state within the union to attend to its specific and exclusive problems.

The specific fields of common action I have in mind are defence, foreign policy and economic development (including a common currency for Africa).

In this way, instead of a charter which operates on the basis of peripatetic or widely separated commissions under the control of an administrative secretariat without political direction, we shall have a government for joint action in three fields of our governmental activity.

It has been suggested from this rostrum, and it is on our agenda also, that we should decide at this conference as to the location of the permanent head-quarters of the OAU and appoint a permanent secretary-general. If, as I hope, we agree in principle, at this conference to move on to the establishment of a union government of Africa, we shall require quite a different set of criteria for selecting the headquarters of the organisation and its permanent officials.

We should also be careful to avoid being drawn into discussions at this stage which could lead to a clash of interests as to which country should have the headquarters or provide a secretary-general. This could harm the very unity which we are trying now to establish. I feel very strongly that the status quo should remain.

I see no objection, however, to the proposal that we should appoint a secretary-general, provided it is agreed that the appointment is made on a provisional basis only. I feel that Addis Ababa should continue as the provisional headquarters of our organisation.

Mr Chairman,

I would like to express on behalf of Ghana our sincere thanks to His Imperial Majesty Haile Selassie I and to the Ethiopian government for maintaining the provisional secretariat up to now. I feel, however, that before we rise we should make appropriate contributions from our various states for the upkeep of this our organisation. The burden should not be Ethiopia's alone.

I would like to state in this connection that Ghana is not interested in either the headquarters or the secretary-generalship of the organisation.

Mr Chairman,

280 million people in strength with a common destiny and a common goal could give progress and development in Africa a new momentum and an impetus which go beyond our wildest dreams. Do not let us speak and act as if we are not aware of the revolutionary forces surging through Africa today. Even the industrialised nations outside Africa recognise this now.

Today, there may be frustration, doubt, and distrust in every part of our continent, but tomorrow will see a new hope and a new march to glory, under a united government capable of speaking with one voice for all Africa.

Mr Chairman,

For a few moments, please permit me to refer to the pattern of economic structure which we inherited from the colonialists in Africa. All of us, under colonial rule, were encouraged to produce a limited number of primary commodities, mainly agricultural and mineral, for export overseas. Capital for development was owned by foreigners and profits were vigorously transferred abroad.

A trade pattern of this sort stagnated the rest of our national economy, and our resources remained undeveloped. In consequence, indigenous capital formation was negligible, leaving all our countries in a state of abject poverty.

Since independence, we have been making energetic efforts to reverse and overhaul these unsatisfactory features in our economy. In some of the independent African states great efforts have been made to relax traditional economic links with the ex-colonial powers, but none of us can say that we have succeeded in breaking those dangerous links completely.

Another handicap which we suffered from colonialism was the restriction of our economies which has hampered economic development in many ways. The very fact that all the independent African states produce and maintain development plans is an indication of our deep concern for realising nationalist aspirations and improving the conditions of living of our people.

But however deep our concern, however strong our determination, these development plans will avail us nothing if the necessary capital is not available. This capital, as we all know, is everywhere desperately short. The men with the know-how are few and scattered. It is by our coming together and pooling our resources that we can find a solution to this problem. In other words, only by unified economic planning on a continental basis with a central political direction within a union government can we hope to meet the economic challenge of our time.

It takes millions of pounds to build the basic industries, irrigation and power plants which will enable us to escape from our present economic stagnation. Our various individual, separate, balkanised states cannot mobilise the enormous amounts of money required for these major projects and industrial complexes. We cannot bargain effectively for the essential funds from foreign sources on the best possible terms.

What we are doing now competing between ourselves for the little capital available from foreign sources. In our scramble to get this capital we grant foreign firms extensive and lucrative concessions for the exploitation of our natural resources. These concessions to secure this capital exacerbate the colonial pattern of our economy. We invest more in raw materials output than in industrial development, and the continued drain abroad of profits which should have been re-invested in economic development retards the progress of our industrialisation plans.

In a continental federal union, we can easily mobilise the amount of capital available to the African states by the establishment of a Central Monetary Development Finance Bank. Already our various states have agreed to form an African Development Bank. This, however, cannot succeed without a continental economic plan and without the necessary political direction which only a union government of Africa can provide.

An African Monetary Development Bank of the kind I envisage will enable us to formulate continental agreements concerning the terms of loans and investments by foreign interests. Together, we can bargain far more effectively with foreign firms and governments for investments and loans for the kinds of industries we desire and not those they desire. We can bargain on the terms of these loans and we can ensure that the increased savings which will arise from continental development of Africa's huge resources will enable us to develop even more rapidly. The unnecessary competition amongst us for capital would cease and moreover we can work up continental tariff policies designed to protect newly developing African industries.

The great risks involved in investing in our individual countries will be reduced, for in an African economic union our development projects would be backed by all the African states together. But even this healthy sign of development is in grave danger of driving us against one another. As the general conditions of our economy are similar in all the independent African states, and as our national development plans are not being co-ordinated, this can only lead to a concomitant expansion of our separate productive capacities in excess of the quantity which can be profitably marketed either internally or abroad. The result of this is obviously the certainty of establishing cut-throat competition among us with heavy financial losses to our respective economies.

The problem of African unity must therefore be examined against the background of the economic position of the independent African states, our aspirations for rapid development and the difficulties with which we are confronted in our separate existence. If we examine these problems carefully, we cannot evade the conclusion that the movement towards African political unity will substantially and immediately contribute to the solution of the economic problems of the independent African states.

Indeed, I will make bold to state that African unity based on a continental union government is the only, I repeat only, possible framework within which the economic difficulties of Africa can be successfully and satisfactorily settled. The appeal for a union government of Africa is therefore not being made merely to satisfy a political end. It is absolutely indispensable for our economic survival in this modern world of ours.

We must remember that just as we had to obtain political independence from colonial rule as a necessary pre-requisite for establishing new and progressive communities for our respective states, so we cannot achieve economic stability in Africa as a whole without the pre-requisite of a continental union government.

Indeed, we cannot hope to sustain the economic development of Africa without first accepting the necessity for a continental division of labour to ensure that particular states specialised in their respective fields for which geographical, economic and social factors make them the most suitable, can develop to their fullest capacity with the best interest of the continent as a whole in mind.

Take, for example, the steel industry. This could be developed to the highest possible limit in Nigeria, Egypt or Mauritania, or Liberia or Ghana, to mention only a few instances. If we do not unite under a federal government, it is clear that each of the states mentioned will wish in their own national interests to pursue the possibility of establishing and expanding its own steel mill. Indeed, this is being done already by some of us to the benefit, profit and gain of foreign concerns.

If, however, our resources were combined to set up steel mills on a continental basis, at strategically chosen points in Africa, we would be in a position to make the greatest possible contribution to the industrial progress of the whole continent. Without a conscious effort based on a common governmental programme, we cannot hope to achieve this end. We might even find ourselves using the resources of one area of Africa to retard the progress and development of one or more other areas by cut-throat competition.

How then, at this moment of history, shall we meet this great challenge?

Certainly, we cannot blink at the harsh facts of life which are all too tragically familiar to us. This is especially true when we consider the economic development of Africa, on which all our other aspirations depend.

The most casual glance at our continent should convince anyone that the price of our disunity is continued exploitation from abroad and foreign interference in our internal matters. No matter where we look in the continent, we will find that, to a greater or lesser degree, the same pattern of exploitation persists.

For example: the economy of the Congo (Leopoldville) is still dominated by three foreign groups which represent Belgian, French, British and American interests. Herein lies the woe and tragedy of our beloved Congo. Two foreign firms – the Rhodesian Anglo-American Corporation and the Rhodesian Selection Trust – control the mining output of Zambia. Copper makes up 80 to 90 per cent of Zambia's exports, yet profits and interest shipped abroad annually often mount to as high as half of Zambia's total export earnings!

Thus, you can see that despite political independence, nearly all of us here today are unable to exploit our agricultural and mineral resources in our own interests. Under a strong union government we would have the material resources for rapid industrialisation, whereby all of us – big or small – would be benefited. But so long as we are divided, we will, to this extent, remain colonies in an economic sense. We shall remain puppets and agents of neo-colonialism.

The truth of this is even more evident when we examine monetary zones and customs unions. Most African states are still in monetary zones linked to the former colonial power. One-fourth of these states are in the sterling zone and one-half are in the franc zone. Owing to this currency arrangement, trade between the independent African states is restricted and hampered. Indeed, trade is practically impossible within this financial environment.

An example of our present economic limitations as separate independent governments may be cited from our experience in our economic relations with our brothers from Upper Volta and Togo. Two years ago, in furtherance of our natural desire for closer collaboration in all fields of development with our sister states, we performed a historic ceremony by breaking down the physical barriers established between Ghana and Upper Volta. The two governments signed a long-term Trade and Payments Agreement under which each government agreed to grant a non-interest bearing 'swing' credit of about £250 000. The Bank of Ghana on behalf of the government of Ghana was appointed as the technical agent to operate the Payments Agreement. In the case of the Upper Volta government, the Banque de l'Afrique Occidentale was nominated by the Upper Volta Government as its agent. To this day, the Banque de l'Afrique Occidentale in Ouagadougou has refused to execute the banking arrangements drawn up by the bank of Ghana to implement the agreement payment instructions which have so far not been honoured.

On the other hand, the Bank of Ghana has been requested by the Banque de l'Afrique Occidentale to transfer sterling in their favour before the payments instructions will be carried out, in spite of the fact that it is expressly laid down in the agreement that all payments to or from either country should be effected through the clearing account to be maintained by the two banks.

If the agreement instituted between Ghana and Upper Volta had worked successfully, the operation of the French currency arrangements, which are the medium of commercial undertakings in Upper Volta, would have been seriously undermined. Is it therefore any wonder that the Banque de l'Afrique Occidentale made the operation of an agreement signed between two sister African states with the best of intentions unworkable and inoperative? Our difficulties with the Republic of Togo arise from the same limitations.

It will be clear from these examples that until we in Africa are able to establish our own independent currency and financial institutions, we shall continue to be at the mercy of the financial arrangements imposed by foreign governments in their own, and not in our, interest.

As long as the states of Africa remain divided, as long as we are forced to compete for foreign capital and to accept economic ties to foreign powers because in our separate entities we are too small, weak and unviable to 'go it alone', we will be unable to break the economic pattern of exploitation established in the days of outright colonialism.

Only if we can unite and carry out co-ordinated economic planning within the framework of African political unity, will it be possible for us to break the bonds of neo-colonialism and reconstruct our economies for the purpose of achieving real economic independence and higher living standards for all our African states, big or small.

Mr Chairman,

After all these arguments that have been advanced, can it still be maintained that a union government for Africa is premature? Have we not got the men? Have we not got the resources? Have we not got the will? What else are we waiting for? I know, and some of you know, that we can, right now, if we have the will and determination to do so. Mere resolutions cannot help us. Not even another charter. The Ghana-Guinea Union, Casablanca Charter, Monrovia Charter and others, have long completed this resolution and charter-writing exercise.

Mr Chairman,

It is therefore with great honour and privilege that I now propose to you, your majesties, brother presidents and prime ministers, the framework for a union government of Africa.

This union government shall consist of an assembly of heads of state and government headed by a president elected from among the heads of state and government of the independent African states. The Executive of the union government will be a Cabinet or Council of Ministers with a chancellor or prime minister as its head, and a Federal House consisting of two chambers – the Senate and a House of Representatives. If you agree, we can appoint our foreign ministers, assisted by experts, to work out a Constitution for a union government of Africa.

Brother presidents and prime ministers: with our common suffering and aspirations, we should be one and a united people. Our continent, surrounded on all sides by oceans, is one of the most compact land masses in the world. Nature has endowed us with the richest and the best of natural resources. Circumstances and our common experience in history have made all of us a people with one destiny. Let us not betray the great promise of our future or disappoint the great hopes of the masses of our people by taking the wrong turning in this critical and momentous hour of decision.

We cannot save ourselves except through the unity of our continent based on common action through a continental union government. Only a united Africa under a union government can cure us of our economic ills and lift us out of our despair and frustration.

I make this sincere and serious appeal in the interest of our common progress, our security and our future well-being. I hope that all of us will accept this appeal with equal sincerity. But I know that, for various reasons, some of us may not be ready or prepared to take this historic and momentous decision now.

Nevertheless, I charge those of us who are ready to do so now – even if we are only a few (and how I wish it could be all of us) – firstly, to come away from Cairo having agreed to the establishment of a union government of Africa.

Secondly, those of us who subscribe to this solemn agreement must designate our foreign ministers to constitute a Working Committee to draft the Constitution for the federal union government of Africa.

Thirdly, those who subscribe to this agreement should, within six months, meet at a place to be agreed upon, to adopt and proclaim to the world the federal union government of Africa.

Mr Chairman, brother presidents and prime ministers: it has been said that 'great things from little causes spring.' How true this saying is, can be judged from the beginnings of some of the world's great powers of today. The USA started within 13 weak economically non-viable colonies exposed to serious political and economic hardships. Yet today, the USA is a world power with not less than fifty constituent states.

The Soviet Union, whose scientists have astounded the world with their interplanetary exploits, began their union amid untold hardships and difficulties with but three states. Today, the Soviet Union is composed of 16 federated states!

We cannot wait, we dare not wait, until we are encompassed by our doom, for failing to seize this grand opportunity rising to the call of Africa's finest hour.

This is the challenge which history has thrust upon us. This is the mandate we have received from our people, that we set about to create a union government for Africa now; and this is also the challenge which providence and destiny has thrust upon us. We cannot, we must not, we dare not fail or falter.

Society and Ideology

In the last chapter, I tried to show, and confirm by test cases, that philosophy always arose from a social milieu, and that a social contention is always present in it either explicitly or implicitly.[54] Social milieu affects the content of philosophy, and the content of philosophy seeks to affect social milieu, either by confirming it or by opposing it. In either case, philosophy implies something of the nature of an ideology. In the case where the philosophy confirms a social milieu, it implies something of the ideology of that society. In the other case in which philosophy opposes a social milieu, it implies something of the ideology of a revolution against that social milieu. Philosophy in its social aspect can therefore be regarded as pointing up an ideology.

On the motto page of my book *Towards Colonial Freedom*, I make the following quotation from Mazzini:

> Every true revolution is a programme; and derived from a new, general, positive, and organic principle. The first thing necessary is to accept that principle. Its development must then be confined to men who are believers in it, and emancipated from every tie or connection with any principle of an opposite nature.

Here Mazzini asserts the connection between a revolution and an ideology. When the revolution has been successful, the ideology comes to characterise the society. It is the ideology which gives a countenance to the ensuing social milieu. Mazzini further states the principle to be general, positive and organic. The statement, elucidation and theoretical defence of such a principle will collectively form a philosophy. Hence, philosophy admits of being an instrument of ideology.

Indeed, it can be said that in every society there is to be found an ideology. In every society, there is at least one militant segment which is the dominant segment of that society. In communalistic societies, this segment coincides with the whole. This dominant segment has its fundamental principles, its beliefs about the nature of man, and the type of society which must be created for man. Its fundamental principles help in designing and controlling the type of organisation which the dominant segment uses. And the same principles give

---

54 *Editor's note*: The author is referring to Kwame Nkrumah, 'Philosophy and Society' in *Consciencism: Philosophy and Ideology for De-colonization and Development with Particular Reference to the African Revolution* (New York: Monthly Review, 1970).

rise to a network of purposes, which fix what compromises are possible or not possible. One can compromise over programme, but not over principle. Any compromise over principle is the same as an abandonment of it.

In societies where there are competing ideologies, it is still usual for one ideology to be dominant. This dominant ideology is that of the ruling group. Though the ideology is the key to the inward identity of its group, it is in intent solidarist. For an ideology does not seek merely to unite a section of the people; it seeks to unite the whole of the society in which it finds itself. In its effects, it certainly reaches the whole society, when it is dominant. For, besides seeking to establish common attitudes and purposes for the society, the dominant ideology is that which in the light of circumstances decides what forms institutions shall take, and in what channels the common effort is to be directed.

Just as there can be competing ideologies in the same society, so there can be opposing ideologies between different societies. However, while societies with different social systems can coexist, their ideologies cannot. There is such a thing as peaceful coexistence between states with different social systems; but as long as oppressive classes exist, there can be no such thing as peaceful coexistence between opposing ideologies.

Imperialism, which is the highest stage of capitalism, will continue to flourish in different forms as long as conditions permit it. Though its end is certain, it can only come about under the pressure of nationalist awakening and an alliance of progressive forces which hasten its end and destroy its conditions of existence. It will end when there are no nations and peoples exploiting others; when there are no vested interests exploiting the earth, its fruits and resources for the benefit of a few against the well-being of the many.

When I say that in every society there is at least one ideology, I do not thereby mean that in every society a fully articulated set of statements is to be found. In fact, it is not ideology alone which can be so pervasive and at the same time largely covert.

In every society, there is to be found a morality; this hardly means that there is an *explicit* set of statements defining the morality. A morality is a network of principles and rules for the guidance and appraisal of conduct. And upon these rules and principles we constantly fall back. It is they which give support to our moral decisions and opinions. Very often we are quite definite about the moral quality of an act, but even when we are so definite, we are not necessarily ready with the reasons for this decision or opinion. It is not to be inferred from any such reticence, however, that there are no such reasons. We share within the same society a body of moral principles and rules garnered from our own experience and that of our forebears. The principles directing these experiences give us skill in forming moral opinions without having to be articulate about the sources of the judgements.

Another example of a similar phenomenon can be found in Freud. Sigmund Freud believed that nothing was ever forgotten by the individual. He did not through this imply that the individual consciously remembered everything. On the one hand, it is because the individual did not consciously remember everything that psychoanalysis was necessary – as a probe into the subconscious and the unconscious; on the other hand, it is because nothing was really forgotten that psychoanalysis is possible at all, for everything is there for it to probe. Thus, according to Freud, all our experiences are stored up, and they affect our overt behaviour even if we have no conscious memory of the experiences themselves.

Just as a morality guides and seeks to connect the actions of millions of persons, so an ideology aims at uniting the actions of millions towards specific and definite goals, notwithstanding that an ideology can be largely implicit. I am aware that in this usage I depart somewhat from the fashionable one. It is often thought that an ideology has to be a body of writing of one individual, or a small group of individuals, directed only at fundamental change in a society. This is an evident mistake. An ideology, even when it is revolutionary, does not merely express the wish that a present social order should be abolished. It seeks also to defend and maintain the new social order which it introduces. But while it is defending its own social order, it is still an ideology, and the same. That is to say, an ideology can remain an ideology while defending an existing progressive society. Nor can the fact that some particular ideology is not explicit on paper prevent it from being one. What is crucial is not the paper, but the thought.

I have said an ideology seeks to bring a specific order into the total life of its society. To achieve this, it needs to employ a number of instruments. The ideology of a society displays itself in political theory, social theory and moral theory, and uses these as instruments. It establishes a particular range of political, social and moral behaviour, such that unless behaviour of this sort fell within the established range, it would be incompatible with the ideology. What I mean may also be expressed in the following terms. Given the ideology of a society, then some political behaviour would be incompatible with it and some other political behaviour would be compatible with it. Given a socialist ideology, for example, the political dictatorship of capital would be incompatible with it. There is always a definite range within which social-political theory and practice must fall if they are to conform to a socialist ideology. Thus, ideology displays itself in moral theory and practice. In the account of some Greek philosophers in the last chapter, I suggested how a humanist ideology held implications for political theory and illustrated this mainly from Aristotle.

The ideology of a society is total. It embraces the whole life of a people, and manifests itself in their class structure, history, literature, art, religion. It also acquires a philosophical statement. If an ideology is integrative in intent, that is to say, if it seeks to introduce a certain order which will unite the actions of millions towards specific and definite goals, then its instruments can also be seen as instruments of social control. It is even possible to look upon 'coercion' as a fundamental idea in society. This way of looking at society readily gives rise to the idea of a social contract. According to this idea, man lived, during certain dark ages in the dim past, outside the ambit of society. During those dark ages, man was alleged to have lived a poor, nasty, brutish, short and fearful life. Life, not surprisingly, soon became intolerable. And so the poor men came together, and subtly agreed upon a contract. By means of this contract they waived certain rights of theirs in order to invest a representative with legislative and executive powers of coercion over themselves.

We know that the social contract is quite unhistorical, for unless men already lived in a society, they could have no common language, and a common language is already a social fact, which is incompatible with the social contract. Nevertheless, howsoever it is that societies arose, the notion of a society implies organised obligation.

I have made mention of the way in which ideology requires definite ranges of behaviour. It is difficult, however, to fix the limits of these ranges. Still the impression is not to be formed from this difficulty that the ranges are not definite. They are as definite as territories, even if, on occasion, border uncertainties arise between territories next to each other. Obviously, there are at least two senses of definiteness. The one sense is mathematical. In this sense, a range of conduct is definite if, and only if, every item of conduct either falls unambiguously inside it or falls unambiguously outside it. In the other sense, a range of conduct is definite if there are items of behaviour unambiguously falling inside it, and items of behaviour unambiguously falling outside it. Any ambiguity that there is must only be at the extremes. It is this possible fluidity at the extremes which makes growth and progress logically possible in human conduct.

Every society stresses its permissible ranges of conduct and evolves instruments whereby it seeks to obtain conformity to such a range. It evolves these instruments because the unity out of diversity which a society represents is hardly automatic, calling as it does for means whereby unity might be secured, and, when secured, maintained. Though, in a formal sense, these means are means of 'coercion', in intent they are means of cohesion. They become means of cohesion by underlining common values, which themselves generate common interests, and hence common attitudes and common reactions. It is this community, this identity in the range of principles and values, in the range of interests, attitudes, and so of reactions, which lies at the bottom of social order. It is also this community which makes social sanction necessary, which inspires the physical institutions of society, like the police force, and decides the purposes for which they are called into being.

Indeed, when I spoke at the Law Conference at Accra in January 1962, I emphasised that law, with its executive arms, must be inspired at every level by the ideals of its society. Nevertheless, a society has a choice of instruments. By this, I do not merely mean that different societies could have different instruments. I mean that a society can for example decide that all its instruments of 'coercion' and unity shall be centralised. The logical extreme of this is where every permissive right is explicitly backed by an enactment, and where every social disapprobation is made explicit in a prohibitive enactment. This logical extreme of centralisation is, needless to say, impossible of attainment. But any society can attempt to approximate to it as much as it desires. A society, however, which approximates too closely to this extreme will engender such an unwieldy bureaucracy that the intention of bureaucracy will be annulled. Of course, ideally the intention of bureaucracy is to achieve impartiality and eschew the arbitrary. But when a society develops an unwieldy bureaucracy, it has allowed this fear of the arbitrary to become pathological, and it is itself autocratic.

And yet, a society must count among its instruments of 'coercion' and cohesion, prohibitions and permissions which are made explicit in a statutory way. In many societies, there is in addition a whole gamut of instruments which are at once subtle and insidious. The sermon in the pulpit, the pressures of trade unionism, the opprobrium inflicted by the press, the ridicule of friends, the ostracism of colleagues; the sneer, the snub and countless other devices, these are all non-statutory instruments by means of which societies exert coercion, by means of which they achieve and preserve unity.

'Coercion' could unfortunately be rather painful, but it is signally effective in ensuring that individual behaviour does not become dangerously irresponsible. The individual is not an anarchic unit. He lives in orderly surroundings, and the achieving of these orderly surroundings calls for methods both explicit and subtle.

One of these subtle methods is to be found in the account of history. The history of Africa, as presented by European scholars, has been encumbered with malicious myths. It was even denied that we were a historical people. It was said that whereas other continents had shaped history, and determined its course, Africa had stood still, held down by inertia; that Africa was only propelled into history by European contact. African history was therefore presented as an extension of European history. [Georg] Hegel's authority was lent to this ahistorical hypothesis concerning Africa, which he himself unhappily helped to promote. And apologists of colonialism lost little time in seizing upon it and writing wildly thereon. In presenting the history of Africa as the history of the collapse of our traditional societies in the presence of the European advent, colonialism and imperialism employed their account of African history and anthropology as an instrument of their oppressive ideology.

Earlier on, such disparaging accounts had been given of African society and culture as to appear to justify slavery, and slavery, posed against these accounts, seemed a positive deliverance of our ancestors. When the slave trade and slavery became illegal, the experts on Africa yielded to the new wind of change, and now began to present African culture and society as being so rudimentary and primitive that colonialism was a duty of Christianity and civilisation. Even if we were no longer, on the evidence of the shape of our skulls, regarded as the missing link, unblessed with the arts of good government, material and spiritual progress, we were still regarded as representing the infancy of mankind. Our highly sophisticated culture was said to be simple and paralysed by inertia, and we had to be encumbered with tutelage. And this tutelage, it was thought, could only be implemented if we were first subjugated politically.

The history of a nation is, unfortunately, too easily written as the history of its dominant class. But if the history of a nation, or a people, cannot be found in the history of a class, how much less can the history of a continent be found in what is not even a part of it – Europe. Africa cannot be validly treated merely as the space in which Europe swelled up. If African history is interpreted in terms of the interests of European merchandise and capital, missionaries and administrators, it is no wonder that African nationalism, in the forms it takes, is regarded as a perversion and neo-colonialism as a virtue.

In the new African renaissance, we place great emphasis on the presentation of history. Our history needs to be written as the history of our society, not as the story of European adventures. African society must be treated as enjoying its own integrity; its history must be a mirror of that society, and European contact must find its place in this history only as an African experience, even if as a crucial one. That is to say, European contact needs to be assessed and judged from the point of view of the principles animating African society, and from the point of view of the harmony and progress of this society.

When history is presented in this way, it can become not an account of how those African students referred to in the introduction became more Europeanised than others; it can become a map of the growing tragedy and the final triumph of our society. In this way, African history can come to guide and direct African action.[55] African history can thus become a pointer at the ideology which should guide and direct African reconstruction.

This connection between an ideological standpoint and the writing of history is a perennial one. A check on the work of the great historians, including Herodotus and Thucydides, quickly exposes their passionate concern with ideology. Their irresistible moral, political, and sociological comments are particular manifestations of more general ideological standpoints. Classically, the great historians have been self-appointed public prosecutors, accusing on behalf of the past, admonishing on behalf of the future. Their accusations and admonishings have been set in a rigid framework of presuppositions, both about the nature of the good man and about the nature of the good society, in such a way that these presuppositions serve as intimations of an implicit ideology.

Even [Leopold] von Ranke, the great 19th century German historian, who boasted that his aim was not to sit in judgement on the past, but only to show

---

55 *Editor's note*: The author is referring to Nkrumah, 'Introduction' in *Consciencism*.

us what really happened, was far from being a mere chronicler of the past. He was, in spite of his claims, an *engagé* historian. The key to the attitude which he strikes in his historical works lies first, in his views on the necessity of strife for progress, and second, in his ideas on the source of the state and the relation of the individual to the state. Dutifully grinding an axe for His Prussian Majesty, on the first point von Ranke holds that it is precisely through one state seeking a hegemony of Europe, and thereby provoking a rivalry, that the civilisation of the European state is maintained; on the second point he holds that the state, in being an idea of God, enjoys a spiritual personality, and hence that neither reform nor revolution is exportable, for this would do violence to the personality of the importing state. He also holds that it is only through the state to which an individual belongs that he can develop and preserve his fullness of being. And the ideal of liberty which he is able to propose to Prussian subjects is a spontaneous subjection to the state. Is it surprising that he should have 'explained' [Martin] Luther's condemnation of the Peasants' War? Von Ranke, writing history, implements an ideological viewpoint which he at the same time seeks to conceal.

I have mentioned art as another of the subtle instruments of ideology. One can illustrate this in various ways. In the Medieval Age of Europe, when religion was considered to be the main preoccupation of life, all other concerns were subordinated to the religious, and actions tended to win approval to the extent that they supported religion, or at least were not in conflict with it. In the second chapter, I illustrated how economic activity was subordinated to the religious concern. Art, too, became infected by this idea.[56] It accordingly specialised in biblical illustration and apocalypses of paradise.

Today, in the socialist countries of Europe, where the range of conduct is fixed by socialist principles, that particular art which glorifies the socialist ideology is encouraged at the expense of that art which the supremacy of aristocrats or the bourgeoisie might inspire. The former in general encouraged a bucolic and a classical kind of art, its subjects appropriated from the class of gods and goddesses, and leisurely flute-playing shepherd boys. The bourgeoisie for their part injected a puritan strain into art, and in general directed it along lines of portraiture. Art has not, however, always propagated ideals within an already accepted ideology. It has sometimes thrived in the vanguard of reform or even revolution. [Francisco] Goya, for example, was responsible for significant conscience-stricken and protest painting in which by paint and brush he lambasted the brutalities of the 19th century ruling classes. Here he was not defending an ideology but was exposing one to attack.

In African art, too, society was often portrayed. It is the moral-philosophical preoccupation in terms of which this portrayal was done which explains its

---

56 *Editor's note*: The author is referring to Nkrumah, 'Philosophy and Society', *Consciencism*.

typical power. It is this also which explains the characteristic distortion of form in African art. In the portrayal of force, whether as forces of the world, of generation and death, or the force of destiny, it was essential that it should not be delineated as something assimilated and overcome. And this is the impression which the soft symmetries of lifelike art would have given. It is to avoid this impression of force overcome that African art resorted to distortion of forms.

By treating of such examples, one may illustrate subtle methods of 'coercion' and cohesion. To cope with the 'teddy boy' problem, many churches in Britain formed clubs.[57] In these clubs they hoped to entice teddy boys by the provision of rock and roll music. Once these youths were so trapped, the churches expected to influence, and so coerce them as to reinstate their behaviour within the range of passable conduct. The churches used a non-subtle instrument which was at the same time not centralise.

In the Soviet Union, too, open and systematic ridicule was resorted to, and when this did not work well enough, teddy boys were moved from one area of the country to another. Through inconveniencing them, Soviet authorities sought by a non-statutory instrument to influence, and so coerce, teddy boys in order to bring their activities within the range of passable behaviour.

These instruments all relate to some conception of 'the desirable society.' This is a conception which is nurtured by ideology. As the conception of 'the desirable society' changes, some of its instruments too change, the subtle ones changing in a quiet and discreet way. When this happens, it is said that new ground is broken.

Philosophy, too, is one of the subtle instruments of ideology and social cohesion. Indeed, it affords a theoretical basis for the cohesion. In *The Republic* of Plato, we are confronted with an example in which philosophy is made the theoretical basis of a proposed social order. In that proposal, philosophy would be an instrument of the ideology belonging to the social order proposed by Plato.

Philosophy performs this function in two ways. It performs it as a general theoretical statement to which a specific social-political theory is parallel. I have illustrated this in the discussion of some early Greek philosophers in the second chapter. Philosophy also performs this ideological function when it takes shape as political philosophy or as ethics. Through political philosophy, it lays down certain ideals for our pursuit and fortification, and it becomes an instrument of unity by laying down the same ideals for all the members of a given society.

As ethics, philosophy proposes to throw light upon the nature of moral principles and moral judgements; it also seeks to expose the source of the

---

57 *Editor's note*: Teddy boys were a rebellious youth subculture in 1950s and 1960s Britain, who were known for wearing tailored suits, sporting distinctive haircuts and listening to rock 'n' roll music. Some segments of the teddy boy community were involved in gang violence and racial aggression towards West Indian and migrant communities.

validity of ethical principles, and so of moral obligation. In ethics, we have an instrument of great fascination which runs parallel to statutory instruments without itself being statutory. Moral laws were never passed; there are no policemen or courts to ensure adherence to them.

There is a certain fascination about morality. When someone asks why he has to take notice of any state law, the intention of the law can be explained to him. If he is not satisfied, it can be pointed out to him that he supported a certain Constitution, or at least that a certain Constitution is binding upon him, and under that Constitution parliament is empowered to enact laws. If this does not satisfy him, then it can be pointed out to him that the laws of the land are to be taken note of, on pain of unpleasant consequences. But if someone should ask why he has to be moral, a similar kind of answer cannot be made to him. Indeed, this fact led David Hume to say that reason could not tell him why he should not prefer the safety of his little finger to the survival of mankind.

Philosophers, grappling with the question of the source of moral obligation, have attempted different sorts of answer. Many have given their answer in terms of the individual psychology, in terms of the pleasure or the pain which certain courses of action entail for their perpetrators. Here, these philosophers have tried to anchor moral obligation in something, in regard to which the question 'why?' would, they hoped, be impossible. They accordingly expected that the question why one likes pleasant things and dislikes painful ones could not be sensibly asked. If, therefore, moral obligation could be founded on pleasure and pain in such a way that morality raised expectations of pleasure and im- morality raised expectations of pain, a final answer would be procured to the question why one should be moral. But this account relates to the individual welfare and not the social.

A few have tried to base moral laws on the nature of the human reason itself. In this way they hoped to give a final answer to the question why one should be moral. If moral laws were purely commands of the reason, to ask why one should be moral would be like asking why one should be consistent. Just as consistency is a requirement of human discourse, so morality would be a requirement of human action.

Yet others, eschewing a psychological or a rationalist answer, explore a sociological one, giving their account in terms of the general welfare or the general consensus. According to the utilitarians, for example, an action is right to the extent that it tends to promote the general welfare, and wrong to the extent that it tends to hinder it. Here they regard as devoid of meaning the question why one ought to seek the general welfare. If this question is devoid of sense, so is the question why one ought to be moral. A consequence of this view is that social welfare officers should be among the most ethical of men.

The need for subtle means of social cohesion lies in the fact that there is a large portion of life which is outside direct central intervention. In order that this portion of life should be filled with order, non-statutory methods are required. These non-statutory methods, by and large, are the subtle means of social cohesion. But different societies lay different emphases on these subtle means even if the range of conformity which they seek is the same. The emphasis which a particular society lays on a given means depends on the experience, social-economic circumstances and the philosophical foundation of that society.

In Africa, this kind of emphasis must take objective account of our present situation at the return of political independence. From this point of view, there are three broad features to be distinguished here. African society has one segment which comprises our traditional way of life; it has a second segment which is filled by the presence of the Islamic tradition in Africa; it has a final segment which represents the infiltration of the Christian tradition and culture of Western Europe into Africa, using colonialism and neo-colonialism as its primary vehicles. These different segments are animated by competing ideologies. But since society implies a certain dynamic unity, there needs to emerge an ideology which, genuinely catering for the needs of all, will take the place of the competing ideologies, and so reflect the dynamic unity of society, and be the guide to society's continual progress.

The traditional face of Africa includes an attitude towards man which can only be described, in its social manifestation, as being socialist. This arises from the fact that man is regarded in Africa as primarily a spiritual being, a being endowed originally with a certain inward dignity, integrity and value. It stands refreshingly opposed to the Christian idea of the original sin and degradation of man.

This idea of the original value of man imposes duties of a socialist kind upon us. Herein lies the theoretical basis of African communalism. This theoretical basis expressed itself on the social level in terms of institutions such as the clan, underlining the initial equality of all and the responsibility of many for one. In this social situation, it was impossible for classes of a Marxian kind to arise. By a Marxian kind of class, I mean one which has a place in a horizontal social stratification. Here classes are related in such a way that there is a disproportion of economic and political power between them. In such a society there exist classes which are crushed, lacerated, and ground down by the encumbrance of exploitation. One class sits upon the neck of another.

In the traditional African society, no sectional interest could be regarded as supreme; nor did legislative and executive power aid the interests of any particular group. The welfare of the people was supreme. But colonialism came and changed all this. First, there were the necessities of the colonial administration to which I referred in the introduction. For its success, the colonial administration needed a cadre of Africans, who, by being introduced to a certain minimum of European education, became infected with European ideals, which they tacitly accepted as being valid for African societies. Because these African instruments of the colonial administration were seen by all to be closely associated with the new sources of power, they acquired a certain prestige and rank to which they were not entitled by the demands of the harmonious development of their own society.

In addition to them, groups of merchants and traders, lawyers, doctors, politicians, and trade unionists emerged, who, armed with skills and levels of affluence which were gratifying to the colonial administration, initiated something parallel to the European middle class. There were also certain feudal-minded elements who became imbued with European ideals either through direct European education or through hobnobbing with the local colonial administration. They gave the impression that they could be relied upon implicitly as repositories of all those staid and conservative virtues indispensable to any exploiter administration. They, as it were, paid the registration fee for membership of a class which was now associated with social power and authority.

Such education as we were all given, put before us right from our infancy, ideals of the metropolitan countries, ideals which could seldom be seen as representing the scheme, the harmony and progress of African society. The scale and type of economic activity, the idea of the accountability of the individual conscience introduced by the Christian religion, countless other silent influences, these have all made an indelible impression upon African society.

But neither economic nor political subjugation could be considered as being in tune with the traditional African egalitarian view of man and society. Colonialism had in any case to be done away with. The African Hercules has his club poised ready to smite any new head which the colonialist hydra may care to put out.

With true independence regained, however, a new harmony needs to be forged, a harmony that will allow the combined presence of traditional Africa, Islamic Africa and Euro-Christian Africa, so that this presence is in tune with the original humanist principles underlying African society. Our society is not the old society, but a new society enlarged by Islamic and Euro-Christian influences. A new emergent ideology is therefore required, an ideology which can solidify in a philosophical statement, but at the same time an ideology which will not abandon the original humanist principles of Africa.

Such a philosophical statement will be born out of the crisis of the African conscience confronted with the three strands of present African society. Such a philosophical statement I propose to name *philosophical consciencism*, for it will give the theoretical basis for an ideology whose aim shall be to contain the African experience of Islamic and Euro-Christian presence as well as the experience of the traditional African society, and, by gestation, employ them for the harmonious growth and development of that society.

Every society is placed in nature. And it seeks to influence nature, to impose such transformations upon nature, as will develop the environment of the society for its better fulfilment. The changed environment, in bringing about a better fulfilment of the society, thereby alters the society. Society placed in nature is therefore caught in the correlation of transformation with development. This correlation represents the toil of man both as a social being and as an individual. This kind of correlation has achieved expression in various social-political theories. For a social-political theory has a section which determines the way in which social forces are to be deployed in order to increase the transformation of society.

Slavery and feudalism represent social-political theories in which the deployment of forces is not a problematic question. In both slavery and feudalism, workers, the people whose toil transforms nature for the development of society, are dissociated from any say in rule. By a vicious division of labour, one class of citizen toils and another reaps where it has not sown. In the slave society, as in the feudal society, that part of society whose labours transform nature is not the same as the part which is better fulfilled as a result of this transformation. If by their fruits we shall know them, they must first grow the fruits. In slave and feudal society, the fruit eaters are not the fruit-growers. This is the cardinal factor in exploitation, that the section of a society whose labours transform nature is not the same as the section which is better fulfilled as a result of this transformation.

In every non-socialist society, there can be found two strata which correspond to that of the oppressor and the oppressed, the exploiter and the exploited. In all such societies, the essential relation between the two strata is the same as that between masters and slaves, lords and serfs. In capitalism, which is only a social-political theory in which the important aspects of slavery and feudalism are refined, a stratified society is required for its proper functioning, a society is required in which the working class is oppressed by the ruling class; for, under capitalism, that portion of society whose labours transform nature and produce goods is not the portion of society which enjoys the fruits of this transformation and productivity. Nor is it the whole of society which is so enhanced.

This might indeed be termed a contradiction. It is a social contradiction in so far as it is contrary to genuine principles of social equity and social justice. It is also an economic contradiction in so far as it is contrary to a harmonious and unlimited economic development.

Capitalism is a development by refinement from feudalism, just as feudalism is a development by refinement from slavery. The essence of reform is to combine a continuity of the fundamental principle, with a tactical change in the manner of expression of the fundamental principle. Reform is not a change in the thought, but one in its manner of expression, not a change in what is said but one in idiom. In capitalism, feudalism suffers, or rather enjoys reform, and the fundamental principle of feudalism merely strikes new levels of subtlety. In slavery, it is thought that exploitation, the alienation of the fruits of the labour of others, requires a certain degree of political and forcible subjection. In feudalism, it is thought that a lesser degree of the same kind of subjection is adequate to the same purpose. In capitalism, it is thought that a still lesser degree is adequate. In this way, psychological irritants to revolution are appeased, and exploitation finds a new lease of life, until the people should discover the *opposition* between reform and revolution.

In this way, capitalism continues with its characteristic pompous plans for niggardly reforms, while it coerces one section of a society somehow into making itself available to another section, which battens on it. That development which capitalism marks over slavery and feudalism consists as much in the methods by means of which labour is coerced as in the mode of production. Capitalism is but the gentleman's method of slavery.

Indeed, a standard ruse of capitalism today is to imitate some of the proposals of socialism and turn this imitation to its own use. Running with the hare and hunting with the hounds is much more than a pastime to capitalism; it is the hub of a complete strategy. In socialism, we seek an increase in levels of production in order solely that the people, by whose exertions production is possible, shall raise their standard of living and attain a new consciousness and level of life. Capitalism does this too, but not for the same purpose. Increased productivity under capitalism does indeed lead to a rise in the standard of living; but when the proportion of distribution of value between exploited and exploiter is kept constant, then any increase in levels of production must mean a greater *quantity*, but nor *proportion*, of value accruing to the exploited. Capitalism thus discovers a new way of seeming to implement reform, while really genuinely avoiding it. It creates the welfare state.

Whereas capitalism is a development by refinement from slavery and feudalism, socialism does not contain the fundamental ingredient of capitalism, the principle of exploitation. Socialism stands for the negation of that very principle wherein capitalism has its being, lives, and thrives, that principle which links capitalism with slavery and feudalism.

If one seeks the social-political ancestor of socialism, one must go to communalism. Socialism has characteristics in common with communalism, just as capitalism is linked with feudalism and slavery. In socialism, the principles underlying communalism are given expression in modern circumstances. Thus, whereas communalism in an untechnical society can be *laissez-faire*, in a technical society where sophisticated means of production are at hand, if the underlying principles of communalism are not given centralised and correlated expression, class cleavages arise, which are the result of economic disparities, and accompanying political inequalities. Socialism, therefore, can be and is the defence of the principles of communalism in a modern setting. Socialism is a form of social organisation which, guided by the principles underlying communism, adopts procedures and measures made necessary by demographic and technological developments.

These considerations throw great light on the bearing of revolution and reform on socialism. The passage from the ancestral line of slavery via feudalism and capitalism to socialism can only lie through revolution: it cannot lie through reform. For in reform, fundamental principles are held constant and the details of their expression modified. In the words of Marx, it leaves the pillars of the building intact. Indeed, sometimes, reform itself may be initiated by the necessities of preserving identical fundamental principles. Reform is a tactic of self-preservation.

Revolution is thus an indispensable avenue to socialism, where the antecedent social-political structure is animated by principles which are a negation of those of socialism, as in a capitalist structure (and therefore also in a colonialist structure, for a colonialist structure is essentially ancillary to capitalism). Indeed, I distinguish between two colonialisms, between a domestic one, and an external one. Capitalism at home is domestic colonialism.

But because the spirit of communalism still exists to some extent in societies with a communalist past, socialism and communism are not in the strict sense of the word 'revolutionary' creeds. They may be described as restatements in contemporary idiom of the principles underlying communalism. On the other hand, in societies with no history of communalism, the creeds of socialism and communism are fully revolutionary, and the passage to socialism must be guided by the principles of scientific socialism.

The nature and cause of the conflict between the ruling class and the exploited class is influenced by the development of productive forces, that is, changes in technology; the economic relations which these forces condition; and the ideologies that reflect the properties and psychology of the people living in that society. The basis of a socialist revolution is created when the class struggle within a given society has resulted in mass consent and mass desire for positive action to change or transform that society. It is then that the foundation is laid for the highest form of political action – when a revolution attains its excellence, and workers and peasants succeed in overthrowing all other classes.

I have explained how society's desire to transform nature reflects itself in different social-political theories. I wish now to suggest how the same desire reflects itself in philosophy. Just as social-political theories, to the extent that they deploy forces for the harnessing and development of nature, fall into two lots, so do philosophies. From this standpoint, the two real social-political alternatives facing society are either that one section should produce, and another section batten thereon, or that all sections should produce and all sections should be fulfilled by the value created by labour.

In the same way, there are two real philosophical alternatives. These alternatives coincide with idealism and materialism. In the preceding chapter, I explained how idealism was connected with a tiered society, how through its mode of explaining nature and social phenomena by reference to spirit, idealism favoured a class structure of a horizontal sort, in which one class sat upon the neck of another.

I also explained there how materialism, on the other hand, was connected with a humanist organisation, how through its being monistic, and referring all natural processes to matter and its laws, it inspired an egalitarian organisation of society. The unity and fundamental identity of nature suggests the unity and fundamental identity of man in society. Idealism favours an oligarchy, materialism favours an egalitarianism.

Individuals have both idealist and materialist tendencies in them. So have societies both idealist and materialist streaks. But these streaks do not exist in equipoise. They are connected by a conflict in which now one streak predominates, now the other.

By reason of the connection of idealism with an oligarchy and of materialism with an egalitarianism, the opposition of idealism and materialism in the same society is paralleled by the opposition of conservative and progressive forces on the social level. When in the dialectical opposition of capitalism to socialism, the former for a time becomes triumphant, social progress is not thereby altogether arrested, though it is seriously attenuated. But since it is not arrested, it is hardly cause for wonder that the workers of today in many respects enjoy better circumstances of life than even a good many feudal lords of the past. To confess to this degree of progress is not to say, however, that capitalism has been without its shanty towns and slums, its captive workers languishing and finally dying in public squares, victims of hunger, cold and disease.

The question is not whether there has been discernible progress under capitalism, but rather whether what progress is admitted can be said to be adequate. Here we discern one of capitalism's deadly sins. Under this social-political system, man's materialist approach to nature loses its bearings. It sheds its humanist stimulus under the impulse of the profit motive. If happiness is defined in the context of society, then happiness becomes that feeling which an individual derives, from a given economic, political and cultural context, that he is in a position to make good his aspirations. Since capitalist development is unfortunately a process in which a rapacious oligarchy is pitted against an exploited mass, happiness, according to this definition, is denied to many. The achievements of the capitalist oligarchy define new limits of what is attainable by the individual, and thereby push outward the frontiers of legitimate aspirations. But capitalism is a system in which these limiting aspirations are by definition denied to the people, and only reserved for a few.

The evil of capitalism consists in its alienation of the fruit of labour from those who with the toil of their body and the sweat of their brow produce this fruit. This aspect of capitalism makes it irreconcilable with those basic principles which animate the traditional African society. Capitalism is unjust; in our newly independent countries it is not only too complicated to be workable, it is also alien.

Under socialism, however, the study and mastery of nature has a humanist impulse, and is directed not towards a profiteering accomplishment, but the affording of ever-increasing satisfaction for the material and spiritual needs of the greatest number. Ideas of transformation and development, in so far as they relate to the purposes of society as a whole and not to an oligarch purpose, are properly speaking appropriate to socialism.

On the philosophical level, too, it is materialism, not idealism, that in one form or another will give the firmest conceptual basis to the restitution of Africa's egalitarian and humanist principles. Idealism breeds an oligarchy, and its social implication, as drawn out in my second chapter, is obnoxious to African society. It is materialism, with its monistic and naturalistic account of nature, which will baulk arbitrariness, inequality and injustice. How materialism suggests a socialist philosophy I have explained in my second chapter.

In sum, the restitution of Africa's humanist and egalitarian principles of society requires socialism. It is materialism that ensures the only effective transformation of nature, and socialism that derives the highest development from this transformation.

Obstacles to Economic Progress

Speaking of West Africa in 1962, the United Nations Economic Commission for Africa pointed out:

> Few other regions of the world show such a multitude of fairly small States both as far as production and population go. The only similar region of some importance is Central America.

West Africa is in fact divided into 19 separate independent states and includes two colonial enclaves possessed by Spain and Portugal. The population of the area is about a third of the total population of Africa, yet the average population of the independent countries, if Nigeria is excluded, is about 2–3 million. It is, however, illusory to regard even Nigeria as an exception to the balkanisation policy practised by the departing colonial rulers. The constitution imposed on Nigeria at independence divided the country into three regions (which have since grown to four) loosely joined on a federal basis but with sufficient powers left to the regions to cripple overall economic planning. If the other states of West Africa are examples of political balkanisation, Nigeria is an example of economic balkanisation. Ghana, with a population of over seven million, only escaped a similar fate by the resistance put up by the Convention People's Party government to a British plan which could have created no less than five regions, some with a population of less than one million, yet each possessing sufficient powers to defeat central planning. Kenya, which was also forced to accept at independence a similar type of constitution, has only recently been able to establish a unified regime.

When France was faced with the possibility of being forced to accept some form of independence, or at least self-government, for the territories of the old colonial federations of French West and Equatorial Africa, a series of balkanisation measures were adopted by the French government. The *Loi-cadre* of 1956 established the frontiers of the present French-speaking states. The dismantling process begun by the *Loi-cadre* was completed by the referendum of 1958 on the Constitution of the French Fifth Republic. Each of the territories established by the *Loi-Cadre* was called upon to decide separately whether it wished to remain an overseas territory of France, an autonomous republic within the French Community, or to be independent.

Teresa Hayter, a research assistant of the British Overseas Development Institute, in the April 1965 issue of the journal of the British Royal Institute of International Affairs has described the process:

> The territories were to make separate decisions; it was therefore they and not the Federations of West and Equatorial Africa which were legally to inherit France's powers; no provision was made for strengthening the Federal institutions and in fact they were dismantled after the referendum and came formally to an end in April 1959. The original purpose of the Federations had been to enable the colonies to pay for themselves, through a reallocation of their revenues; ... Senghor in particular has bitterly accused France of "balkanising" Africa in the *Loi-Cadre* ...With the choice so loaded, only Guinea voted against the Constitution; all the others became autonomous republics, members of the Franco-African Community.

Fearing that the example of Guinea might be followed by other states which had decided to join the Community, the French government removed everything of value from the territory. Administrators and teachers were withdrawn. Documents and even electric light bulbs were removed from government buildings. Financial assistance, trade support and the payment of pensions to Guinean war veterans were discontinued.

Despite the pressure placed on Guinea in this way, the remaining French states were forced by internal pressure to seek political independence. This destroyed the conception usually associated with General [Charles] de Gaulle, the originator of the French Community, of a non-sovereign group of African states each separately linked to France. One after another the 'autonomous Republics' obtained international sovereignty but under such adverse conditions that they had in fact to maintain all the military, financial, commercial, and economic links of the previous colonial period. In order to exist at all as independent states, these former French territories were forced to accept French 'aid' even to meet their recurrent expenses.

French 'aid' to developing countries is, in proportion to the French national income, the highest in the world and is, in absolute terms, the second highest. Nearly all of this 'aid' is absorbed by commitments in Africa, and nearly half of it goes to the fourteen states which were previously autonomous republics and whose combined population is only slightly larger than that of Nigeria. Aid of this type can dictate African relations with the developed world and, as experience has shown, can be extremely dangerous to the recipients.

French African aid originally arose from the advantage which French firms and individuals derived from the African franc zone and this has determined the framework in which the aid is still provided. So long as the relationship which the aid provided was profitable to France it naturally continued. It was in effect a levy on French taxpayers for the benefit of French individuals and firms.

The overall value of the policy to France was that in return for guaranteed markets and prices for colonial primary products, such as coffee, cocoa, groundnuts, bananas, and cotton, the African states had to import from France fixed quantities of certain goods, such as machinery, textiles, sugar, and flour, which were then uncompetitive in price or surplus in Europe, and in addition the states were forced to limit their imports from countries outside the franc zone. While this scheme made nonsense of any plan for inter-African trade, it was for a period highly profitable to France. With the fall in the world price of primary commodities these profits began to diminish, as did enthusiasm for 'aid' in France. At the present moment the most which can be said in favour of French aid is that it does not now, as it did in the past, make an actual profit for France from the less developed states of its former African empire. Teresa Hayter sums it up:

> France does not gain in its transactions with the States nor does it lose; aid, private investment, French Government expenditures and imports from them are balanced by exports to them, repatriation of capital and remittances of profits and salaries.

This state of affairs is considered to be no longer of value to France. The Jeanneney Report published in 1964 and expressing the official French view, pointed out that the protective system of the French zone was no longer in the interests of France and the report therefore advocated the re-deployment of French aid. In any event, France had to comply with her obligations to the European Common Market. Under the new Convention of Association which came into force in the summer of 1964, the six members of the European Common Market are to achieve in stages a free trade area and this will no longer make it possible for France to discriminate in favour of the African states nor for these states to discriminate against France's common market partners. Exports from these states will by the end of a five-year period have to be aligned to world prices. In consequence the primary production which they have built up on the strength of the promise of guaranteed markets and prices is likely to fail to be competitive in world conditions. It is difficult to see how Senegal in particular can manage without a French subsidy for her groundnuts, and President [Léopold] Senghor has already called attention to the serious economic position into which this puts his country.

In fact, the limited neo-colonialism of the French period is now being merged in the collective neo-colonialism of the European Common Market which enables other states, hitherto outside the French preserve, to profit by the system. It also rationalises the division of Africa into economic zones based upon Europe, by drawing in four other states. The Congo (Leopoldville), Burundi, and Rwanda are, as previous Belgian colonies, tied to the Belgian economic system and Somalia through its previous association with Italy is also brought in as an associated state of the common market.

A grouping such as this raises the wider problems of African neo-colonialism and emphasises its irresponsible nature. Of the states carved out of the former French colonies one, Guinea, has been able, with great suffering and losses it is true, to cut free from the type of neo-colonialist control imposed on the others. Mali has been forced to accept some of the rules and regulations which govern the relations of the former French colonies to France, but at least she has set up her own currency, limits transfers of money abroad and receives from France only a partial guarantee of the parity of her currency with the French franc.

In the case of all the other states their currencies have been stabilised on a fixed parity with the French franc and have a total guarantee from the French treasury. These states pay their receipts of French francs into operation accounts in the French treasury. These accounts can be overdrawn and the states can draw on them against their own currencies to an unlimited extent. Obviously, however, whatever the theoretical position, the international financial position of these countries is subject to control in that at any time their operation accounts in the French treasury could be blocked, as was done in the case of Guinea. Most, at any rate, of the states concerned lack the strength to stand up against such pressure as did Guinea.

Why then, it may be asked, are these powers not sufficient to enable France to persuade these states to follow present French foreign policy which is based upon a 'third force' concept? France did not support the USA and Belgium in their 'humanitarian' intervention at Stanleyville in the Congo. Unlike Britain and the other common market countries, France has openly opposed the US's policy in Santo Domingo, has recognised the People's Republic of China, and has recommended the neutralisation of Vietnam.

Yet only a minority of the African states which would appear to be under French neo-colonial control have followed the French line. The majority of them refuse to recognise China or in any way criticise USA policy. Indeed, they behave in a fashion suggestive of being under USA rather than French influence. The answer to this apparent paradox will, I believe, be found in the following chapters of this book in which I attempt to explain the power and ramifications of international financial control.[58] Here one has a super state which can at times even override the policy wishes of the nominal neo-colonial master.

The control of the funds of the French neo-colonial African states is exercised by the administrative council of their central banks, which are composed partly of Frenchmen without whose agreement no decision in monetary policy can be taken. This French banking complex, with its absolute control of the currencies and external payments of the French neo-colonial states, could, in theory, dictate that these states follow a French policy. However, the complex is itself subject,

---

58 *Editor's note*: The author is referring to Nkrumah, *Neo-Colonialism, the Last Stage of Imperialism* (London: Thomas Nelson & Sons, 1965)

in the manner later described, to external pressures which support USA rather than French policies where a difference of opinion arises.

Part of the value of commencing a study of neo-colonialism in its African context is that it provides examples of every type of the system. It is impossible to define the African situation in terms of independent states, divided into the non-aligned and the neo-colonialist camp, colonies and racialist states such as South Africa. In Africa, all former colonies which have now become independent, including particularly South Africa, are subject in some degree to neo-colonialist pressures which however much they wish to resist they cannot entirely escape, struggle as they may. The difference in reality is between those states that accept neo-colonialism as a policy and those which resist it. Similarly, the colonial problem of Africa is in many ways really neo-colonial.

The Portuguese African territories appear at first sight only to raise the issue of freedom from colonial rule but in fact they exist as colonies only because Portugal is itself a neo-colonial state. For the last 50 years the Great Powers have regarded the Portuguese colonies as counters which they can exchange between themselves in order to readjust the balance of power. In 1913, the British and Germans had initialled an agreement for their division and this was only prevented by the outbreak of WWI. In the appeasement period prior to WWII, when it was thought that [Adolf] Hitler could be bought off by an offer of colonial territory, the Portuguese colonies were again regarded as the suitable bribe.

If Portugal controls these colonies now it is only because of the military strength which she derives through her NATO alliance. Portugal is however not a member of NATO because of any military assistance which she could render the alliance but because this is a convenient way by which Portuguese territory can be made available to the forces of other members of the alliance.

At the other end of the scale is the French colony of Somalia. It continues to exist as a colony not because France would resist pressure to grant it independence but because of African disunity. It is a point of dispute between Somalia and Ethiopia. African disunity maintains this colony. If it were to go to either of its neighbours, it would almost inevitably provoke a conflict between them.

Rhodesia, while theoretically a colony, is really a fossilised form of the earliest type of neo-colonialism which was practised in southern Africa until the formation of the Union of South Africa. The essence of the Rhodesia system is not to employ individuals drawn from the people of the territory itself to run the country, as in the newer type of neo-colonial state, but to utilise instead an alien minority. The majority of the European ruling class of Rhodesia only came to the colony after WWII , but it is they and not the African inhabitants, who outnumber them 16 to 1, that Britain regards as 'the Government.' This racialist state is protected from outside pressure because under international law it is a British colony, while Britain herself excuses her failure to exercise her legal rights to prevent the oppression and exploitation of the African inhabitants (of which of course she officially disapproves) because of a supposed

British parliamentary convention. In other words, by maintaining Rhodesia nominally as a colony, Britain in fact gives her official protection as a second South Africa and the European racialists are left free to treat the African inhabitants as they will.

The Rhodesian system thus has all the hallmarks of the neo-colonial model. The patron power, Britain, awards to a local government over which it claims to have no control unlimited rights and exploitation within the territory. Yet Britain still retains powers to exclude other countries from intervening either to liberate its African population or to bring its economy into some other zone of influence. The manoeuvring over Rhodesia's 'independence' is an excellent example of the workings of neo-colonialism and of the practical difficulties to which the system gives rise. A European minority of less than a quarter of a million could not maintain, in the conditions of Africa today, rule over four million Africans without external support from somewhere. When the settlers talk of 'independence' they are not thinking of standing on their own feet but merely of seeking a new neo-colonialist master who would, in their view, be more reliable than Britain.

As will be seen from the chapters which follow, modern neo-colonialism is based upon the control of nominally independent states by giant financial interests. These interests often act through or on behalf of a particular capitalist state, but they are quite capable of acting on their own and forcing those imperial countries in which they have a dominant interest to follow their lead. There is, however, an older type of neo-colonialism which is based primarily on military considerations.

A world power, having decided on principles of global strategy that it is necessary to have a military base in this or that nominally independent country, must ensure that the country where the base is situated is friendly. Here is another reason for balkanisation. If the base can be situated in a country which is so constituted economically that it cannot survive without substantial 'aid' from the military power which owns the base, then, so it is argued, the security of the base can be assured. Like so many of the other assumptions on which neo-colonialism is based this one is false. The presence of foreign bases arouses popular hostility to the neo-colonial arrangements which permit them more quickly and more surely than does anything else, and throughout Africa these bases are disappearing. Libya may be quoted as an example of how this policy has failed.

Libya has had a long colonial history. From the 16th century onwards it was a Turkish colony, but in 1900, in the heyday of colonialism, France and Italy agreed that if Italy would not oppose France occupying Morocco, France would not oppose Italy occupying Libya. So, when in 1911 and 1912 France was occupying Morocco, Italy went to war with Turkey and, defeating her, annexed Libya.

Despite promises during WWII to the people of Libya that they would never again be subjected to Italian rule, France tried at the peace settlement to have

Italy reinstalled in order to support her own position in Tunisia. This solution proving impossible, Libya became nominally independent but actually under British neo-colonial control.

According to the figures collated by the British Overseas Development Institute, during the period 1945 to 1963 Libya received no less than 17 per cent of the total bilateral aid which Britain gave to all foreign countries outside the Commonwealth in that period. The Overseas Development Institute notes that although these payments to Libya are counted as 'aid' there IS no doubt that they are in essence straightforward payments to the Libyan government in return for the use of bases. Nevertheless, popular pressure in Libya has now made it necessary for the Libyan government to terminate the military agreement for British bases.

These limitations on the real independence of many countries in Africa should not be allowed to obscure the very great achievements already gained in the struggle for African independence and unity. In 1945, Africa largely comprised the colonial territories of European powers, and the idea that the greater part of the continent would be independent within 20 years would have seemed impossible to any political observer in the immediate post-war period. Yet, not only has independence been achieved but considerable progress has been made towards the establishment of African unity. To this unity there are still powerful obstacles but they are no greater than the obstacles already overcome and, if their nature is understood, they are clearly surmountable.

Already, and this will ultimately be the decisive factor, the mass of the African people support unity in the same way as they previously supported the various local movements for political independence. Many of the political leaders of French West Africa, for example, did not at first support independence. In 1946, in the French National Assembly, of which he was then a member, Félix Houphouet-Boigny, the president of the Ivory Coast, claimed 'there are no separatists on these benches ... there is a powerful bond, capable of resisting all tests, a moral bond which unites us. It is the ideal of liberty, fraternity, equality, for whose triumph France has never hesitated to sacrifice its most noble blood.' The same policy of the maintenance of unity with France was also supported at that time by President Senghor of Senegal, who said, 'The French union must be a conjunction of civilisations, a melting-pot of culture ... it is a marriage rather than an association.'

It was mass pressure for independence which forced these leaders to reverse their previous positions and to declare themselves in favour of national sovereignty. In the same way mass pressure made it impossible for an African leader to oppose independence, so today mass pressure makes it impossible for them openly to oppose African unity. Those who are against it can only show their opposition in indirect ways; by suggesting that the pace towards it is too fast; that this or that plan is impracticable or that there are procedural difficulties which prevent them assisting in formulating a practical plan for it. The case for African unity is very strong and the instinct of the mass of the people is right.

It is only when the artificial boundaries that divide her are broken down so as to provide for viable economic units, and ultimately a single African unit, that Africa will be able to develop industrially, for her own sake, and ultimately for the sake of a healthy world economy. A common currency is needed and communications of all kinds must be developed to allow the free flow of goods and services.

The Economic Commission for Africa (ECA) has repeatedly emphasised the need for economic planning on a continental scale. The inadequacy of national planning can be demonstrated by a glance at the economies of, for example, Mali, the Upper Volta, Niger, and Uganda. These land-locked states, which export large quantities of food products to other African states, cannot remain indifferent to the agricultural self-sufficiency schemes adopted by their neighbours. Similarly, a national government planning the establishment of a new industry may find that a neighbouring state is developing one like it. Such duplication would probably result in wasted resources if each was depending on exporting its surplus to its neighbour.

Few would argue against the need for economic planning on a national scale. How much stronger is the argument for continental planning. The modern trend is towards larger economic and political units as interdependence of nations and peoples grows. No country can be completely self-sufficient or afford to ignore political events outside its borders. Africa is clearly fragmented into too many small, uneconomic and non-viable states, many of whom are having a very hard struggle to survive. As already noted, others have had to cling to old ties with former colonial rulers and have become easy prey to neo-colonialist forces. Some of them have found themselves, whether they liked it or not, drawn into the Cold War and into the rivalries between foreign powers. The Congo is a notable example.

Naturally, each national government is concerned primarily with the welfare of its own citizens. It could only be expected to agree to a policy of unification if the immediate and long-term benefits became so apparent that it would be positively damaging to its citizens not to co-operate. We are faced here with the problem of uneven economic growth. Some African countries are richer in natural resources than others. The less fortunate will need reassuring that their interests will not suffer at the hands of the more developed states.

Past economic union experience has not been encouraging. The linking of the Rhodesias and Nyasaland benefited chiefly Southern Rhodesia. Kenya has gained principally from the East African Common Market, Uganda and Tanganyika being at best only marginal gainers. In the former French colonial federations, the benefits of economic unity tended to centre in Brazzaville, Abidjan, and Dakar. These examples further strengthen the argument for continentally planned economic growth so that all states can benefit from industrialisation and other improvements made possible by unified direction. The richer countries will be able to help the poorer. Resources can be pooled and development projects co-ordinated to raise the living standards of every African.

The time factor is important. As ECA has pointed out, now is the time to act, before each state gets too deeply involved in major investment and structural decisions based on narrow, national markets. With each month that passes, the foreign interests of neo-colonialism get a tighter grip on Africa's economic life.

The comparatively recent penetration of American big business into Africa points once again to the danger from neo-colonialism. So also does the combining of large firms to form powerful monopolies. How can some of our smaller states hope to bargain successfully with powerful foreign combines some of which control financial empires worth more than the state's total revenue? The smaller the state, and the more formidable the foreign interests, the less likely are the conditions for economic independence to be met. For example, Ghana, because of its economic size and alternative industries, has been in a stronger position for bargaining with the aluminium companies than much smaller, and economically more limited Togo can hope to be in dealing with French phosphate interests. The domination of Africa's economy by foreign firms must be ended if we are to achieve rounded economic growth, and this can only be done through unified action.

Something in the nature of an economic revolution is required. Our development has been held back for too long by the colonial type of economy. We need to reorganise entirely so that each country can specialise in producing the goods and crops for which it is best suited.

With economic unity, those countries in Africa which are beginning to establish modern industries would benefit from wider markets. We would all be in a better bargaining position to obtain higher prices for our goods and to establish adequate taxation of foreign factor earnings. In fact, a whole new pattern of economic development would be made possible. Agriculture could be modernised more quickly with more capital at its disposal. Industries on a larger and more economic scale could be planned. These could afford to make use of new techniques involving heavy capital outlay. Smaller plants planned to meet only national needs are likely to have higher costs, and are eventually less able to reduce costs than optimum sized limits.

National planning bodies would still have a very important part to play in a unified Africa. They would, for example, supply essential information about local conditions, but their work would be made easier with the experienced advice and help of a single planning body keeping an eye on Africa's interests as a whole. The research and training in development projects already being carried out by the ECA Development Institute in Dakar would be strengthened to serve both the continental and national bodies. Expensive failures due to lack of co-ordination would be avoided. A case in point is the Inga dam project which is to provide power for a sugar refinery, a plastics and hardboard (from sugar cane waste) complex in Bangui, which in turn will ship bulk plastics to a plastic products industry in Brazzaville. Obviously, there should be a planning body able to phase and harmonise construction timing for the Brazzaville and Bangui plants, the power lines from Inga to Bangui and Brazzaville, and the transportation services between Bangui and Brazzaville and the dam itself.

In the process of obtaining economic unity there is bound to be much hard bargaining between the various states. Integration of different aspects of economic policy will proceed at different rates, and there may be disappointing delays and compromises to be worked out. But given the will to succeed, difficulties can be resolved.

In general, the broader the front on which economic unity is launched the quicker the goals and policies of a fully developed Africa can be achieved. An all-African planning body could take immediate steps towards the development of large-scale industry and power; for the removal of barriers to inter-African trade; and for the creation of a central bank and the formation of a unified policy on all aspects of export control, tariff and quota arrangements. The ECA has carried out several surveys designed to provide information to help in the making of decisions on these points.

Among immediate needs are the manufacture in Africa of agricultural machinery of all kinds to speed up the modernisation of agriculture. We need supplies of electrical equipment for use in the growing electric power production essential for industrial growth. Mining and industrial machinery must be produced in Africa to lower the costs of developing our mineral resources. Construction machinery and supplies, chemicals, fertilisers, plastics, are all urgently required, and Africa must produce them for her own requirements.

Reports of the ECA Industrial Co-ordination Missions to different regions in Africa suggest that the production of iron and steel, non-ferrous metals, engineering supplies, chemicals and fertilisers, cement, paper and textiles should be developed on an inter-African basis since their efficiency depends on large-scale production. Other industries which can run efficiently on a smaller scale can be planned nationally.

The location of the various industries will, of course, depend on many factors such as the availability of power, mineral deposits, nearness to processing plants, markets and so on. Production of aluminium and copper, for example, will have to be developed in those countries where the essential resources, ore and cheap power, are available. The manufacturing of aluminium and copper products, however, need not take place in the countries producing the metals. Similarly, the production of cotton is limited to certain climatic regions, while cotton textile industries can be developed further afield.

Every African state has some contribution to make to the economic whole. There are, for instance, no known deposits of potash in West Africa, but requirements can be met from North Africa, Ethiopia and possibly also from the Congo (Brazzaville) and Gabon. Plans for nitrogenous fertiliser production in

Zambia have already been worked out. The plant could be supplied with coal from Rhodesia (Zimbabwe) and low-cost power from the Victoria Falls. Kenya, with its large forest reserves, could become the centre of a wood distillation complex able to supply the countries of East and Central Africa with gas, acetone, methanol and tar. There are many other examples too numerous to describe.

The urgent need to plan industrial development on a continental scale must not, however, blind us to the equally important need to do the same for agriculture, fishing and forestry. In *The Role of Industry in Development: Some Fallacies*, Dudley Seers has pointed out the inter-dependence of agriculture and industry:

> Materials are needed for growing industries; more important, the swelling town labour force needs to be fed, and this implies that a rising surplus of food has to be produced in the countryside ... To over-emphasise industry, as some countries have found to their cost, leads paradoxically in the end to a slower rate of industrialisation.

African states are importing larger amounts of food than ever before from abroad. This trend must be stopped by a carefully planned expansion of our own agriculture.

As an industry, there can be specialisation so that each region or state concentrates on producing the agricultural products for which it is best suited. For instance, it is wasteful for each West African state to try to be self-sufficient in rice when Senegal's Casamance district would be well able to supply the need. Equally, Mali and the Upper Volta are obvious exporters of fresh, tinned and processed meat, while coastal states would supply fresh, tinned and smoked fish.

A further argument for a unified agricultural policy is implied in the need to step up efforts to combat many of the obstacles to economic growth. Locusts, the tsetse fly and plant diseases are no respecters of political frontiers. Research into their control would benefit from a pooling of brain power and technical know-how. So also would medicine and social services. How much greater the chance of wiping out major epidemic diseases like river blindness and sleeping sickness if action against them is co-ordinated and unified.

The advantage of unified military and diplomatic policies, both for our own security and to achieve freedom for every part of Africa, are so obvious as to need no comment.

Transport and communications are also sectors where unified planning is needed. Roads, railways, waterways, airlines must be made to serve Africa's needs, not the requirements of foreign interests. Communications between African states are quite inadequate. In many cases it is still easier to travel from an airport in Africa to Europe or America than to go from one African state to another.

Economic unity to be effective must be accompanied by political unity. The two are inseparable, each necessary for the future greatness of our continent, and the full development of our resources. There are several examples of major unions of states in the world today. In *Africa Must Unite*, I described some of the more important ones, and warned against the danger of regional federations in Africa.

Africa today is the main stamping ground of the neo-colonialist forces that seek the domination of the world for the imperialism they serve. Spreading from South Africa, the Congo, the Rhodesias, Angola, Mozambique, they form a maze-like connection with the mightiest international financial monopolies in the world. These monopolies are extending their banking and industrial organisations throughout the African continent. Their spokesmen push their interests in the parliaments and governments of the world and sit on the international bodies that are supposed to exist for the promotion of world peace and the welfare of the less-developed countries. Against such a formidable phalanx of forces, how can we move? Certainly not singly, but in a combination that will give strength to our bargaining power and eliminate so many of the duplications that give greater force and greater advantage to the imperialists and their strategy of neo-colonialism.

Decolonisation is a word much and unctuously used by imperialist spokesmen to describe the transfer of political control from colonialist to African sovereignty. The motive spring of colonialism, however, still controls the sovereignty. The young countries are still the providers of raw materials, the old of manufactured goods. The change in the economic relationship between the new sovereign states and the erstwhile masters is only one of form. Colonialism has achieved a new guise. It has become neo-colonialism, the last stage of imperialism; its final bid for existence, as monopoly capitalism or imperialism is the last stage of capitalism. And neo-colonialism is fast entrenching itself within the body of Africa today through the consortia and monopoly combinations that are the carpetbaggers of the African revolt against colonialism and the urge for continental unity.

These interests are centred on the mining companies of South and Central Africa. From mining they ramify into an involved pattern of investment companies, manufacturing concerns, transport, public utility organisations, oil and chemical industries, nuclear installations and many other undertakings too numerous to mention. Their enterprises spill across the vast African continent and over the oceans into North America, Australia, New Zealand, Asia, the Caribbean, South America, the United Kingdom, Scandinavia, and most of western Europe.

Connections, direct and indirect, are maintained with many of the giants of American industry and finance. They are supported by leading bankers, financiers and industrialists in the United Kingdom, France, Belgium, Germany, America, and elsewhere. The rotas of their directorates are filled with names that have a familiar ring for those who have the least knowledge of international finance and industry. Names like Oppenheimer, Hambro, Drayton, Rothschild, d'Erlanger, Gillet, Lafond, Robiliart, van der Straeten, Hochschild, Chester Beatty, Patino, Engelhard, Timmins are ubiquitous. Others, equally powerful in the interests they dominate, avoid the publicity of lengthy lists of their directorships, either by complete absence from the pages of directories anxious to advertise their glories, or by coyly hiding their eminence behind a lonely announcement with name and address.

These intricate inter-connections of the great imperialist monopolies expose the real forces that are behind world events. They indicate also the pattern which links those events to the developing countries at different points of the globe. They reveal the duality of the interests that force the developing countries to import goods and services which are the products of companies combined in the monopoly groups directly exploiting their natural resources or intimately associated with them. This is the double edge to the guillotine that cuts off Africa's wealth from Africa, to the greater enrichment of the countries which absorb her primary materials and return them to her in the form of finished products.

In their newfound independence, it is to these very same monopolistic groups that the new African states are obliged to turn to supply the requirements arising from the need to lay the foundations for their economic transformation. The policy of non-alignment, whenever it is exercised, imposes the obligation to 'shop around', but since capitalism has come to the peak of monopoly, it is impossible for any of us to avoid dealing with monopoly in some form or another. But it is in the nature of our arrangements with the monopolies that the freedom or otherwise of the African states lies. Where we establish and maintain the integrity of our financial institutions and keep our basic projects free from imperialist control, we leave ourselves room to manoeuvre away from the neo-colonialism that, unfortunately, has closed its grip upon countries whose independence is overshadowed by a heavy reliance upon extra-African associations. In this atmosphere of relative freedom, the giant combines that open up industrial enterprises on our soil do so on arrangements that are well screened and are part of nationally planned advancement. The national banks are really national banks, formed and run out of the country's own resources, and our other financial and economic institutions are guarded against neo-colonialist infiltration.

Unhappily, these conditions are rare in Africa. Most of the territories pass into the state of national sovereignty in unviable circumstances that inhibit even a modicum of free movement within national limits. They could be overcome, but only within the combined strength that continental unity and a central connective socialist policy, free of attachments to other continents, could give. As things are, most of our new states, alarmed at the prospect of the harsh world of poverty, disease, ignorance, and lack of financial and technical resources into which they are thrust from the womb of colonialism, are reluctant to cut the cord that holds them to the imperialist mother. Their hesitancy is fostered by the sugared water of aid, which is the stopgap between avid hunger and the hoped-for greater nourishment that never comes. As a result, we find that imperialism, having quickly adopted its outlook to the loss of direct political control, has retained and extended its economic grip (and thereby its political compulsion) by the artfulness of neo-colonialist insinuation.

The increasing expansion of productive capacity and potential output of the advanced capitalist countries has its corollary in the necessity to export on a geometrically increasing scale the finished products of industry and the excess capital that could only further inflate competition at home, but brings rapid and high returns from the industrially-starved new nations. Hence the fevered jostling for position in these areas as well as in that of raw materials monopoly, which is using Africa as the playground, not only of the cold war (an aspect of the fight of capitalism for existence against socialism), but of the competitive struggle of international monopoly. North American imports into Africa rose from 10–3 per cent in 1959 to 13–7 per cent in 1962, while those from other western countries and Japan remained the same or declined slightly. This corresponds with the increasing American investments in the continent's extractive industries and the growth of USA's participation in financial establishments on this continent. American banking houses are making inroads into territories formerly catered for solely by European and British banks. The French banks still dominate in the former French countries and the Belgians in the Congo; but this is frequently a front for American participation.

European financial advisers constantly counsel the African countries on the advantages that they can receive from remaining in association with the erstwhile 'mother country', while depreciating the possibilities of inter-African association. Much subtlety is employed by Lombard, the commentator of the *Financial Times*.[59] In an article which appeared in the issue of 6 February 1964 of this influential London newspaper, a product of an industrial holding company which also produces *The Economist*, Lombard asserted that 'there is not much that African countries can do directly to help one another financially at this stage of their economic evolution.' He is therefore,

> glad to see that the independent African countries are now coming to rec-
> ognise that it is very much in their own interests to preserve the monetary
> ties with leading European countries they inherited from their colonial days
> ... They obviously entertained strong suspicion that the enthusiasm their

---

59 *Editor's note*: The author refers to Lombard, a British business column in the
    Financial Times. It borrowed its name from *Lombard Street: A Description of the
    Money Market*, an 1873 book by Walter Bagehot, the editor of *The Economist*,
    which was a full study of the Bank of England.

old mother countries were displaying for allowing them to remain within their monetary areas was motivated largely, if not wholly, by consideration of self-interest. And they are inclined to assume that this implied that their own purpose would be served best by following up political independence with its financial equivalent at the earliest possible opportunity.

Lombard assured his readers that the Africans showed wisdom when the secretariat of ECA, assisting the OAU to implement its resolution on the possibility of establishing an African clearing house and payments union, had the good sense 'to seek the advice of the distinguished American monetary authority Professor Triflin of Yale University.' Need we be surprised that in his report the distinguished American professor pointed out that 'it would be most unwise lightly to condemn or break up financial arrangements with major trading companies and financial centres.'

This, of course, we might consider neo-colonialist penetration, but to Lombard it is only one side of the picture. For there are two worlds, and the African countries 'should now strive to get the best of both worlds, by maintaining and even further developing the relations they have with the major international monetary areas and at the same time building their own financial self-help mechanisms.' How it is possible to resolve two contradictions Lombard does not volunteer to explain, but what he does confess is that this unresolvable two-way procedure 'would meet with nothing but the fullest approval from their (African) present monetary area associates.'

This says plenty and we have no difficulty in believing what it says, for the simple fact is that those who control the major international monetary areas are placing their time bombs within the 'self-help mechanisms' of the African countries. For these mechanisms are controlled by the financial monopolists of imperialism, the bankers and financiers who have been very busy in the past few years setting up establishments throughout Africa, infiltrating into the economic heart of many countries and linking with the most important enterprises that are being established to exploit the continent's natural resources on a larger scale than ever before for their own private gain.

Though the aim of the neo-colonialists is economic domination, they do not confine their operations to the economic sphere. They use the old colonialist methods of religious, educational, and cultural infiltration. For example, in the independent states, many expatriate teachers and 'cultural ambassadors' influence the minds of the young against their own country and people. They do this by undermining confidence in the national government and social system through exalting their own notions of how a state should be run, and forget that there is no monopoly of political wisdom.

But all this indirect subversion is as nothing compared with the brazen onslaught of international capitalists. Here is empire, the empire of finance capital, in fact if not in name, a vast sprawling network of inter-continental activity on a highly diversified scale that controls the lives of millions of people in the most widely separated parts of the world, manipulating whole industries and exploiting the labour and riches of nations for the greedy satisfaction of a few. Here resides the mainspring of power, the direction of policies that stand against the advancing tide of freedom of the exploited people of Africa and the world. Here is the adamantine enemy of African independence and unity, braced in an international chain of common interest that regards the likely coming together of the new nations as a major blow at its continued domination of the resources and economies of others. Here, indeed, are the real workings of neo-colonialism. Here indeed are the economic ramifications of the monopolies and combines. Their financial and economic empires are pan-African and they can only be challenged on a pan-African basis. Only a united Africa through an All-African Union Government can defeat them.

The Mechanisms of Neo-colonialism

In order to halt foreign interference in the affairs of developing countries it is necessary to study, understand, expose and actively combat neo-colonialism in whatever guise it may appear. For the methods of neo-colonialists are subtle and varied. They operate not only in the economic field, but also in the political, religious, ideological and cultural spheres.

Faced with the militant peoples of the ex-colonial territories in Asia, Africa, the Caribbean, and Latin America, imperialism simply switches tactics. Without a qualm it dispenses with its flags, and even with certain of its more hated expatriate officials. This means, so it claims, that it is 'giving' independence to its former subjects, to be followed by 'aid' for their development. Under cover of such phrases, however, it devises innumerable ways to accomplish objectives formerly achieved by naked colonialism. It is this sum total of these modern attempts to perpetuate colonialism while at the same time talking about 'freedom', which has come to be known as neo-colonialism.

Foremost among the neo-colonialists is the USA, which has long exercised its power in Latin America. Fumblingly at first, she turned towards Europe, and then with more certainty after WWII when most countries of that continent were indebted to her. Since then, with methodical thoroughness and touching attention to detail, the Pentagon set about consolidating its ascendancy, evidence of which can be seen all around the world.

Who really rules in such places as Great Britain, West Germany, Japan, Spain, Portugal, or Italy? If General de Gaulle is 'defecting' from U.S. monopoly control, what interpretation can be placed on his 'experiments' in the Sahara Desert, his paratroopers in Gabon, or his trips to Cambodia and Latin America?

Lurking behind such questions are the extended tentacles of the Wall Street octopus. And its suction cups and muscular strength are provided by a phenomenon dubbed 'The Invisible Government', arising from Wall Street's connection with the Pentagon and various intelligence services. I quote:

The Invisible Government ... is a loose amorphous grouping of individuals and agencies drawn from many parts of the visible government. It is not limited to the Central Intelligence Agency, although the CIA is at its heart. Nor is it confined to the nine other agencies which comprise what is known as the intelligence community: the National Security Council, the Defence Intelligence Agency, the National Security Agency, Army Intelligence, Navy

Intelligence and Research, the Atomic Energy Commission, and the Federal Bureau of Investigation.

The Invisible Government includes also many other units and agencies, as well as individuals, that appear outwardly to be a normal part of the conventional government. It even encompasses business firms and institutions that are seemingly private.

To an extent that is only beginning to be perceived, this shadow government is shaping the lives of 190,000,000 Americans. An informed citizen might come to suspect that the foreign policy of the United States often works publicly in one direction and secretly through the Invisible Government in just the opposite direction.

This Invisible Government is a relatively new institution. It came into being as a result of two related factors: the rise of the United States after World War II to a position of pre-eminent world power, and the challenge to that power by Soviet Communism ...

By 1964 the intelligence network had grown into a massive hidden apparatus, secretly employing about 200,000 persons and spending billions of dollars a year.[60]

Here, from the very citadel of neo-colonialism, is a description of the apparatus which now directs all other Western intelligence set-ups either by persuasion or by force. Results were achieved in Algeria during the April 1961 plot of anti-de Gaulle generals; as also in Guatemala, Iraq, Iran, Suez, and the famous U2 spy intrusion of Soviet air space which wrecked the approaching summit, then in West Germany and again in East Germany in the riots of 1953, in Hungary's abortive crisis of 1959, Poland's of September 1956, and in Korea, Burma, Formosa, Laos, Cambodia, and South Vietnam; they are evident in the trouble in Congo (Leopoldville) which began with [Patrice] Lumumba's murder, and continues till now; in events in Cuba, Turkey, Cyprus, Greece, and in other places too numerous to catalogue completely.[61]

And with what aim have these innumerable incidents occurred? The general objective has been mentioned: to achieve colonialism in fact while preaching independence.

---

60 David Wise and Thomas B. Ross, *The Invisible Government* (New York: Random House, 1964).

61 *Editor's note*: In May 1960, some Western nations and the USSR had planned to meet in Paris, France to discuss issues of disarmament and the perils of nuclear war. On 1 May, a US U-2 spy plane was shot down over the USSR and the Paris Summit ended within a few hours.

On the economic front, a strong factor favouring Western monopolies and acting against the developing world is international capital's control of the world market, as well as of the prices of commodities bought and sold there. From 1951 to 1961, without taking oil into consideration, the general level of prices for primary products fell by 33.1 per cent, while prices of manufactured goods rose 3.5 per cent (within which, machinery and equipment prices rose 31.3 per cent). In that same decade this caused a loss to the Asian, African, and Latin American countries, using 1951 prices as a basis, of some $41,400 million. In the same period, while the volume of exports from these countries rose, their earnings in foreign exchange from such exports decreased.

Another technique of neo-colonialism is the use of high rates of interest. Figures from the World Bank for 1962 showed that seventy-one Asian, African, and Latin American countries owed foreign debts of some $27,000 million, on which they paid in interest and service charges some $5,000 million. Since then, such foreign debts have been estimated as more than $30,000 million in these areas. In 1961, the interest rates on almost three-quarters of the loans offered by the major imperialist powers amounted to more than five per cent, in some cases up to seven or eight per cent, while the call-in periods of such loans have been burdensomely short.

While capital worth $30,000 million was exported to some 56 developing countries between 1956 and 1962, it is estimated that interest and profit alone extracted on this sum from the debtor countries amounted to more than 15,000 million. This method of penetration by economic aid recently soared into prominence when a number of countries began rejecting it. Ceylon, Indonesia, and Cambodia are among those who turned it down. Such 'aid' is estimated on the annual average to have amounted to $2,600 million between 1951 and 1955; $4,007 million between 1956 and 1959, and $6,000 million between 1960 and 1962. But the average sums taken out of the aided countries by such donors in a sample year, 1961, are estimated to amount to $5,000 million in profits, $1,000 million in interest, and $5,800 million from non-equivalent exchange, or a total of $11,800 million extracted against $6,000 million put in. Thus, 'aid' turns out to be another means of exploitation, a modern method of capital export under a more cosmetic name.

Still another neo-colonialist trap on the economic front has come to be known as 'multilateral aid' through international organisations: the IMF, the International Bank for Reconstruction and Development (known as the World Bank), the International Finance Corporation and the International Development Association are examples, all, significantly, having US capital as their major backing. These agencies have the habit of forcing would-be borrowers to submit to various offensive conditions, such as supplying information about their economies, submitting their policy and plans to review by the World Bank, and accepting agency supervision of their use of loans. As for the alleged development, between 1960 and mid-1963 the International

Development Association promised a total of $500 million to applicants, out of which only $70 million was actually received.

In more recent years, as pointed out by Monitor in *The Times*, 1 July 1965, there has been a substantial increase in communist technical and economic aid activities in developing countries. During 1964 the total amount of assistance offered was approximately $600 million. This was almost a third of the total communist aid given during the previous decade. The Middle East received about 40 per cent of the total, Asia 36 per cent, Africa 22 per cent, and Latin America the rest.

Increased Chinese activity was responsible to some extent for the larger amount of aid offered in 1964, though China contributed only a quarter of the total aid committed; the Soviet Union provided a half, and the East European countries a quarter. Although aid from socialist countries still falls far short of that offered from the West, it is often more impressive, since it is swift and flexible, and interest rates on communist loans are only about two per cent compared with five to six per cent charged on loans from Western countries.

Nor is the whole story of 'aid' contained in figures, for there are conditions which hedge it around: the conclusion of commerce and navigation treaties; agreements for economic co-operation; the right to meddle in internal finances, including currency and foreign exchange, to lower trade barriers in favour of the donor country's goods and capital; to protect the interests of private investments; determination of how the funds are to be used; forcing the recipient to set up counterpart funds; to supply raw materials to the donor; and use of such funds – a majority of it, in fact – to buy goods from the donor nation. These conditions apply to industry, commerce, agriculture, shipping. and insurance, apart from others which are political and military.

So-called 'invisible trade' furnishes Western monopolies with yet another means of economic penetration. Over 90 per cent of world ocean shipping is controlled by the imperialist countries. They control shipping rates and, between 1951 and 1961, they increased them some five times in a total rise of about 60 per cent, the upward trend continuing. Thus, net annual freight expenses incurred by Asia, Africa, and Latin America amount to no less than an estimated $1,600 million. This is over and above all other profits and interest payments. As for insurance payments, in 1961 alone these amounted to an unfavourable balance in Asia, Africa and Latin America of some additional $370 million.

Having waded through all this, however, we have begun to understand only the basic methods of neo-colonialism. The full extent of its inventiveness is far from exhausted.

In the labour field, for example, imperialism operates through labour arms like the social democratic parties of Europe led by the British Labour Party, and through such instruments as the International Confederation of Free Trade Unions (ICFTU), now apparently being superseded by the New York Africa-American Labour Centre (AALC) under American Federation of Labor and Congress of Industrial Organisations (AFL-CIO) chief George Meany and the well-known CIA man in labour's top echelons, Irving Brown.

In 1945, out of the euphoria of anti-fascist victory, the World Federation of Trade Unions (WFTU) had been formed, including all world labour except the US's AFL. By 1949, however, led by the British Trade Union Congress (TUC), a number of pro-imperialist labour bodies in the West broke away from the WFTU over the issue of anti-colonialist liberation, and set up the ICFTU.

For ten years it continued under British TUC leadership. Its record in Africa, Asia, and Latin America could gratify only the big international monopolies which were extracting super-profits from those areas.

In 1959, at Brussels, the United States AFL-CIO union centre fought for and won control of the ICFTU executive board. From then on a flood of typewriters, mimeograph machines, cars, supplies, buildings, salaries and, so it is still averred, outright bribes for labour leaders in various parts of the developing world rapidly linked ICFTU in the minds of the rank and file with the CIA. To such an extent did its prestige suffer under these American bosses that, in 1964, the AFL-CIO brains felt it necessary to establish a fresh outfit. They set up the AALC in New York right across the river from the UN.

'As a steadfast champion of national independence, democracy, and social justice', unblushingly stated the April 1965 Bulletin put out by this Centre, 'the AFL-CIO will strengthen its efforts to assist the advancement of the economic conditions of the African peoples. Toward this end, steps have been taken to expand assistance to the African free trade unions by organising the African-American Labour Centre. Such assistance will help African labour play a vital role in the economic and democratic upbuilding of their countries.'

The March issue of this bulletin, however, gave the game away: 'In mobilising capital resources for investment in Workers Education, Vocational Training, Co-operatives, Health Clinics, and Housing, the Centre will work with both private and public institutions. It will also *encourage labour management co-operation to expand American capital investment in the African nations.*' The italics are mine. Could anything be plainer?

Following a pattern previously set by the ICFTU, it has already started classes: one for drivers and mechanics in Nigeria, one in tailoring in Kenya. Labour scholarships are being offered to Africans who want to study trade unionism in – of all places – Austria, ostensibly by the Austrian unions. Elsewhere, labour, organised into political parties of which the British Labour Party is a leading and typical example, has shown a similar aptitude for encouraging 'Labour-management co-operation to expand ... capital investment in African nations.'

But as the struggle sharpens, even these measures of neo-colonialism are proving too mild. Africa, Asia, and Latin America have begun to experience a round of *coups d'état* or would-be coups, together with a series of political assassinations which have destroyed in their political primes some of the newly emerging nations' best leaders. To ensure success in these endeavours, the imperialists have made widespread and wily use of ideological and cultural weapons in the form of intrigues, manoeuvres, and slander campaigns.

Some of these methods used by neo-colonialists to slip past our guard must now be examined. The first is retention by the departing colonialists of various kinds of privileges which infringe on our sovereignty: that of setting up military bases or stationing troops in former colonies and the supplying of 'advisers' of one sort or another. Sometimes a number of 'rights' are demanded: land concessions, prospecting rights for minerals and/or oil; the 'right' to collect customs, to carry out administration, to issue paper money; to be exempt from customs duties and/or taxes for expatriate enterprises; and, above all, the 'right' to provide 'aid.' Also demanded and granted are privileges in the cultural field; that Western information services be exclusive; and that those from socialist countries be excluded.

Even the cinema stories of fabulous Hollywood are loaded. One has only to listen to the cheers of an African audience as Hollywood's heroes slaughter red Indians or Asiatics to understand the effectiveness of this weapon. For, in the developing continents, where the colonialist heritage has left a vast majority still illiterate, even the smallest child gets the message contained in the blood and thunder stories emanating from California. And along with murder and the Wild West goes an incessant barrage of anti-socialist propaganda, in which the trade union man, the revolutionary, or the man of dark skin is generally cast as the villain, while the policeman, the gum-shoe, the federal agent – in a word, the CIA-type spy – is ever the hero. Here, truly, is the ideological underbelly of those political murders which so often use local people as their instruments.

While Hollywood takes care of fiction, the enormous monopoly press, together with the outflow of slick, clever, expensive magazines, attends to what it chooses to call 'news.' Within separate countries, one or two news agencies control the news handouts, so that a deadly uniformity is achieved, regardless of the number of separate newspapers or magazines; while internationally, the financial preponderance of the USA is felt more and more through its foreign correspondents and offices abroad, as well as through its influence over international capitalist journalism. Under this guise, a flood of anti-liberation propaganda emanates from the capital cities of the West, directed against China, Vietnam, Indonesia, Algeria, Ghana and all countries which hack out their own independent path to freedom. Prejudice is rife. For example, wherever there is armed struggle against the forces of reaction, the nationalists are referred to as rebels, terrorists, or frequently 'communist terrorists'!

Perhaps one of the most insidious methods of the neo- colonialists is evangelism. Following the liberation movement there has been a veritable riptide of religious sects, the overwhelming majority of them American. Typical of these are Jehovah's Witnesses who recently created trouble in certain developing countries by busily teaching their citizens not to salute the new national flags.

'Religion' was too thin to smother the outcry that arose against this activity, and a temporary lull followed. But the number of evangelists continues to grow.

Yet even evangelism and the cinema are only two twigs on a much bigger tree. Dating from the end of 1961, the U.S. has actively developed a huge ideological plan for invading the so-called Third World, utilising all its facilities from press and radio to the Peace Corps.

During 1962 and 1963 a number of international conferences to this end were held in several places, such as Nicosia in Cyprus, San Jose in Costa Rica, and Lagos in Nigeria. Participants included the CIA, the U.S. Information Agency (USIA), the Pentagon, the International Development Agency, the Peace Corps, and others. Programmes were drawn up which included the systematic use of USA citizens abroad in virtual intelligence activities and propaganda work. Methods of recruiting political agents and of forcing 'alliances' with the USA, were worked out. At the centre of its programmes lay the demand for an absolute US monopoly in the field of propaganda, as well as for counteracting any independent efforts by developing states in the realm of information.

The US sought, and still seeks, with considerable success, to co-ordinate on the basis of its own strategy the propaganda activities of all Western countries. In October 1961, a conference of NATO countries was held in Rome to discuss problems of psychological warfare. It appealed for the organisation of combined ideological operations in Afro-Asian countries by all participants.

In May and June 1962, a seminar was convened by the USA in Vienna on ideological warfare. It adopted a secret decision to engage in a propaganda offensive against the developing countries along lines laid down by the USA. It was agreed that NATO propaganda agencies would, in practice if not in the public eye, keep in close contact with US embassies in their respective countries.

Among instruments of such Western psychological warfare are numbered the intelligence agencies of Western countries headed by those of the USA's 'Invisible Government.' But most significant among them all are Moral Re-Armament (MRA), the Peace Corps and the USIA.

MRA is an organisation founded in 1938 by the American, Frank Buchman. In the last days before WWII, it advocated the appeasement of Hitler, often extolling [Heinrich] Himmler, the Gestapo chief. In Africa, MRA incursions began at the end of World War II. Against the big anti-colonial upsurge that followed victory in 1945, MRA spent millions advocating collaboration between the forces oppressing the African peoples and those same peoples. It is not without significance that Moïse Tshombe and Joseph Kasavubu of Congo (Leopoldville) are both MRA supporters. George Seldes, in his book *One Thousand Americans*, characterised MRA as a fascist organisation 'subsidised by ... Fascists, and with a long record of collaboration with Fascists the world over ...' This description is supported by the active participation in MRA of people like General [Gervais] Carpentier, former commander of NATO land forces, and General Ho Ying-chin, one of Chiang Kai-shek's top generals. To cap this, several newspapers, some of them in the Western world, have claimed that MRA is actually subsidised by the CIA.

When MRA's influence began to fail, some new instrument to cover the ideological arena was desired. It came in the establishment of the American Peace Corps in 1961 by President John F. Kennedy, with Sargent Shriver, Jr., his brother-in-law, in charge. Shriver, a millionaire who made his pile in land speculation in Chicago, was also known as the friend, confidant, and co-worker of the former head of the CIA, Allen Dulles. These two had worked together in both the Office of Strategic Services, USA wartime intelligence agency, and in the CIA.

Shriver's record makes a mockery of President Kennedy's alleged instruction to Shriver to 'keep the CIA out of the Peace Corps.' So does the fact that, although the Peace Corps is advertised as a voluntary organisation, all its members are carefully screened by the USA Federal Bureau of Investigation. Since its creation in 1961, members of the Peace Corps have been exposed and expelled from many African, Middle Eastern, and Asian countries for acts of subversion or prejudice. Indonesia, Tanzania, the Philippines, and even pro-West countries like Turkey and Iran, have complained of its activities.

However, perhaps the chief executor of U.S. psychological warfare is the USIA. Even for the wealthiest nation on earth, the USA lavishes an unusual amount of men, materials, and money on this vehicle for its neo-colonial aims.

The USIA is staffed by some 12 000 persons to the tune of more than $130 million a year. It has more than 70 editorial staffers working on publications abroad. Of its network comprising 110 radio stations, 60 are outside the USA. Programmes are broadcast for Africa by American stations in Morocco, Eritrea, Liberia, Crete, and Barcelona, Spain, as well as from offshore stations on American ships. In Africa alone, the USIA transmits about 30 territorial and national radio programmes whose content glorifies the USA while attempting to discredit countries with an independent foreign policy. The USIA boasts more than 120 branches in about 100 countries, 50 of which are in Africa alone. It has 250 centres in foreign countries, each of which is usually associated with a library. It employs about 200 cinemas and 8 000 projectors which draw upon its nearly 300 film libraries.

This agency is directed by a central body which operates in the name of the president, planning and co-ordinating its activities in close touch with the Pentagon, CIA and other Cold War agencies, including even armed forces intelligence centres. In developing countries, the USIA actively tries to prevent expansion of national media of information so as itself to capture the market-place of ideas. It spends huge sums for publication and distribution of about 60 newspapers and magazines in Africa, Asia, and Latin America.

The American government backs the USIA through direct pressures on developing nations. To ensure its agency a complete monopoly in propaganda, for instance, many agreements for economic co-operation offered by the USA include a demand that Americans be granted preferential rights to disseminate information. At the same time, in trying to close the new nations to other sources of information, it employs other pressures. For instance, after agreeing to set up USIA information centres in their countries, both Togo and Congo (Leopoldville) originally hoped to follow a non-aligned path and permit Russian information centres as a balance. But Washington threatened to stop all aid, thereby forcing these two countries to renounce their plan.

Unbiassed studies of the USIA by such authorities as Dr R. Holt of Princeton University, retired Colonel R. Van de Velde, former intelligence agents Murril Dayer, Wilson Dizard, and others, have all called attention to the close ties between this agency and US Intelligence. For example. Deputy Director Donald M. Wilson was a political intelligence agent in the US Army. Assistant Director for Europe, Joseph Philips, was a successful espionage agent in several Eastern European countries.

Some USIA duties further expose its nature as a top intelligence arm of the US imperialists. In the first place, it is expected to analyse the situation in each country, making recommendations to its embassy, thereby to its government, about changes that can tip the local balance in US favour. Secondly, it organises networks of monitors for radio broadcasts and telephone. conversations, while recruiting informers from government offices. It also hires people to distribute US propaganda. Thirdly, it collects secret information with special reference to defence and economy, as a means of eliminating its international military and economic competitors. Fourthly, it buys its way into local publications to influence their policies, of which Latin America furnishes numerous examples. It has been active in bribing public figures, for example in Kenya and Tunisia. Finally, it finances, directs and often supplies with arms all anti-neutralist forces in the developing countries, witness Tshombe in Congo (Leopoldville) and Pak Hung Ji in South Korea. In a word, with virtually unlimited finances, there seems no bounds to its inventiveness in subversion.

One of the most recent developments in neo-colonialist strategy is the suggested establishment of a businessmen corps which will, like the Peace Corps, act in developing countries. In an article on 'U.S. Intelligence and the Monopolies' in *International Affairs* (Moscow, January 1965), V. Chernyavsky writes: 'There can hardly be any doubt that this Corps is a new U.S. intelligence organisation created on the initiative of the American monopolies to use Big Business for espionage.'

It is by no means unusual for US Intelligence to set up its own business firms which are merely thinly disguised espionage centres. For example, according to Chernyavsky, the CIA. has set up a firm in Taiwan known as Western Enterprises Inc. Under this cover it sends spies and saboteurs to South China. The New Asia Trading Company, a CIA firm in India, has also helped to camouflage US intelligence agents operating in South-east Asia.

Such is the catalogue of neo-colonialism's activities and methods in our time. Upon reading it, the faint-hearted might come to feel that they must give up in despair before such an array of apparent power and seemingly inexhaustible resources. Fortunately, however, history furnishes innumerable proofs of one of its own major laws: that the budding future is always stronger than the withering past. This has been amply demonstrated during every major revolution throughout history.

The American Revolution of 1776 struggled through to victory over a tangle of inefficiency, mismanagement, corruption, outright subversion, and counter-revolution the like of which has been repeated to some degree in every subsequent revolution to date.

The Russian Revolution during the period of [Allied] Intervention, 1917 to 1922, appeared to be dying on its feet. The Chinese Revolution at one time was forced to pull out of its existing bases, lock, stock and barrel, and make the unprecedented Long March; yet it triumphed. Imperialist white mercenaries who dropped so confidently out of the skies on Stanleyville after a plane trip from Ascension Island thought that their job would be 'duck soup.' Yet, till now, the nationalist forces of Congo (Leopoldville) continue to fight their way forward. They do not talk of if they will win, but only of when.

Asia provides a further example of the strength of a people's will to determine their own future. In South Vietnam 'special warfare' is being fought to hold back the tide of revolutionary change. 'Special warfare' is a concept of General Maxwell Taylor and a military extension of the creed of John Foster Dulles: let Asians fight Asians. Briefly, the technique is for the foreign power to supply the money, aircraft, military equipment of all kinds, and the strategic and tactical command from general staff down to officer 'advisers', while the troops of the puppet government bear the brunt of the fighting. Yet in spite of bombing raids and the immense build-up of foreign strength in the area, the people of both North and South Vietnam are proving to be unconquerable.

In other parts of Asia, in Cambodia, Laos, Indonesia, and now the Philippines, Thailand and Burma, the peoples of ex-colonial countries have stood firm and are winning battles against the allegedly superior imperialist enemy. In Latin America, despite 'final' punitive expeditions, the growing armed insurrections in Colombia, Venezuela, and other countries continue to consolidate gains.

In Africa, we in Ghana have withstood all efforts by imperialism and its agents; Tanzania has nipped subversive plots in the bud, as have Brazzaville, Uganda, and Kenya. The struggle rages back and forth. The surging popular forces may still be hampered by colonialist legacies, but nonetheless they advance inexorably.

All these examples prove beyond doubt that neo-colonialism is not a sign of imperialism's strength but rather of its last hideous gasp. It testifies to its inability to rule any longer by old methods. Independence is a luxury it can no longer afford to permit its subject peoples, so that even what it claims to have 'given' it now seeks to take away.

This means that neo-colonialism *can* and *will* be defeated. How can this be done?

Thus far, all the methods of neo-colonialists have pointed in one direction, the ancient, accepted one of all minority ruling classes throughout history – *divide and rule*.

Quite obviously, therefore, *unity* is the first requisite for destroying neo-colonialism. Primary and basic is the need for an all-union government on the much-divided continent of Africa. Along with that, a strengthening of the Afro-Asian Solidarity Organisation and the spirit of Bandung is already under way. To it, we must seek the adherence on an increasingly formal basis of our Latin American brothers. Furthermore, all these liberatory forces have, on all major issues and at every possible instance, the support of the growing socialist sector of the world.

Finally, we must encourage and utilise to the full those still all too few yet growing instances of support for liberation and anti-colonialism inside the imperialist world itself.

To carry out such a political programme, we must all back it with national plans designed to strengthen ourselves as independent nations. An external condition for such independent development is neutrality or *political non-alignment*. This has been expressed in two conferences of Non-Aligned Nations during the recent past, the last of which, in Cairo in 1964, clearly and inevitably showed itself at one with the rising forces of liberation and human dignity.

And the preconditions for all this, to which lip service is often paid but activity seldom directed, is to develop ideological clarity among the anti-imperialist, anti-colonialist, pro-liberation masses of our continents. They, and they alone, make, maintain or break revolutions.

With the utmost speed, neo-colonialism must be analysed in clear and simple terms for the full mass understanding by the surging organisations of the African peoples. The AATUF has already made a start in this direction, while the Pan-African Youth Movement, the women, journalists, farmers, and others are not far behind. Bolstered with ideological clarity, these organisations, closely linked with the ruling parties where liberatory forces are in power, will prove that neo-colonialism is the symptom of imperialism's weakness and that it is defeatable. For, when all is said and done, it is the so-called little man, the bent-backed, exploited, malnourished, blood-covered fighter for independence who decides. And he invariably decides for freedom.

African Socialism Revisited, 1967

This paper was presented at the Africa Seminar held in Cairo. Nkrumah was invited there by the two organs, At-Talia and Problems of Peace and Socialism.

The term 'socialism' has become a necessity in the platform diction and political writings of African leaders. It is a term which unites us in the recognition that the restoration of Africa's humanist and egalitarian principles of society calls for socialism. All of us, therefore, even though pursuing widely contrasting policies in the task of reconstructing our various nation-states, still use 'socialism' to describe our respective efforts. The question must therefore be faced: What real meaning does the term retain in the context of contemporary African politics?

I warned about this in my book *Consciencism*. And yet, socialism in Africa today tends to lose its objective content in favour of a distracting terminology and in favour of general confusion. Discussion centres more on the various conceivable types of socialism than upon the need for socialist development.

Some African political leaders and thinkers certainly use the term 'socialism' as it should in my opinion be used: to describe a complex of social purposes and the consequential social and economic policies, organisational patterns, state structure, and ideologies which can lead to the attainment of those purposes. For such leaders, the aim is to remould African society in the socialist direction; to reconsider African society in such a manner that the humanism of traditional African life re-asserts itself in a modern technical community.

Consequently, socialism in Africa introduces a new social synthesis in which modern technology is reconciled with human values, in which the advanced technical society is realised without the staggering social malefactions and deep schisms of capitalist industrial society. For true economic and social development cannot be promoted without the real socialisation of productive and distributive processes. Those African leaders who believe these principles are the socialists in Africa.

There are, however, other African political leaders and thinkers who use the term socialism because they believe that socialism would, in the words of Chandler Morse, 'smooth the road to economic development.' It becomes necessary for them to employ the term in a 'charismatic effort to rally support' for policies that do not really promote economic and social development. Those African leaders who believe these principles are supposed to be the 'African socialists.'

It is interesting to recall that before the split in the Second International, Marxism was almost indistinguishable from social democracy. Indeed, the German Social Democratic Party was more or less the guardian of the doctrine of Marxism, and both Marx and Engels supported that Party. Lenin, too, became a member of the Social Democratic Party. After the break-up of the Second International, however, the meaning of the term 'social democracy' altered, and it became possible to draw a real distinction between socialism and social democracy.

A similar situation has arisen in Africa. Some years ago, African political leaders and writers used the term 'African socialism' in order to label the concrete forms that socialism might assume in Africa. But the realities of the diverse and irreconcilable social, political, and economic policies being pursued by African states today have made the term 'African socialism' meaningless and irrelevant. It appears to be much more closely associated with anthropology than with political economy. African socialism has now come to acquire some of its greatest publicists in Europe and North America precisely because of its predominant anthropological charm. Its foreign publicists include not only the surviving social democrats of Europe and North America, but other intellectuals and liberals who themselves are steeped in the ideology of social democracy.

It was no accident, let me add, that the 1962 Dakar Colloquium made such capital of African socialism but the uncertainties concerning the meaning and specific policies of African socialism have led some of us to abandon the term because it fails to express its original meaning and because it tends to obscure our fundamental socialist commitment.

Today, the phrase African socialism seems to espouse the view that the traditional African society was a classless society imbued with the spirit of humanism and to express a nostalgia for that spirit. Such a conception of socialism makes a fetish of the communal African society. But an idyllic, African classless society (in which there were no rich and no poor) enjoying a drugged serenity is certainly a facile simplification; there is no historical or even anthropological evidence for any such society. I am afraid the realities of African society were somewhat more sordid.

All available evidence from the history of Africa up to the eve of the European colonisation, shows that African society was neither classless nor devoid of a social hierarchy. Feudalism existed in some parts of Africa before colonisation; and feudalism involves a deep and exploitative social stratification, founded on the ownership of land. It must also be noted that slavery existed in Africa before European colonisation, although the earlier European contact gave slavery in Africa some of its most vicious characteristics. The truth remains, however, that before colonisation, which became widespread in Africa only in the 19th century, Africans were prepared to sell, often for no more than 30 pieces of silver, fellow tribesmen and even members of the same 'extended family' and clan. Colonialism deserves to be blamed for many evils in Africa, but surely it was not preceded by an African Golden Age or paradise. A return to the pre-colonial African society is evidently not worthy of the ingenuity and efforts of our people.

All this notwithstanding, one could still argue that the basic organisation of many African societies in different periods of history manifested a certain communalism and that the philosophy and humanist purposes behind that organisation are worthy of recapture. A community in which each saw his well-being in the welfare of the group certainly was praiseworthy, even if the manner in which the well-being of the group was pursued makes no contribution to our purposes.

Thus, what socialist thought in Africa must recapture is not the structure of the traditional African society but its spirit, for the spirit of communalism is crystallised in its humanism and in its reconciliation of individual advancement with group welfare. Even if there is incomplete anthropological evidence to reconstruct the traditional African society with accuracy, we can still recapture the rich human values of that society. In short, an anthropological approach to the traditional African society is too much unproven; but a philosophical approach stands on much firmer ground and makes generalisation feasible.

One predicament in the anthropological approach is that there is some disparity of views concerning the manifestations of the classlessness of the traditional African society. While some hold that the society was based on the equality of its members, others hold that it contained a hierarchy and division of labour in which the hierarchy – and therefore power – was founded on spiritual and democratic values. Of course, no society can be founded on the equality of its members although societies are founded on egalitarianism, which is something quite different. Similarly, a classless society that at the same time rejoices in a hierarchy of power (as distinct from authority) must be accounted a marvel of socio-political finesse.

We know that the traditional African society was founded on principles of egalitarianism. In its actual workings, however, it had various shortcomings. Its humanist impulse, nevertheless, is something that continues to urge us towards our all-African socialist reconstruction. We postulate each man to be an end in himself, not merely a means; and we accept the necessity of guaranteeing each man equal opportunities for his development. The implications of this for socio-political practice have to be worked out scientifically, and the necessary social and economic policies pursued with resolution. Any meaningful humanism must begin from egalitarianism and must lead to objectively chosen policies for safeguarding and sustaining egalitarianism. Hence, socialism. Hence, also, scientific socialism.

A further difficulty that arises from the anthropological approach to socialism, or African socialism, is the glaring division between existing African societies and the communalistic society that was. I warned in my book *Consciencism* that 'our society is not the old society, but a new society enlarged by Islamic and Euro-Christian influences.' This is a fact that any socio-economic policies must recognise and take into account. Yet the literature of African socialism comes close to suggesting that today's African societies are communalistic. The two societies are not coterminous; and such an equation cannot be supported by any attentive observation. It is true that this disparity is acknowledged in some of the literature of African socialism; thus, my friend and colleague Julius Nyerere, in acknowledging the disequilibrium between what was and what is in terms of African societies, attributes the differences to the importations of European colonialism.

We know, of course, that the defeat of colonialism and even neo-colonialism will not result in the automatic disappearance of the imported patterns of thought and social organisation. For those patterns have taken root, and are in varying degree sociological features of our contemporary society. Nor will a simple return to the communalistic society of ancient Africa offer a solution either. To advocate a return, as it were, to the rock from which we were hewn is a charming thought, but we are faced with contemporary problems, which have arisen from political subjugation, economic exploitation, educational and social backwardness, increases in population, familiarity with the methods and products of industrialisation and modern agricultural techniques. These – as well as a host of other complexities – can be resolved by no mere communalistic society, however sophisticated, and anyone who so advocates must be caught in insoluble dilemmas of the most excruciating kind. All available evidence from socio-political history discloses that such a return to a status quo ante is quite unexampled in the evolution of societies. There is, indeed, no theoretical or historical reason to indicate that it is at all possible.

When one society meets another, the observed historical trend is that acculturation results in a balance of forward movement, a movement in which each society assimilates certain useful attributes of the other. Social evolution is a dialectical process; it has ups and downs, but, on balance, it always represents an upward trend.

Islamic civilisation and European colonialism are both historical experiences of the traditional African society, profound experiences that have permanently changed the complexion of the traditional African society. They have introduced new values and a social, cultural, and economic organisation into African life. Modern African societies are not traditional, even if backward, and they are clearly in a state of socio-economic disequilibrium. They are in this state because they are not anchored to a steadying ideology.

The way out is certainly not to regurgitate all Islamic or Euro-colonial influences in a futile attempt to recreate a past that cannot be resurrected. The way out is only forward, forward to a higher and reconciled form of society, in which the quintessence of the human purposes of traditional African society reasserts itself in a modern context forward, in short, to socialism, through policies that are scientifically devised and correctly applied.

The inevitability of a forward way out is felt by all; thus, Leopold Sedar Senghor, although favouring some kind of return to African communalism, insists that the refashioned African society must accommodate the 'positive contribution' of colonial rule, 'such as the economic and technical infrastructure and the French educational system.' The economic and technical infrastructure of even French colonialism and the French educational system must be assumed, though this can be shown to be imbued with a particular socio-political philosophy. This philosophy, as should be known, is not compatible with the philosophy underlying communalism, and the desired accommodation would prove only a socio-political mirage.

Senghor has, indeed, given an account of the nature of the return to Africa. His account is highlighted by statements using some of his own words: that 'the African is a field of pure sensation'; that he does not measure or observe, but 'lives' a situation; and that this way of acquiring 'knowledge' by confrontation and intuition is 'negro-African'; the acquisition of knowledge by reason, 'Hellenic.' In *African Socialism*, he proposes:

> that we consider the Negro-African as he faces the Other: God, man, animal, tree or pebble, natural or social phenomenon. In contrast to the classic European, the Negro-African does not draw a line between himself and the object, he does not hold it at a distance, nor does he merely look at it and analyse it. After holding it at a distance, after scanning it without analysing it, he takes it vibrant in his hands, careful not to kill or fix it. He touches it, feels it, smells it. The Negro-African is like one of those Third Day Worms, a pure field of sensations ... Thus the Negro-African sympathises, abandons his personality to become identified with the Other, dies to be reborn in the Other. He does not assimilate; he is assimilated. He lives a common life with the Other; he lives in a symbiosis.[62]

It is clear that socialism cannot be founded on this kind of metaphysics of knowledge.

To be sure, there is a connection between communalism and socialism. Socialism stands to communalism as capitalism stands to slavery. In socialism, the principles underlying communalism are given expression in modern circumstances. Thus, whereas communalism in a non-technical society can be laissez-faire, in a technical society where sophisticated means of production are at hand, the situation is different; for if the underlying principles of communalism are not given correlated expression, class cleavages will arise, which are connected with economic disparities and thereby with political inequalities. Socialism, therefore, can be, and is, the defence of the principles

---

62 Leopold Sedar Senghor, *African Socialism* (Praeger Publishers: London and New York, 1964), p.72–73.

of communalism in a modern setting; it is a form of social organisation that, guided by the principles underlying communalism, adopts procedures and measures made necessary by demographic and technological developments. Only under socialism can we reliably accumulate the capital we need for our development and also ensure that the gains of investment are applied for the general welfare.

Socialism is not spontaneous. It does not arise of itself. It has abiding principles according to which the major means of production and distribution ought to be socialised if exploitation of the many by the few is to be prevented; if, that is to say, egalitarianism in the economy is to be protected. Socialist countries in Africa may differ in this or that detail of their policies, but such differences themselves ought not to be arbitrary or subject to vagaries of taste. They must be scientifically explained, as necessities arising from differences in the particular circumstances of the countries themselves.

There is only one way of achieving socialism; by the devising of policies aimed at the general socialist goals, each of which takes its particular form from the specific circumstances of a particular state at a definite historical period. Socialism depends on dialectical and historical materialism, upon the view that there is only one nature, subject in all its manifestations to natural laws and that human society is, in this sense, part of nature and subject to its own laws of development.

It is the elimination of fancifulness from socialist action that makes socialism scientific. To suppose that there are tribal, national, or racial socialisms is to abandon objectivity in favour of chauvinism.

Peking to Conakry

The word 'coup' should not be used to describe what took place in Ghana on 24 February 1966. On that day, Ghana was captured by traitors among the army and police who were inspired and helped by neo-colonialists and certain reactionary elements among our own population. It was an act of aggression, an 'invasion', planned to take place in my absence and to be maintained by force. Seldom in history has a more cowardly and criminally stupid attempt been made to destroy the independence of a nation.

When the action took place, I was on my way to Hanoi, at the invitation of President Ho Chi Minh, with proposals for ending the war in Vietnam. I had almost reached Peking, the furthest point in my journey. The cowards who seized power by force of arms behind my back, knew they did not have the support of the people of Ghana, and therefore thought it safer to wait until I was not only out of the country, but well beyond the range of a quick return.

The news was brought to me by the Chinese Ambassador in Accra who had gone on ahead to Peking to meet me, and to be with me during my visit to China. He had just accompanied Prime Minister Chou En-Lai, Liu Shao-qi, and other officials when they welcomed us at the airport, and he had come straight on out to the government house where I was staying. I remember his exact words:

'Mr. President, I have bad news. There has been a *coup d'état* in Ghana.'

l was taking a brief rest after the long flight from Rangoon and wondered if I had heard him correctly.

'What did you say?'

'A *coup d'état* in Ghana.'

'Impossible,' I said. 'But yes, it is possible. These things do happen. They are in the nature of the revolutionary struggle.'

I learned later that the Chinese welcoming party had known about events in Ghana when I stepped from the aircraft at Peking, but with characteristic courtesy had waited to break the news to me privately. My first reaction was to return immediately to Accra. If the VC10 of Ghana Airways in which we had travelled most of the way had been at Peking I would have embarked at once. But we had left it behind in Rangoon and had continued to Peking in an aircraft sent by the Chinese government.

I knew that to avoid unnecessary bloodshed I would have to be back in Ghana within 24 hours, and this was clearly impossible. I decided, therefore, to make an immediate statement to the Ghanaian people, and to fight back on African soil just as soon as my hosts could make the necessary travel arrangements.

What had happened in Ghana was no more than a tactical set-back in the African revolutionary struggle of a type which I had often predicted. At the very first conference of the OAU in Addis Ababa, I had warned my fellow heads of state that none of us was safe if we remained disunited. For this reason, I considered that the overall strategy remained unchanged but what had happened in Ghana made it all the more necessary to press on by revolutionary means to secure a united Africa.

The following is the text of the statement I released to the press:

> On my arrival in Peking, my attention has been drawn to reports from press agencies which allege that some members of the Ghana armed forces supported by some members of the police have attempted to overthrow my government—the government of the Convention People's Party.
>
> I know that the Ghanaian people are always loyal to me, the Party and the Government, and all I expect of everyone at this hour of trial is to remain calm, but firm in determination and resistance.
>
> Officers and men in the Ghana armed forces who are involved in this attempt, are ordered to return to their barracks and wait for my return.
>
> I am the constitutional head of the Republic of Ghana, and the supreme commander of the armed forces.
>
> I am returning to Ghana soon.

I followed this up with a cable to all Ghanaian embassies:

'Be calm and remain firm at your posts. Send all messages and reports to me through the Ghana Embassy, Peking, and not, repeat not, through Accra until further notice.'

As I discussed the news from Ghana with the 22 officials accompanying me, among them A. Quaison-Sackey (Foreign Minister), Kwesi Armah (Minister of Trade), M. F. Dei-Anang (Ambassador Extraordinary, in charge of the African Affairs Secretariat), J. E. Bossman (Ambassador to the UK), and F. Arkhurst (Ghana's Permanent Representative at the United Nations), I was somewhat disappointed to note their reaction. At a time like this, I would have expected them to show courage and fortitude. But most of them were frightened. Quaison-Sackey, for example, developed diarrhoea, and must have visited the lavatory about 20 times that day. Their obvious dismay was in striking contrast to the calmness and courage of the 66 other personnel – the security officers and members of my personal secretariat. These were men. Compared with them, the politicians were old women.

With Alex Quaison-Sackey, I will deal later. Kwesi Armah settled down in London where it appeared that he had considerable funds of money available to him. The rebel regime, on the basis of this, attempted to have him extradited on the grounds that he had stolen the money in question. His many trials before the English courts exposed at least the falsity of the allegations which these authorities had made. I am glad that he was acquitted since I am sure that the particular charges made against him were false. Nonetheless, I believe that he brought his misfortunes on himself by failing to take a positive political stand. His various court cases however prove the nonsense contained in many of the allegations of corruption against my government.

Enoch Okoh and Michael Dei-Anang were old British trained civil servants. They had made their way up through the colonial structure. They had been among my most trusted officials but they chose to return to Ghana, presumably in the hope that they would be accepted by the counterrevolutionaries.

Enoch Okoh, as head of the civil service and as the person who knew therefore which promotions had been made and why was treated with leniency and was appointed to be in charge of the Housing Corporation. Since the new regime did not intend to build any houses for the people this was perhaps the appropriate punishment for his desertion.

Michael Dei-Anang was not so treated and, much to his surprise, was thrown into prison.

Fred Arkhurst, after his treachery, returned to his former position at the United Nations but was eventually removed by the 'NLC' who could not trust someone who had, at least, ability.

Naturally we were all of us anxious about the safety of our families in Ghana, but I suppose the official members of the party were also thinking about their bank accounts and their property. It is said that a man's heart lies where his treasure is. But even allowing for the fact that they had more to lose than the other personnel, I still find it hard to understand how they could have lost grip of themselves so easily. It was as though they had put their hands up at the first whiff of danger.

However, they did manage to pull themselves together sufficiently for me to be able to discuss the next moves with them. It was not until later, after they had left Peking, and were on their own, that the full depth of their defeatism became apparent, and they deserted.

We agreed that for the next day or two, while arrangements were being made, I should carry out official engagements as planned. This was also the wish of the Chinese government. The Chinese made it clear that they regarded the military and police action in Ghana as no more than a temporary obstacle in the long struggle against imperialism, the kind of event to be expected, but which had no effect whatsoever on the final outcome. 'You are a young man,' Chou En-Lai told me, 'you have another forty years ahead of you!'

At the banquet held in my honour on 24 February, Liu Shao-qi spoke of Afro-Asian solidarity, and the African peoples' revolutionary struggle:

> Most of the African countries have won independence, but the African peoples' revolutionary struggle against imperialism is by no means completed. They still have to carry on this struggle in greater depth. The imperialists headed by the United States are more active than ever in pressing forward with their policies of neo-colonialism in an attempt to subvert independent African countries and suppress the anti-imperialist revolutionary struggle of the African peoples. In his latest book, *Neo-Colonialism—The Last Stage of Imperialism*, President Nkrumah gave a detailed description of neo-colonialism and explicitly pointed out that 'foremost among the neo-colonialists' is the United States, which is 'the very citadel of neo-colonialism.' However hard the imperialists may whip up revolutionary adverse currents, the anti-imperialist revolutionary struggles of the African peoples can never be suppressed but are bound to win final victory. The Chinese people have unswervingly stood on the side of the African peoples and resolutely support their just struggles.

He went on to condemn US policy in Vietnam, and to expose the hypocrisy of American so-called peace moves. No direct mention was made of the news from Ghana, or the possibility that I might not proceed to Hanoi. In my reply, I also attacked neo-colonialism, and said that final victory would rest with the common man. I went on to condemn US aggression in Vietnam and called for the complete withdrawal of all American forces from Vietnam so that peace negotiations could begin.

I knew that I could not now go to Hanoi. My duty lay first with the people of Ghana, and I was determined to return to Africa as quickly as possible. But I was sorry to have to abandon my mission as it was the second time that President Ho Chi Minh had asked me to go, and I wanted to do anything I could to help end the war. I was, and as far as I know, still remain the only head of state or government that the President of North Vietnam has invited to Hanoi to discuss the war since the American phase began. When I informed him of my decision, he replied that I would be welcome in Hanoi at any future date.

During the next two days, while I continued to carry out official engagements and to deal with the messages which began to pour in from abroad, the Chinese could not have shown greater care for my safety. If anyone near to me so much as put his hand in his pocket he was instantly pounced upon by security officers. They trusted no one, not even the Ghanaians who were with me.

Messages of encouragement and support continued to arrive from heads of state and governments all over the world. Many African leaders offered me immediate hospitality. Among them were President Sékou Touré of Guinea, President Gamal Abdel Nasser of Egypt, President Nyerere of Tanzania, and

President Modibo Keita of Mali. I was very touched that they should declare their solidarity so quickly and with such generosity, and it was only after deep thought that I decided to accept the invitation of President Sékou Touré and the Political Bureau of the Guinean Democratic Party. I sent the following note to President Sékou Touré:

PEKING.

25th February 1966

My dear Brother and President,

I have been deeply touched by your message of solidarity and support I have received today. It is true, as you say, that this incident in Ghana is a plot by the imperialists, neo-colonialists and their agents in Africa. As these imperialist forces grow more militant and insidious, using traitors to the African cause against the freedom and independence of our people, we must strengthen our resolution and fight for the dignity of our people to the last man, and for the unity of Africa. It is heartening to know that in this struggle we can count on the support and understanding of Africa's well-tried leaders like yourself.

I know that our cause will triumph and that we can look forward to the day when Africa shall be really united and free from foreign interference and the intrigues of saboteurs and puppets.

I am safe and well here in Peking, and I have sent my special emissary who will deliver this message to you to let you know the plans I am making for my early return to Africa. I trust that you will give him every possible assistance for the fulfilment of his mission.

I shall visit you in Guinea soon.

With sincere and brotherly affection.

Shortly afterwards. I received a further message from President Sékou Touré:

The Political Bureau and the Government after a thorough analysis of the African situation following the seizure of power by the instruments of imperialism have decided:

1. To organise a national day of solidarity with the Ghanaian people next Sunday. Throughout the length and breadth of the country there will take place popular demonstrations on the theme of anti-imperialism.

2. To call on all progressive African countries to hold a special conference and take all adequate measures.

We think that the time factor is vital here, since it is important to make a riposte without further delay, by every means. Your immediate presence would be very opportune, it seems to us, and we are therefore impatiently waiting for you.

Yours very fraternally,
Ahmed Sékou Touré.

I do not propose to publish in full all the messages I received from heads of state and governments. But I would like to quote from the messages of two other African leaders. First, the note from President Modibo Keita of Mali:

I am happy to hear that you are well. Please thank our comrades of the People's Republic of China for this important contribution to Africa's struggle for liberty and progress.

Yesterday, the 24th of February, we learned of the serious events which took place in Ghana and which do no credit to those who have provoked them.

For us, the authors of the *coup d'état* have committed an act of high treason ...

... This is one phase of the unremitting struggle waged by neo-colonialists and imperialists against Africa which wishes to live in freedom and dignity and in friendship with all peoples who are peace-loving and who wish to build a just society. All Africans, conscious of the grave dangers posed to our peoples and our continent, should mobilise themselves to bar the way to neo-colonialism and imperialism.

The Malian people consider themselves engaged in this struggle.

Secondly, I quote from the message from Albert Margai, then Prime Minister of Sierra Leone:

Whilst we are conscious of the many and diverse forces working in Africa which daily and constantly strive to foil our struggle for the final emancipation of those still subject to colonial rule and our ultimate claims to unity, I have nevertheless formed great hope and fortitude in the courage of your convictions and determined efforts to defy all odds in refusing to accept the results of the recent revolt as a fait accompli. Please accept, my dear Brother, the assurance of my highest consideration, esteem and prayers for your personal well-being and safety.

Apart from the fact that Guinea and Ghana formed a union in 1961, and a strong bond of friendship exists between President Sékou Touré, the Political Bureau of the Guinea Democratic Party, the people of Guinea and myself, I wanted to go to a country as near to Ghana as possible.

This would leave no one in any doubt about my intention to take up the neo-colonialist challenge and to restore legal government in Ghana. Guinea is only some 300 miles from Ghana. Jet flying time between the two countries is a mere 30–40 minutes. From Guinea I knew I would be in a good position to carry on the African revolutionary struggle. I decided that we should all, with the exception of Quaison-Sackey and Bossman, go to Guinea via Moscow.

Quaison-Sackey as foreign minister was entrusted with a very important mission. He was to go to Addis Ababa to represent the legal government of Ghana at the OAU conference of foreign ministers due to open there within a few days. Instead of rising to the occasion, and accepting this great challenge and responsibility, he went to Accra and offered his services to the neo-colonialist puppets, the so-called NLC. The latter, it seems, made little use of him. Traitors have no friends.

I heard of his betrayal when I arrived in Moscow on 1 March, and it was there that I was also told of Bossman's defection. By then, Kwesi Armah and other officials had left Moscow to deal, as they said, with 'urgent private matters.' They were to return to Moscow, and we were all to travel together to Conakry. Instead, they defected. I then decided to proceed at once to Guinea with my personal entourage and members of my guard department. I wanted no one with me who was faint-hearted or two-faced. Every member of my party knew he was free to leave at any time. The security officers and other members of my personal staff decided to remain with me.

The Russian government sent an aircraft to Peking to fetch me, and I left from an airstrip near Peking on 28 February. Before leaving, I made the following statement to the press:

I think you all know that certain members of my armed forces have attempted to usurp political power in Ghana while I was on the way to Hanoi. What they have done, in fact, is to commit an act of rebellion against the Government of the Republic. I am determined to crush it without delay, and to do this I rely upon the support of the Ghanaian people and of Ghana's friends in the world.

By the arrest, detention and assassination of ministers, the Party's civil servants, and trade unionists, and by the massacre of defenceless men and women, the authors of these insane acts of robbery, violence and anarchy have added brutality to their treason.

Never in the history of our new Ghana have citizens, men and women been assassinated in cold blood. Never have their children become orphans for political reasons. Never before have Ghanaians, our people, been shot because of their political convictions.

This is a tragedy of monstrous proportions. The excessive personal ambition and the insane acts of these military adventurers, if not stifled now, will not only destroy the political, economic and social achievements of the last few years, but will also obstruct the course of the African revolution.

AU that has been achieved by the Ghanaian people with the assistance of all our friends is in jeopardy.

I am returning to Ghana; I know that the friendly nations and people of goodwill everywhere will support me in restoring the constitutional government of Ghana.

I take this opportunity to express my sincere condolences to all the families whose valiant sons and daughters have given their lives in the defence of Ghana.

At this moment, as I leave Peking, the capital city of the People's Republic of China, I express my profound gratitude to the Chinese people and to their leaders for their support and their kind hospitality.

We landed near Moscow at dawn on 1 March, after a brief stop at Irkutsk in Siberia, and were met by leading Soviet government officials. After a busy day of talks I re-embarked at midnight for the flight to Guinea.

We touched down briefly in Yugoslavia, and in Algeria, and reached Conakry in the afternoon of Wednesday 2 March. It was wonderful to be on African soil again. Guinea was agog with excitement. President Sékou Touré and members of the Political Bureau of the Democratic Party were among the huge crowd at the airport to welcome me. A 21 gun salute was fired.

At a mass rally in the packed sports stadium in Conakry the following day, President Sekou Touré announced that I had been made Secretary-General of the Guinean Democratic Party and Head of State of Guinea. 'The Ghanaian traitors,' he said 'have been mistaken in thinking that Nkrumah is simply a Ghanaian ... He is a universal man.' It looked as though the entire population of Conakry was in the stadium that afternoon and I shall never forget the reception they gave to Sékou Touré and myself as we were driven round the arena in an open car. The crowds rose to their feet, cheering, shouting anti-imperialist and anti-neo-colonialist slogans, and waving placards: 'Long live the African Revolution', 'Long live Kwame Nkrumah', 'Long live Sékou Touré', 'Down with neo-colonialists', etc. It was a deeply moving experience, and I found my thoughts turning to similar mass rallies held in the Polo Ground, Accra. The people of Ghana were now being made to suffer for something which was not of their own making. They had been overcome by powerful external forces, and by the plotting and deception of a few selfish and ambitious reactionaries.

President Sékou Touré made a long speech. I did not know at the time exactly what he said. He spoke in French, and my knowledge of that language was then sketchy. I understood that I had been presented to the people of Guinea, but had no idea that I had been made president. It was not until after the ceremony, when I heard the press reports, that the full realisation of my new appointment became clear to me.

Such a gesture of political solidarity must surely be without historical precedent. When our historians come to record the events of 1966, they will doubtless consider the action of the Guinean Government as a great landmark in the practical expression of pan-Africanism.

In this way began one of the most fruitful and happiest periods of my life – the time I spent in Conakry, about which I shall write later in this book.[63]

---

63 *Editor's note*: Nkrumah is referring to *Dark Days in Ghana* (London: Lawrence and Wishart, 1968), p. 20–32.

24 February 1966

One of the first things I did after my arrival in Guinea was to establish an efficient communications system so that I could be kept fully informed of what was happening inside Ghana. Almost at once I began to receive detailed eyewitness accounts of what actually took place on 24 February and in the dark days which followed the army and police usurpation of power. At the same time there began a steady flow of Ghanaians to visit me in Conakry, to tell me about what had happened in Ghana and to express their loyalty. Some of them had walked all the way; others had found quicker means of travel. But all came at great personal risk to themselves and their families. Letters also began to pour in, and gradually the full, terrible story of violence and bloodshed took shape, and has since been confirmed to me over and over again by innumerable people who were there at the time of the military and police action and saw what took place. Several of the eyewitnesses who came to me still bore the marks of the brutal attacks made on them.

The true account of the seizure of power in Ghana by traitors and neo-colonialists does not make pleasant reading. But the facts must be faced and put on record so that the enormity of the crime committed against the people of Ghana can be accurately assessed.

I left Accra on 21 February 1966. I was seen off at the airport by most of the leading government and party officials, and by service chiefs. I recall the handshakes and the expressions of good wishes from John Willie Kofi Harlley, Deku, Yakubu, and others. These men, smiling and ingratiating, had all the time treason and treachery in their minds. They had even planned my assassination on that day, though they later abandoned the idea. I remember shaking hands with Major-General Barwah – to be murdered in cold blood three days later when he refused to surrender to the rebel army soldiers. I little thought then that I would never see him again, or that Zanerigu, commander of the Presidential Guard Regiment, Kojo Botsio, Kofi Baako and other ministers who were there at the airport, would be shortly seized by renegade soldiers and policemen and thrown into prison.

After a week of so-called 'manoeuvres', the operation began early in the morning of Wednesday 23 February 1966 when the garrison at Kumasi, numbering 600 men, was ordered to move southwards to Accra. On the way, the convoy of some 35 vehicles was met and halted by the two arch-traitors Colonel Emmanuel Kwesi Kotoka, Commander of the Second Infantry Brigade Group, and Major Akwasi Amankwa Afrifa of the Second Brigade. Kotoka had only recently been put in charge of the Kumasi garrison, and I had not yet confirmed his appointment.

Afrifa was left in command while Kotoka went to Accra to report progress to the commissioner of police, Harlley and to find some soldier better known than himself to be the nominal head of the revolt. The man chosen was Major-General Ankrah even though the conspirators had thought so little of his abilities than they had not previously troubled to consult him. He was, however, one of the few officers who had held even the rank of major in colonial days and had seen service in the world war if only as a quartermaster. In the Congo he had shown some bravery and, at least, routine ability and I had decorated him for his services but essentially he was of mediocre calibre. He held the post of second in command in the armed forces after independence through seniority, not ability. He would not have been appointed even to this post but for the death shortly before of another senior officer. In 1965 I retired him. Undoubtedly, it was his lack of understanding of what was going on around him which recommended him as a figurehead to those manipulating the 'coup.'

The troops were then told that I intended sending them to fight in Vietnam and in Rhodesia, and that I had deserted Ghana taking with me £8 million. There was, they were told, there was no government left in Ghana, and it was their duty to assume control of the country to maintain law and order. Already, it was said, Russian planes were landing on a secret airstrip in northern Ghana. Furthermore, a secret tunnel had been made from Flagstaff House, the presidential residence, to Accra airport, and for days Russians had been arriving. The only way to save Ghana, and to avoid being sent to fight in Vietnam, the troops were told, was to take Flagstaff House.

Several days after the military seizure of power, Kotoka and Afrifa appeared on Ghana TV congratulating themselves on their easy success. One remark stood out unmistakable and clear: 'And you know, we didn't find any Russians at all – not one! Nor could we find any trace of that tunnel.' This was followed by peals of laughter at the poor soldiers who had believed their story.

The first object of the military operation was to force the surrender of Major-General Barwah, Army Chief of Staff and Deputy Chief of Defence Staff, who was in command of the Ghana Army in the absence from the country of the Chief of Defence Staff, General Aferi. At the same time, Brigadier Hasan, head of Military Intelligence, and Colonel Zanerigu, commander of the Presidential Guard Regiment, and Owusu-Sekyere, former head of the CID and in charge of the Special Branch, were to be arrested.

This stage of the operation was badly bungled. Hasan was arrested, but Zanerigu, when confronted, escaped through a window of his house and drove to Flagstaff House to warn the Presidential Guard Regiment. Barwah could not be intimidated. Woken from his sleep in the early hours of the morning of the 24th by the arrival of Kotoka and some 25 men, he courageously refused either to join the traitors or to surrender. Thereupon, Kotoka shot him dead at point-black range in cold blood in the presence of his wife and children. The seven security officers who were stationed at Barwah's house were also murdered on the spot on Kotoka's orders.

Kotoka subsequently boasted of his killing of Barwah but said because he was protected by a 'juju' he was able to catch the bullets which Barwah fired in his defence and to throw them back at him. When the counter coup of April 1967 took place Kotoka's 'magic' could not save him. Unlike Barwah he surrendered without protest or struggle to those who had captured him at his headquarters. His 'juju' did not prevent him being shot in his tum.

Barwah's murder was one of the most disgraceful and ghastly crimes ever committed in Ghana's history. In an attempt to wipe the blood from their hands the so-called National Liberation Council (NLC) gave Barwah and the security officers a military burial a few days later. What a mockery, and what hypocrisy! Yet these terrible, cold-blooded murders were only the first of many which occurred on 24 February and during subsequent days. They set the tone, as it were, of the whole operation which was characterised throughout by cowardice, bloodshed, and criminal stupidity.

By 6 am on the 24th, the Accra police, acting on Harlley's orders, had rounded up most of the ministers and other key political figures, and fighting had broken out at Flagstaff House between members of the Presidential Guard Regiment and rebel army units. There were about 30 members of the Guard Regiment at Flagstaff House when the alarm was raised. These were soon joined by others who managed to slip in by a back entrance to reinforce their comrades. Although heavily outnumbered they successfully held up the rebel detachment sent to seize the Ghana radio station a short distance from Flagstaff House. Only eight of the 124 detailed for this operation managed to get through. These captured the radio station, apparently without incident, and at 6 am Kotoka arrived to broadcast that the army and police had taken over the government of Ghana.

The announcement was premature. At 7 am resistance was actually increasing at Flagstaff House, as the defenders, less than a hundred of them, fought fiercely back against some 600 rebel troops. By this time a battalion in Accra under Ocran had joined them, not knowing what the fighting was all about. Thus, the rebels were able to gain control of the airport, cable office, radio station, and all the approach roads to Accra.

Kotoka had established a combined HQ with the police at Police Headquarters, and from there the order was given for the 2nd Battalion to go into action at Flagstaff House. The Guard Regiment fought on, though their position was now hopeless. The outside walls of Flagstaff House had been blasted open, and the defenders had retreated behind the second gate. Still, they refused to surrender. It was only after the rebels threatened to blow up the family residence at Flagstaff House in which my wife and three young children were sheltering that they finally gave in.

The fierce fighting at Flagstaff House at this time was in striking contrast to the failure at the time of the April 1967 counter-coup of Kotoka's bodyguard to defend his headquarters. He had made Flagstaff House into a strong point from which he commanded the army. Yet when it was attacked by a small detachment of some 25 men the garrison immediately surrendered as did that of the Broadcasting Station which was also only attacked by a force of similar size. Again, a small group of soldiers, not more than 50 in all, were sufficient to capture the Castle at Osu from which the 'NLC' conducted their government. Ankrah 'the Chairman' of the 'NLC' was the first of its defenders to run away, jumping over the Castle wall, plunging into the sea and wading down the shore.

What followed the fall of Flagstaff House on 24 February 1966, has been concealed from the world. But the people of Ghana know and will never forget.

It may be explained in part by the fact that the soldiers who had carried out the 'coup' were frightened men. They had been told that there was a great store of arms beneath Flagstaff House and a hidden Russian army was concealed there which would suddenly emerge to attack them. They were jittery and fired on anyone on the slightest suspicion. They so frightened officials of the Japanese embassy that they put placards on all their cars saying, 'We are NOT Chinese.' There was also potential indiscipline. Despite the fact that Ghanaian armed forces in the Congo were regarded as the best of the African troops stationed there, the habit of drug-taking and excessive drinking which some of the soldiers had acquired there led to a mutiny in one battalion in which the commanding officer was so badly injured that he was left for dead, and in which the mutinous soldiers took over for two or three days complete control of the camp. In order to restore discipline, it had been necessary to disband this battalion.

The officers who organised the 'coup', having deceived their men, were now in no position to discipline them.

Rebel troops, many of them almost mad from the effects of Indian hemp which had been issued to them, others intoxicated with alcohol looted from ransacked houses and trigger-happy. carried out the most cruel and senseless attacks on innocent men, women, and children. Thousands of pounds worth of damage was done to government property, and valuable historical documents and records were destroyed.

At Flagstaff House itself, troops dashed from one room to another, smashing windows and furniture, tearing up papers, ripping telephones from desks, and destroying anything they could lay their hands on. My own office was singled out for special treatment. The full extent of the loss of books and manuscripts I shall discover on my return. I am hoping that by some miracle the precious notes I was compiling for a history of Africa may have been spared. If not, years of work will have been wasted, and the labour of collecting and sorting material and writing it up will have to begin again from scratch. The stupidity of this needless destruction of government property, and the failure of the rebel officers to exercise any control over their men, demonstrates the quality of their leadership.

In the six-roomed two-storey house where I lived with my family, troops were allowed to run riot, seizing clothes and other intimate personal possessions, including rare old books and manuscripts. My wife and children, although not physically harmed, were not permitted to take a single thing with them when they were turned out of the house and forced to take refuge in the Egyptian embassy.

My mother, 80 years old and almost blind, who was staying at Flagstaff House, was forcibly ejected and told to go 'where you belong.' I understand some friends took her to Nkroful where I was born. Later, the actual house in which I was born was burnt down on 'NLC' orders. My mother was forced to appear before a 'commission of enquiry' with the idea of making her admit that I was not her son and indeed was not a Ghanaian at all. I am proud to know that she resolutely refused to say anything of the sort and conducted herself with the utmost dignity.

From Flagstaff House, the troops went to Kanda Estate where many security officers have their quarters. There they hurled grenades into the compound, broke into houses and flats, tossed furniture out of the windows, and carried off radios, refrigerators and other property. Anyone who resisted them was brutally shot. Women, children, and old people were driven out into the streets. Many of the women were raped. Even young children were hit with rifle butts. A woman with a child on her back was shot, and both mother and child were thrown to the ground from a three-storey window. The rank-and-file police who had taken no part in the 'coup' were horrified at what was taking place and did their best to restrain the soldiers and this led in some cases to actual fighting between the two forces.

Meanwhile, the soldiers had been reinforced by a new element. It was part of the propaganda against Ghana abroad and internally that my government had detained thousands of individuals. There were, of course, political detainees but their number, for state security, was fortunately small. Most of these detainees under the Preventive Detention Act were the so-called 'criminal' detainees. As industrialisation developed in Ghana so, as in all countries, organised crime increased and at one stage in the immediate post-independence period we were faced with a situation which, if we had not dealt with it, would have resulted in the country being terrorised by organised criminal gangs. The view of the police was that it was not possible in many cases, any more than it was in the US at some periods of its history, to secure convictions in courts of the gang leaders or of their supporters. The Preventive Detention Act was therefore extended to cover habitual criminals suspected of gangsterism.

If the rebels had only released the genuine political detainees the total would have been so small as to discredit them and, in any case, they required the prison accommodation occupied by the criminal detainees in order to lock up anyone suspected of being a CPP member or supporter. In the days following the 'coup' the criminal detainees were not only released but were able to represent themselves as 'the heroes of the counter-revolution.' By day they joined, naturally, in the demonstrations against my government and at night returned to their old activities to such an extent that even the strictly controlled 'NLC' press demanded that they should be returned to prison.

Accra was handed over to lawless elements which the rank-and-file police had no means of controlling. Bar owners were forced at gun point to sell free beer to soldiers and to the 'heroes of the counter-revolution,' the criminal detainees. These people assaulted women, thieved, and looted. It will be only after the return to legal government in Ghana that it will be possible to assess exactly the number of those who died in fighting against the rebel soldiers or were subsequently killed in the looting and robbery which followed. The casualties in the fighting were certainly heavy. The number of civilians killed, it is more difficult to estimate. Two members of parliament certainly lost their lives and a number of people in no way connected with politics died. Among those shot dead near Flagstaff House was an air hostess on her way to the airport. In all, the total was probably around 1,600 dead and many more injured. So much for the 'bloodless coup'!

One thing is clear. Never before in the cherished history of our new Ghana had citizens, defenceless men and women, been assassinated in cold blood by their own soldiers. Not a single Ghanaian life was taken during the whole 15 years of my administration. There are few, if any, governments in the world which can say as much. Yet here was this handful of traitors at one blow spoiling our proud record and dragging Ghana's name through the mud.

In the days which followed the insurrection, hundreds of patriotic Ghanaians were thrown into prison. All ministers, MPs, officials of the party and of all its subsidiary and associate organisations including the trade unions were arrested and detained. The same applied to branch officers throughout the country. In fact, the entire leadership, except for the few who managed to escape or go into hiding, was at one swoop rounded up and thrown into prison.

The prison authorities, with some exceptions, continued to act in the humane and considerate way which we had insisted upon in the prison service, since the establishment of independence. The Director of Prisons, in particular, saw to it that no one, insofar as he could prevent it, once inside the prison, was ill-treated. It is significant that subsequently he was pronounced by the 'NLC' to have become insane and taken to a lunatic asylum where he died, mysteriously electrocuted.

Professor Kojo Abraham, Fellow of All Souls, Oxford, and a former governor of the School of Oriental and African Studies in London, was mercilessly beaten when soldiers arrived to arrest him. He was flung unconscious into the police van. Abraham, at the time of his arrest, was an MP and acting Vice-Chancellor of the University of Ghana. His only crime was that he was a leading member of the party. The manuscript of a new book he was writing was among the first of a pile of papers and books publicly burnt, Nazi-style, by the mutinous soldiers who arrested him.

Geoffrey Bing, Q.C., a distinguished British lawyer, and one of my legal advisers, who had come to Ghana at government invitation to help in our legal and constitutional work, had his clothes and shoes torn off him and was made to walk up and down barefoot and to stand up and sit down in repeated succession without being able to use his hands. Bayonets were stuck into his back, and it was not until a commander of the Ghana Navy arrived on the scene that they stopped torturing him.

Typical of the sort of thing which happened was the wounding of the deputy manager of one of the hotels in Accra. He was being driven by his driver on hotel business but suddenly was shot by a soldier. The explanation subsequently given was that as he was sitting at the back of the car the soldier thought he must have been a minister in my government.

These are only a few examples of the countless acts of brutality carried out within the first week or so, by the traitorous renegades and cowards who seized power in Ghana on 24 February 1966. The people of Ghana were stunned. Nobody outside Accra knew what had happened, or was happening. In some cases, particularly in the remoter districts, it was days before they realised what had taken place. Even then, the full implications of the army and police action dawned only slowly as they began gradually to see through the lies poured out over the radio and in the press, and saw with their own eyes the way in which the independence and progress of their beloved country was being destroyed, and its assets sold to foreign interests.

In Accra, military police and soldiers in full battle dress and armed with sub-machine guns patrolled the streets. In such circumstances, and with all the party leadership arrested, it was not surprising that there was no immediate and open resistance. But secret, underground resistance began at once.

It grew by leaps and bounds.

While a number of the ministers hastened to ingratiate themselves with the rebels, others remained firm. Nothing for example has been heard of N. A. Welbeck, Minister of Information and Party Propaganda who resolutely refused to make any cringing retraction of his past political activities. And the same is true of other ministers such as I. K. Chinebuah, Minister of Education and former headmaster of Achimota School. The most heartening demonstration, however, came from the resolute attitude adopted by many of those in the intermediate and lower ranks of the party.

The journalists, regional commissioners, district commissioners, and party secretaries were imprisoned in the central block of Ussher Fort prison. Almost from the first day of their imprisonment onward they were singing in chorus party songs so loudly that they could be heard well outside the prison and this despite the fact that their block was patrolled by armed soldiers.

Ghanaians are not a timid people as has been suggested in the foreign press. Far from it. They may be slow to anger and may take time to organise and act. But once they are ready, they strike, and strike hard. It pays no one to tamper with Ghanaian freedom and dignity. Ghana is out of the gambling house of colonialism and will never return to it.

The American, British, and European press has made much of the 'demonstrations' which occurred in Accra in celebration of the 'coup.' It is interesting, however, that even in the Ghanaian papers there were no reports of any such demonstrations in the villages or in the countryside where one would have expected them, if the revolt had been genuinely popular. It is understandable however that certain elements, particularly in Accra, should demonstrate in favour of the new regime. The criminal detainees naturally led the celebrations but they were joined by more sober citizens. The Intellectuals and the professional classes had always been against my government which they felt, quite rightly, was challenging their position of privilege. The lawyer and the clergyman thus found themselves joining in the same processions through the streets as the criminal. There was a section of the market women who had been exploiting the shortage of goods due to the measures which we had to take for the control of non-essential imports. They had been exposed by the Abraham Commission and they naturally were delighted that its chairman should have now been thrown into jail. In addition to this there were at the start a number of people who were genuinely deceived by the revolt.

The disastrous fall in the world price of cocoa had led to inevitable import shortages of consumer goods. These people really believed that the 'coup' would change all this, and so they joined the gangs in the streets. Others joined them out of curiosity. Even so it was necessary for the army to force children from their school rooms and to dragoon demonstrators in order to make a satisfactory show. A small number of students from the University at Legon, wanting to demonstrate in favour of the new regime, asked for and were given police protection, so fearful were they of the reaction of the people of Accra. It was not until instructions were issued from police headquarters that the first street 'demonstrations' took place.

Banners and posters, most of them prepared beforehand in the US embassy, were pushed into the hands of the unwilling 'demonstrators.' Many of the slogans and words used on them were quite foreign to the Ghanaian people, and in some cases completely incomprehensible. The same kind of thing was noticeable in the newspapers and news bulletins issued immediately after the seizure of power. Words and phrases were used which had never been seen in a Ghanaian newspaper before. The same discrepancy occurred on the radio as bulletins and news flashes were broadcast. The voice was Ghanaian, but the unfamiliar words and the glib expressions were foreign, and often caused the announcer to hesitate and falter.

Clearly, the polished editorials, news bulletins and unfamiliar slogans had been devised by experts trained in the art of overthrowing 'undesirable governments,' but who had not taken the trouble to familiarise themselves with the Ghanaian way of thinking or expression.

I understand that the Uganda government in its investigations following the abortive coup which took place in Kampala on 26 February, only two days after the action in Accra, discovered prepared news bulletins, posters, and newspaper editorials which were strikingly similar in style and content to those actually used in Ghana. I leave the reader to draw the obvious conclusions.

In the Makola market, a woman who had a large picture of myself above her stall was shot dead by an army officer after refusing three times to hand it over for destruction. This kind of incident, not seen by foreign journalists, who obediently and very willingly photographed and reported only the staged demonstrations and rigged press interviews, was typical of many other pathetic but deeply moving acts of heroism performed by the ordinary men and women of Ghana during those dark days.

Much publicity was given in the imperialist press and on TV to the pulling down of the statue of myself in front of the National Assembly building in Accra. It was made to appear as though angry crowds had torn the statue from its pedestal and had carried off chunks of it. But it was not for nothing that no photographs could be produced to show the actual pulling down of the statue; and the few women seen carrying away portions of the statue on their heads were photographed from the back view. In fact, when the statue was pulled down the parliament building where it stood had been cordoned off by the military and no unauthorised person was allowed into the area. All those who were there at the time had been those brought in by the military, who had closed to all civilians the whole of the high street onto which the statue faced. When the statue had been pulled down about half-a-dozen terrified young children were forced to sit on it as it lay on the ground. Even the jubilant imperialist press evidently saw nothing strange in publishing photographs of bewildered toddlers, tears running down their cheeks, sitting on a headless statue, while the same imperialist press extolled what it described as a 'most popular coup.' Since even the women shown carrying away pieces of it on their heads were photographed from behind, it is impossible to be certain whether they were from a group of the market women condemned by the Abraham Commission or, as was widely rumoured in Accra, 'soldiers dressed up as women.'

There are many other incidents which could be recorded, but sufficient has been written to show the manner in which the military and police action of 24 February 1966 was carried out.

The Big Lie

It has been said that the fabrication of the 'big lie' is essential in the planning of any usurpation of political power. In the case of Ghana, the big lie told to the world was that Ghana needed to be rescued from 'economic chaos.' Various other lies were hinged to this central lie. The country was said to be hopelessly in debt and the people on the verge of starvation. Among the lies aimed against me personally was the one that I had accumulated a large private fortune; this was to form the basis for an all-out character assassination attempt. But these lies were subsidiary to the one big lie of 'economic mismanagement', which was to provide an umbrella excuse for the seizure of power by neo-colonialist inspired traitors.

If Ghana was in such a serious economic condition, why was there no lack of investment in her growing industries? Investors do not put their money into mismanaged enterprises and unstable economies. Why did the imperialist powers try to exert an economic squeeze on Ghana? No one in his right mind bothers to attack an already-dying concern. Who made up the figures of Ghana's supposed 'debt'? Why was only one side of the ledger shown – why no mention of assets? How can the obvious evidence of the modernisation and industrialisation of Ghana, such as the new roads, factories, schools and hospitals, the harbour and town of Tema, the Volta and Teffie bridges and the Volta Dam be reconciled with the charge of wasted expenditure?

If the Ghanaian people were starving, why no evidence of this, and why no popular participation in the 'coup'? How was it that Ghana had the highest living standard in Africa per capita, the highest literacy rate, and was the nearest to achieving genuine economic independence? All these questions, and many related to them, are now being asked. An examination of our development plans and of their implementation reveals the truth – that it was their success and not their failure which spurred our enemies into action. Ghana, on the threshold of economic independence, and in the vanguard of the African revolutionary struggle to achieve continental liberation and unity, was too dangerous an example to the rest of Africa to be allowed to continue under a socialist-directed government.

In the first ten years of its administration, the Ghana government drew up the First and Second Five Year Development Plans (1951–1956 and 1959–1964), and the Consolidation Plan, which covered the two-year gap between these Plans (1957–1959). Under these plans, the foundations were to be laid for the modernisation and industrialisation of Ghana. A skilled labour force was to be trained and an adequate complement of public services built up such as transport, electricity, water, and telecommunications.

We had to work fast. Under colonial rule, foreign monopoly interests had tied up our whole economy to suit themselves. We had not a single industry. Our economy was dependent on one cash crop – cocoa. Although our output of cocoa is the largest in the world, there was not a single cocoa processing factory.

Before we took office in 1951 there was no direct railway between Accra and Takoradi, in those days our main port. Passengers and freight had to travel by way of Kumasi. This was because Kumasi was the centre of the timber and mining industries, both of which served foreign interests and were therefore well supplied with the necessary communications. There were few roads, and only a very rudimentary public transport system. For the most part, people walked from place to place. There were very few hospitals, schools, or clinics. Most of our villages lacked a piped water supply. In fact, the nakedness of the land when my government began in 1951 has to have been experienced to be believed.

Failure to promote the interests of our people was due to the insatiable demands of colonial exploitation. It was not until we had grasped political power that we were in a position to challenge this, and to develop our resources for the benefit of the Ghanaian people. Those who would judge us merely by the heights we have achieved would do well to remember the depths from which we started.

The condition of Ghana in 1964 showed that our first two development plans had been carried out with a high degree of success. We had one of the most modern networks of roads in Africa. Takoradi harbour had been extended, and the great artificial harbour at Tema, the largest in Africa, built from scratch. Large extensions to the supply of water and to the telecommunication network had been constructed, and further extensions were under construction. Our agriculture was being diversified and mechanised. Above all, the Volta River Project, which was designed to provide the electrical power for our great social, agricultural and industrialisation programme, was almost completed.

In education, progress was equally impressive. In ten years, we had achieved more than in the whole period of colonial rule. The figures below show the great increase in the numbers of children in primary and middle schools, and of students in secondary and technical schools and in colleges of higher education.

	1951	1961	% Increase
Primary Schools	154,360	481,500	211.9
Middle Shools	66,175	160,000	141.7
Secondary and Technical Schools	3,559	19,143	437.8
Teacher Training Colleges	1,916	4,552	137.5
University Students	208	1,204	478.8

The building of schools and colleges was given top priority in our development plans. We took the unprecedented step in Africa of making all education free, from primary to university level. In addition, textbooks were supplied free to all pupils in primary, middle and secondary schools.

In the 1964–1965 school year there were 9,988 primary and middle schools with an enrolment of 1,286,486. There were 89 secondary schools with 32,971 pupils; 47 teacher training colleges with an enrolment of 10,168; 11 technical schools and 3 universities. All this, in a population of 7,500,000 put Ghana in the lead among independent African states. At the same time, a mass literacy campaign has made Ghana the most literate country in the whole of Africa. A look at some of the other social achievements during the Party's first ten years of office reveals a similar rate of progress.

Basic Services	1951	1961	% Increase
Health			
Number of Hospital Beds	2,368	6,155	159.9
Rural and Urban Clinics	1	30	–
Doctors and Dentists	156	500	220.5
Transport and Communications			
Roads (in Miles)			
Class 1 (Bitumen)	1,398	2,050	46.7
Class 2 (Gravel)	2,093	3,346	59.8
(Since 1961 the mileage of motor roads has risen to 19,236. Feeder roads connect most villages to the trunk road network.)			
Post Offices	444	779	75.4
Telephones	7,383	25,488	245.2
Electricity			
Installed Electrical Capacity (kW)	84,708	120,860	42.7
Electrical Power Generated (kW '000)	281,983	390,174	38.4

In 1962 the government adopted what was known as the Party's *Programme of Work and Happiness*. It proclaimed our fundamental objective as the building of a socialist state devoted to the welfare of the masses.

The concrete programme of action for this was worked out in the Seven Year Development Plan launched on 11 March 1964. In presenting the plan to the national assembly, I said that its main tasks were first, to speed up the rate of growth of our national economy; secondly, to enable us to embark upon the socialist transformation of our economy through the rapid development of the state and co-operative sectors; thirdly, to eradicate completely the colonial structure of our economy.

The plan embodied measures meant to achieve a self-sustaining economy founded on socialist production and distribution – an economy balanced between agriculture and industry, providing sufficient food for the people and supporting secondary industries based on the products of our agriculture. Ghana was to be as soon as possible a socialist state. The people, through the state, would have an effective share in the economy of the country and an effective control over it. Thus, the principles of scientific socialism would be applied to suit our own particular situation.

The party has always proclaimed socialism as its objective. But socialism cannot be achieved without socialists, much hard work and sacrifice, and detailed economic planning to provide a vast improvement in the level of material wealth of the country, and distribution of this wealth among the population. It was decided in the Seven Year Plan that Ghana's economy would for the time being remain a mixed one, with a vigorous public and co-operative sector operating alongside the private sector. Our socialist objectives demanded, however, that the public and co-operative sectors should expand faster than the private sector, especially those strategic areas of production upon which the economy of the country essentially depended.

Various state corporations and enterprises were to be established as a means of securing our economic independence and assisting in the national control of the economy. They were, like all business undertakings, expected to maintain themselves efficiently, and to show profits which could be used for further investment and to help finance public services. A State Management Committee was set up to ensure their efficient and profitable management.

Many state enterprises were quick to show results. The Ghana National Trading Corporation (GNTC) made a net profit of £4,885,900 in 1965 and had become the largest trading concern in the country. Other state enterprises, by their very nature, took a longer time to develop, and by February 1966 were only just beginning to make a profit. A few, notably in the agricultural sector, were in their infancy and were not expected to yield significant results for some time to come. A certain period of adaptation is necessary for all young industries, particularly in developing countries where the patterns of production are still mainly agricultural and elementary.

But it is noteworthy that the traitors of February 1966 found no less than 63 state enterprises which they could put on the market.

In our Seven Year Plan, we recognised the value of foreign investment in the private sector, particularly in the production of consumer goods, the local processing of Ghanaian raw materials and the utilisation of Ghana's natural resources in the areas of economic activity where a large volume of investment was required. But we welcomed foreign investors in a spirit of partnership. We did not intend to allow them to operate in such a way as to exploit our people. They were to assist in the expansion of our economy in line with our general objectives, an agreed portion of their profits being allocated to promote the welfare and happiness of the Ghanaian people.

The state retained control of the strategic branches of the economy, including public utilities, raw materials, and heavy industry. The state also participated in light and consumer goods industries in which the rates of return on capital were highest. We intended that those industries which provided the basic living needs of the people should be state-owned in order to prevent any exploitation.

It was estimated that during the seven years there would be a total expenditure of £1,016 million. Total government investment in the plan was to be £476 million. Foreign investors, individual Ghanaians, local authorities, and the co-operative sector were expected to invest about £440 million. Ghanaians, it was hoped, would contribute nearly £100 million of direct labour in the construction of buildings, in community development and in the extension of their farms.

Special attention was given to the modernising of agriculture, so that a greater yield and a diversity of crops could be produced. We needed to produce more food locally so that we could reduce our imports of foodstuffs and at the same time improve the health of the people by increasing the protein content in the average diet. Most developing countries face nutritional problems of one kind or another. In our case, the great need was for more fish and meat to provide a properly balanced diet. We planned to increase the output of fish from an estimated 70,000 tons in 1963 to 250,000 tons in 1969. Livestock production, including poultry and eggs, was to increase from 20,080 tons to 37,800 tons.

Immediate steps were taken to expand the fishing fleet and to develop fish processing and marketing facilities. We bought 29 fishing trawlers from Russia. The immense man-made lake formed as part of the Volta River Project was being stocked with fish, and this too was about to bring a big improvement in the diet of the Ghanaian people.

As for meat and poultry, the government subsidised the development of many poultry farms, and the rearing of large herds of cattle. In colonial days, fresh meat, milk, and eggs were available to Europeans only. Before the setback of February 1966, however, they were becoming part of the regular diet of the Ghanaian masses.

The task of correcting the imbalance in our food economy was regarded as the greatest challenge to the agricultural sector of the plan. Far-reaching schemes were initiated for major improvements in irrigation and water conservation in the northern and upper regions of Ghana. Peasant farmers throughout the country were informed that they would be able to make use of the agricultural machinery of state and co-operative farms. It was not the government's intention to squeeze out the peasant farmer. Far from it, we needed the maximum effort of every individual farmer if we were to achieve our agricultural targets.

During the period of the plan, Ghana's production of raw materials was to be considerably increased. Cocoa, our main export, earned the country 1,680 million cedis between 1951 and 1961. Of this, the farmers received 1,008 million cedis and the remainder was used by the government and the Cocoa Marketing

Board for maintaining public services and for the general development of the country. We increased our cocoa production from 264,000 tons in 1956–1957, to 590,000 tons in 1963–1964 and huge silos had been built, able to store half the cocoa crop, to enable us to restrict exports and so ensure a fair price for our cocoa in the world market.

Plans were also far advanced to increase exports of timber, and to develop new species of wood for buildings, furniture and other wood products, and for use in paper factories. Efforts were being made to revive our once-flourishing export crop of palm oil. Rubber production was being increased. In the Western Region, a vast new plantation, 18 miles long, had been sown. Within two to three years Ghana was to be one of the greatest rubber producers in Africa. The production of palm oil, cotton, sugar cane, and tobacco was being stepped up. By 1970, there were to be four factories in operation producing 100,000 tons of sugar a year, more than sufficient to eliminate the item from our list of imports.

Greatest of all our development projects was the Volta Dam. When the Seven Year Plan was launched, the Volta Project was expected to begin to generate electrical power by September 1965. Completion of the project would enable us to develop the full industrial potential of Ghana. It would increase by nearly 600 per cent the installed electrical capacity of the country. Nearly one-half of this new capacity would be taken up by the aluminium smelter in Tema; it is estimated that Ghana has sufficient bauxite to last for 200 years. But apart from this the Volta Project would have an ample reserve of power for other users, and Ghana would have liberated herself decisively from the possibility of a power shortage becoming a brake on the rate of economic progress.

Construction targets for the various parts of the Volta River Project were achieved, some of them ahead of schedule, and the official inauguration ceremony took place on 23 January 1966. At that time, building was about to start on a large subsidiary dam at Bui. Plans were also well advanced for the construction of an aluminium plant which would have given Ghanaians control of the whole process of aluminium production. As it was, we were exporting bauxite to the UK for processing while we were importing alumina manufactured in the US from bauxite mined in Jamaica for our aluminium smelter.

In keeping with my government's policy of linking Ghana's progress with Africa's total development, provision was made in the plan for economic co-operation with other African states. As I said in my address to the national assembly on 11th March 1964:

While we wait for the setting up of a Union Government for Africa, we must begin immediately to harmonise our plans for Africa's total development. For example, I see no reason why the independent African states should not, with advantage to each other, join together in an economic union and draw up together a joint Development Plan which will give us greater scope and flexibility to our mutual advantage. By the same token, I see no reason why the independent African states should not have common shipping and air lines in the interests of improved services and economy. With such rationalisation of our economic policies, we could have common objectives and thus eliminate unnecessary competition and frontier barriers and disputes.

When in fact I inaugurated the completed Volta River Project on 23 January 1966, I said: 'We are ready and prepared to supply power to our neighbours in Togo, Dahomey, Ivory Coast and Upper Volta. As far as I am concerned this project is not for Ghana alone. Indeed, I have already offered to share our power resources with our sister African states.'

On that day at Akosombo, some 60 miles north-east of Accra, when I switched on illuminating lights signifying the official opening of hydro-electric power from the Volta, one of my greatest dreams had come true. I had witnessed the wide-scale electrification of Ghana and the breakthrough into a new era of economic and social advance. The Volta Dam permitted not only a large aluminium plant at Tema processing the country's rich bauxite deposits, but a broad range of other industrial projects. The initial power output is 512,00 kW (588,00 kW at full load) and the ultimate power output will be 768,00 kW (882,000 kW at full load). There are 500 miles of transmission lines. The main grid carries 161,000 volts.

The water building up behind the dam is forming the largest man-made lake in the world. It will cover an area of 3,275 square miles with a capacity of 120 million acre feet of water, and will be 250 miles long, with a shoreline of 4,500 miles. Approximately 80,000 people had to be moved from the area submerged by the lake. This necessitated the construction of 50 new villages and for us to accommodate them, the provision of modem housing, schools, piped water, electricity, medical facilities and new forms of employment. Thousands of acres of land had to be cleared, and people settled on farms and smallholdings with up-to-date methods of cultivation and animal husbandry. All this was achieved.

The creation of the Volta Lake has already provided facilities for an important freshwater fishing industry. The Volta River contained numerous excellent indigenous fish; and research has shown which fish to breed to increase the supply, and how to control weed growth. A number of ports and fishing villages being formed round the lakeside provide bases for a cheap means of transport from the north to the south of Ghana. Furthermore, the lake forms a vast reservoir, making possible the improvement of water supplies to towns and villages and the irrigation of land for agriculture. The natural seasonal fluctuation in the level of the lake immediately affect 650 square miles of land, permitting the cultivation of rice and other crops. Lake Volta was also to be developed as a holiday and tourist attraction.

Ghanaians are justifiably proud that their own government provided £35,000,000 that is half of the cost of the Volta River Project as well as meeting the cost of the new port and township of Tema, which was an essential part of the scheme. The balance of the £70,000,000 required was to be raised by international loans as follows:

International Bank for Reconstruction and Development	£16,790,000
Agency for International Development of the United States Government	£9,640,000
Export-Import Bank of the United Kingdom Government	£3,570,00
United Kingdom Board of Trade acting for the Export Credits Gaurantee Department	£5,000,00

Incidentally, at a time when our detractors talk much of bribery and corruption in the developing countries, it is noteworthy that not a single penny went astray or was misappropriated in the entire Volta undertaking, which involved countless contracts over many years.

Apart from completing the Volta River Project, the Seven Year Development Plan provided for certain further improvements in the physical services. These were mostly intended to improve upon the existing system of transport, communications, water supply and electricity services in order to make them fully capable of supporting the proposed level of industrial and agricultural development.

A considerable proportion of the increase in material wealth that was expected to accrue to the country during the seven years of the plan's operation was to be used to promote public welfare services. Education, the health services, and housing were all to benefit. As far as health services were concerned, the plan proposed to change the main orientation which had hitherto been more curative than preventative. Rural health services were developed in such a way that the rate of infant mortality was lowered, and maternity and post-natal care improved. The main cause of poor health in Ghana is the prevalence of endemic diseases such as malaria. The plan put emphasis on the fight against these endemic diseases.

New regional hospitals, equipped with all specialist facilities, were under construction in Tamale, Koforidua, Ho, and Sunyani, and existing hospitals were being improved. Arrangements had been made to build six new district hospitals and four more urban polyclinics to assist in the decentralisation of out-patient work. In addition, five new mental hospitals with accommodation for 1,200 patients were designed to be ready by 1970. They were to be backed up by psychiatric units providing treatment for as many mental patients as possible.

The urgent need for more doctors was being met by sending Ghanaian medical students to study abroad, and by the setting up of our own medical school. In 1962, 51 pre-medical students were enrolled at the University of Ghana. When our own medical school is functioning fully it will be empowered to provide a screening system for all doctors trained abroad who wish to practise in Ghana.

The medical programme under the Seven Year Development Plan was intended to achieve the following ratios:

1 doctor to 10,000 people

1 nurse to 5,000 patients (including patients in public health centres)

1 technician (laboratory, X-ray, etc.) to 5,000 patients

1 health inspector to 15,000 people

1 health auxiliary (vaccinators, dressing-room attendants, etc.) to 1,000 people.

A large network of health centres was being built all over Ghana to serve the rural population, and regional health officers were being provided with training and facilities to enable them to carry out their important work. The only nursing school which existed in 1945 produced only 8 nurses a year by 1950. In 1961–62 six schools of nursing turned out 265 new nurses and midwives.

Perhaps the most outstanding contribution to public health has come from the Medical Field Unit. This unit was formed to seek out and control trypanosomiasis, and it has been successful in containing the disease. It has also carried out a massive vaccination programme and played a leading role in the control of epidemics of cerebrospinal meningitis. It is currently actively engaged in combating malaria, leprosy, and tuberculosis.

In launching the Seven Year Development Plan, with all its detailed programmes for our country's economic and social progress, I warned about the existence of Ghanaian private enterprise in our midst. It was necessary, I told members of the national assembly, to distinguish between the two types of business which had grown up within recent years. The first was the type which it was the government's intention to encourage, that of the small businessman who employed his capital in an industry or trade with which he was familiar, and which fulfilled a public need. The second consisted of that class of Ghanaian businesses, which were modelled on the old colonial pattern of exploitation. In this category were those who used their capital, not in productive endeavour, but to purchase and resell, at high prices, commodities such as salt, fish, and other items of food and consumer goods which were in demand by the people. This type of business served no social purpose, and steps would be taken to see that the nation's banking resources were not used to provide credit for them.

Even more harmful to the economy was another type of enterprise in which some Ghanaians had been participating. This was the setting up of bogus agencies for foreign companies which were in fact nothing more than organisations for distributing bribes and for exerting improper pressures on behalf of foreign companies. The government intended to carry out a thorough investigation into the activities of these agencies and to suppress them.

The initiative of Ghanaian businessmen would not be cramped, but we intended to take steps to see that it was channelled towards desirable social ends and was not expended in the exploitation of the community. We would discourage anything which threatened our socialist objectives. For this reason, no Ghanaian would be allowed to take up shares in any enterprise under foreign investment. Instead, our people would be encouraged to save by investing in the state sector and in co-operative undertakings.

This, in essence, was our Seven Year Development Plan, a plan scientifically worked out with the participation of some of the world's leading experts on economic and social planning. It was to integrate educational, industrial, and agricultural programmes to bring full employment and to make possible the achievement of economic independence and a big rise in our living standards. And this was the plan the rebel military regime scrapped as soon as it usurped power.

No possible justification can be given for its abandonment and the sell-out of Ghana's increasing assets. The first phase of the plan was going well, and according to schedule. During the first year, £48,900,000 was spent on development projects, and of this amount, £16 million went into the key sectors, agriculture, and industry. In agriculture, the emphasis was on diversification. State farms cultivated 24,00 acres of rubber, oil palm, banana, urena, lobata, coconut, and citrus. Together with the agricultural wing of the Workers' Brigade, which alone had 12,500 acres, the two institutions cultivated large areas for cereals and vegetables. During this period also, improvements were made in the modernisation and productivity of private and co-operative farms.

In the industrial sphere, during this period, nearly all the initiative was in the public sector. The construction of many new industrial plants was undertaken. These included a steel works(30,000 tons), two cocoa processing plants, one at Takoradi (28,000 tons) and the other at Tema (68,600 tons), two sugar refineries, a textile printing plant, a glass factory, a chocolate factory, a meat processing plant, a radio assembly plant, and a large printing works at Tema. All these factories were brought into production during the first phase of the plan.

In addition, work was well advanced on a textile mill and a complex of food industries at Tema, a gold refinery at Tarkwa, and asbestos, cement, shoe, and rubber tyre factories at Kumasi. The buildings for an atomic reactor at Kwabinya were almost finished. So also was a plant for the manufacture of prefabricated houses. In fact, the basic policy underlying the Seven Year Development Plan, to change the structure of our mainly agricultural economy into a balanced modern economy, was going ahead with great speed and efficiency. We were successfully managing to use our local raw materials for establishing industries and were beginning to satisfy local demand for certain consumer goods. For example, we produced matches, shoes, nails, sweets, chocolate, soft drinks, whisky, beer, gin, cigarettes, biscuits, paints, canned fruit, insecticides and other chemicals. An indication of the build-up of our industrial strength may be seen in the fact that at the beginning of January 1966 imports of raw materials amounted to about 9 per cent of Ghana's total imports.

Before the February action, the government was investing £25 million annually in manufacturing projects, and the country's main exports:

Cocoa	680 million cedis annually
Timber	31.2 million cedis annually
Minerals	48 million cedis annually

On an average, Ghana annually imports about 264 million cedis of semi-finished and finished products consisting mainly of food and drinks, textiles and clothing, construction materials, and capital equipment. Annual exports average some 254.4 million cedis of primary produce, mainly cocoa, timber, gold, diamonds, and manganese. Our growing industries were to make possible a cut in imports, particularly of consumer goods, and an increase in our exports, not only of primary produce but of our own locally manufactured products.

A look at the orientation of Ghana's investment policy during recent years throws further light on the direction in which Ghana was moving. In 1951–1959, 90 per cent (£127.8 million) of government expenditure was allocated to provide social services and to create the infrastructure of economic growth, while 10 per cent (£13.4 million) went to the productive sector. During the 1951–1962 period, an average amount of £15.5 million was allocated yearly to the public sector during the First Development Plan, and during the Consolidated Plan an average of £21.4 million yearly. Under the Second Development Plan an average amount of £50 million yearly went to the public sector. Under the Seven Year Development Plan an average of £68 million was going to the public sector yearly, representing a total investment of £442 million for development projects belonging to the public sector. To the above-mentioned £68 million, £34 million were added for the Volta complex – in all £476 million for the public sector.

Investments during the Seven Year Development Plan period (1964–1970) were therefore distributed between social services and infrastructure (62%) and the directly productive sector (38%). This represented for Ghanaians an investment of £10 per head, per year (to be compared with the maximum investment of 8 shillings per head, per year, in countries associated with the Common Market during the 1958–1962 period). It may also be noted that Ghana has a 240 cedis per capita income, that is to say, practically the highest in independent Africa – and in real terms, the highest in Africa, since it cannot be considered that the distribution of gross national product is equitable in countries like South Africa, Rhodesia and most of the neo-colonialist states.

The qualitative aspect of Ghana's imports reveals that while consumer goods dropped from one-half of total imports in 1961 to two-fifths in 1963, industrial equipment and goods increased from 50.6 per cent of total imports in 1961 to 60.6 per cent in 1963.

On the question of ownership, it is worth noting that in 1965 the state controlled between 60 per cent and 65 per cent of the national production (this percentage was to rise in 1970), and that since 1963, the total gold and foreign exchange assets of Ghana, and total capital exports, were likewise under state financial control.

Apart from a 41 per cent control over consumer goods imports, the state was controlling in 1965 over 60 per cent of the exports in the most important sectors such as gold, diamonds, cocoa. In the case of timber, the Timber Marketing Board had increased its foreign exchange earnings from £5.7 million in 1962 to £8 million in 1964, and was able during the same period, to grant revolving loans of £2 million to Ghanaian producers organised into co-operatives.

When the party came to power in 1951, all imported goods were in the hands of a few big foreign firms, especially the monopolist United Africa Company, part of the Unilever complex. Foreign firms dominated Ghana's trade and virtually controlled the economy. By 1965, however, the grip was being broken. The nationalised Ghana National Trading Corporation was distributing 32 per cent of all imports.

My government was also breaking through the stranglehold of the big international banking houses. In 1958, foreign banks held one-third of Ghana's foreign currency reserves; in 1965 they held none.

Our success in breaking the web of economic control which Western capitalism has imposed across the whole of the African continent, and our clear socialist policies, provoked the hostility of the imperialist powers. They knew that as long as I was alive and at the head of the party in Ghana the process could not be halted and neo-colonialist exploitation could not be re-imposed. Ours was a system they could neither penetrate nor manipulate.

Significantly, one of the first acts of the 'National Liberation Council' (NLC) was to announce the abandonment of the Seven Year Development Plan, which would have given the Ghanaian people the only worthwhile independence – real economic independence. The 'NLC' replaced it with a two-year 'review period' during which the socialised industries would be dismantled and the door opened once more to unrestricted 'private enterprise' – in fact, they were establishing a neo-colonialist economic subjugation of Ghana.

The only Ghanaians to benefit from such a sell-out were the African middle-class hangers-on to neo-colonialist privilege and the neo-colonialist trading firms. For the mass of workers, peasants and farmers, the victims of the capitalist free-for-all, it meant a return to the position of 'drawers of water and hewers of wood' to Western capitalism.

Of course, the Ghanaian economy was not without its problems, but is this not true of all national economies, and particularly those of developing countries in the context of the growing gap between rich and poor nations? In any event, these difficulties were not determinant. It was no mean achievement that in January 1965, after five years as a republic, Ghana had 63 state enterprises and a budget of £200 million, including a supplementary budget, for its population of nearly eight million; while Nigeria, richer in national resources and with a population of 55 million, had a budget of £78 million.

Imperialist circles have talked much about Ghana's external debt, given as £250 million. Apart from the dubious accounting which arrived at this conveniently round sum, a figure such is this means nothing unless it is set in the context of the overall Ghanaian economic situation. To implement our various development plans it was necessary to borrow considerable sums of money, but it was borrowed on the basis of building capital assets such as the Volta Dam, and over 100 industries established in Ghana since independence. The government made sure that the international agreements signed were based on economic feasibility, and that the money borrowed could create something lasting and beneficial not only for us in our lifetime but for the generations to follow. Seen in the light of Ghana's growing industries and increasing exports, her 'indebtedness' is put in proper perspective – as an index of the investors' confidence in the enterprise and the management they helped to finance. In addition, it should be noted that only some £20 million was due to be paid in 1967, and this did not prevent the government from refusing the political conditions attached to a loan from the IMF).

Long faces are pulled at the drop in our foreign reserves since independence. In 1957, Ghana had a sterling balance of £200 million. This has not been 'squandered' as the imperialist press would have its readers believe. It has been used to pay off successive balance of payments deficits due to the rise in prices of imported consumer goods, and the drastic fall in the price of our main export crop – cocoa. It should be remembered that the sterling balance was in fact a forced loan not negligible interest which Britain acquired from Ghana during and after the WWII. Its accumulation was made possible by the Cocoa Marketing Board which prevented Ghanaian cocoa growers from receiving the bulk of the proceeds from the sale of their cocoa. The capital the growers might have amassed from cocoa profits and later might have invested in industry was locked up in London 'to maintain the confidence of the foreign investor.'

Our imperialist critics would be better employed examining the economic situation in their own countries, many of which are in grave financial difficulties. In Britain, for example, the £1 is devalued, there is a continuous 'balance of payments crisis' and unemployment is a serious problem.

In Ghana, before 24 February 1966, unemployment was virtually unknown. All salaries were regularly paid and new jobs were constantly being created as the Seven Year Development Plan was being implemented. It was estimated that more than one million new workers would be needed to fill the new jobs which would be created, and also to replace those who left the labour force during the plan period. More than 500,000 of them would be employed in industry and agriculture, and another 400,000 would be needed in government services, commerce and construction. The remainder were to be employed in transport, mining and the public utility services. In fact, plans were being made to import labour.

When neo-colonialist inspired traitors seized power in February 1966, we were expanding our educational system to provide the necessary numbers of qualified people to meet these new demands. Changes were made to shorten and to improve educational courses. For example, there was a reduction made in the number of school years so that university graduates would be ready for employment at the age of 21 or 22 instead of 24 or 25 as used to be the case. Under the new plan, the time spent in middle school was reduced by two years and the secondary school period by one year. Primary education took six years and was followed by two years of vocationally oriented training for those who did not intend to proceed to secondary schools. The reduction by two years of the ten-year middle school programme was designed to permit 300,000 additional young people to join the labour force during the seven-year period, and to equip them with basic training in technical and agricultural skills.

The figures below illustrate the planned growth in school enrolment 1963–1970:

	Total Enrolment	
	1963	1970
Primary–Middle	1,200,000	2,200,00
Secondary	23,000	78,000–
Teacher Training	6,000	21,000
Technical Schools	4,000	6,000
Clerical Training	100	5,000
Universities	2,000	5,000

The intake would be such that from 1968 nearly 250,000 children would complete primary-middle school and 20,000 others would leave secondary school each year. For the entire plan period, the output from all educational institutions was id have been approximately as follows:

Middle and Continuing Schools	750,00
Secondary Schools	46,000
Universities	9,000
Technical Schools	14,000
Secretarial Schools	11,000
Teacher Training	31,000

The tremendous rate of our educational growth created certain difficulties. We needed many more trained teachers, find more school and college buildings.

We were successfully in overcoming these problems. The government allocated 153.6 million cedis (£64 million) for the construction of post-primary school buildings to feed the new secondary and higher educational institutions. The University of Ghana, the Kwame Nkrumah University of Science and Technology, and Cape Coast University College were supplying a large number of teachers; and expatriate teachers had been recruited to fill other vacancies until our own output of teachers was sufficient io cope with the demand. The Cape Coast University College was to have become a fully-fledged University in September 1966, but the 'NLC' has abandoned the plan.

Local authorities and individual communities were primarily responsible for the provision of elementary school facilities, though the government provided teachers, textbooks and other services for primary schools. Special subsidies were given to less favoured parts of the country to help in the development of primary education.

To assist in solving the manpower problem, the TUC, the Ministry of Labour and employers' associations launched and rapidly expanded in-service training schemes to augment the knowledge and technical skills of all new employees. Adult education facilities were also being improved to provide part-time and evening classes for craftsmen, foremen, technicians, and managers. The Institute of Public Education, the Workers' College, the universities, and other specialised institutions were redoubling their efforts to make this type of education available throughout the country.

Ghana was going ahead. The nation's economy was almost completely controlled by Ghanaians, and our educational planning was producing educated and skilled personnel to meet the demand. Likewise, thorough-going machinery had been established for the political education of the masses so that our socialist objectives, and Ghana's role in the wider African revolution, might be clearly understood. This was the purpose of the Young Pioneers, the TUC educational programme, and the Ideological Institute of Winneba where cadres were being trained. It was to make possible the unfolding of the next phase of the Ghanaian revolution: the establishment of a socialist republic, the principle of which was enshrined in the 1961 Constitution of the Republic of Ghana.

This process was well on its way when in 1965, the imperialists and neo-colonialists stepped up their pressure on Ghana in the form of an economic squeeze. In that year, the price of cocoa on the world market was artificially forced down from £476 in 1954 to £87 10s. a ton. This meant that although Ghana exported 500,000 tons of cocoa, she earned only £77 million, or less than her receipts in the mid-1950s for 250,000 tons.

When the Seven Year Development Plan was drawn up, it was assumed that the price of cocoa on the world market would be at least £200 a ton. This was not an unreasonable assumption. Between 1953 and 1963, prices fell only once below £190 a ton. In 1954 the price was £476, and in 1957–1958 it was £352. But the very year the Seven Year Development Plan was launched, cocoa prices began to fall steeply. At the same time, the prices of capital and manufactured goods needed for industrial and agricultural projects under the plan were rapidly rising. Between 1950 and 1961 they had risen by over 25 per cent.

In 1964, the imperialist powers, the principal consumers of cocoa, promised at the Geneva meeting of the UNCTAD that they would 'lift barriers in the form of tariffs and duties on primary products, either raw, processed or semi-processed.' This would have meant that cocoa-grindings, cocoa butter, and chocolate products whose price was firm, could have been sold in the metropolitan markets to cushion the effects of the low cocoa prices. But Britain and the USA did not keep their promise to lower trade barriers against processed and semi-processed primary products. Ghana, regarded by them as a pacesetter in Africa, could not be allowed to succeed in building socialism.

When I spoke to the Ghana cocoa farmers on 22 September 1965, I drew attention to the breach of faith of the cocoa consumers and said that if tariff walls prevented us from selling our chocolate abroad, we could still sell it in Ghana and in other African countries at a price well within the means of all. I announced that cocoa powder was being distributed to schoolchildren, and that the production of cocoa butter, in demand for the manufacture of cosmetics and pharmaceuticals, was being expanded.

We constructed silos which, when completed, would enable us to withhold more than half of our cocoa crop from the world market. This amount would be more than the combined world cocoa surplus of production over consumption. We were, in fact, breaking through the cocoa price squeeze. The USA, however, was stockpiling a record quantity of cocoa to be used to keep prices down. In its 1966 Commodity Review, the United Nations' FAO, reported that the total stocks of cocoa beans in consuming countries at the end of 1964 amounted to 500,000 tons, and that by December 1965 this total was further increased.

The USA and Britain could, if they had wanted, have fixed a reasonable price for cocoa and so have eased the economic situation in Ghana. They had no wish to do so. On the contrary, the forcing down of the price of cocoa was part of their policy of preparing the economic ground for political action in the form of a 'coup' and a change of government.

Throughout 1965, and before then, the U.S. government exerted various other forms of economic pressure on Ghana. It withheld investment and credit guarantees from potential investors, put pressure on existing providers of credit to the Ghanaian economy, and negated applications for loans made by Ghana to American-dominated financial institutions such as the IMF. This pressure ended smartly after 24 February 1966 when the US State Department's political objective had been achieved. The price of cocoa suddenly rose on the world market, and the IMF rushed to the aid of the 'NLC.'

If further proof were needed of America's political motives it may be seen in the U.S. government's hysterical reaction to the publication of my book, *Neo-Colonialism – The Last Stage of Imperialism* in October 1965. In this book I exposed the economic stranglehold exercised by foreign monopolistic complexes such as the Anglo-American Corporation, and illustrated the ways in which this financial grip perpetuated the paradox of Africa: poverty in the midst of plenty. The American government sent me a note of protest, and promptly refused Ghana $35 million of 'aid.'

The fact that our enemies decided finality on subversion and violence as the only effective way in which to achieve their objective of halting the Ghanaian revolution and bringing Ghana into the neo-colonialist fold, is a measure of the success of our economic policies. We had proved that we were strong enough to develop independently, not only without foreign tutelage, but also in the context of active imperialist and neo-colonialist resistance.

Voice from Conakry, 6 March 1966

The first broadcast to the people of Ghana on Radio Guinea's Voice of the African Revolution broadcast.

I expect you all at this hour of trial to remain firm in determination and resistance despite intimidation. Fellow countrymen, chiefs, and people, I am speaking to you from Radio Guinea, Conakry. On the eve of 6 March, Ghana's Independence Day, I send to you all, greetings, and warm regards.

It was on this day that the combined forces of the Ghana people secured independence from British imperialism. This achievement was not an easy task. It involved sacrifice, suffering, and deprivation on the part of all of us.

It was only when I arrived in Peking in China that I was informed that some members of my armed forces, supported by some members of my police, had attempted to overthrow my government. I know that you are always loyal to me, the party, and the government, and I expect you all at this hour of trial to remain firm in determination and resistance despite intimidation.

The people of Ghana built up the CPP which became the vanguard of the national liberation movement in Ghana. By indomitable will, the CPP overcame all difficulties, triumphed over adversities and won independence and planned for the economic, political and social construction of our dear Ghana. The party and government fought not only for political independence but evolved a work and happiness programme of reconstruction. We also joined in the great movement for the liberation and political unification of Africa.

The achievement of the CPP under my leadership is an open book. It can be seen by all, and today, anyone who visits Ghana can be a witness of this great achievement. Internationally, independent Ghana has been playing her role in world affairs. She has supported peace and will always continue to support any movement that can lead to the peace and security of the world.

In all this struggle, the CPP, and its government, have not shed a single drop of Ghanaians' blood. I shuddered when I learned of the shooting and killing of defenceless men and women, and the arrest, intimidation, and imprisonment of many of the leading patriots of the country. The blood of these gallant men and women cries to heaven for redress. Their blood shall not be shed in vain. Those who have died, may they rest in peace.

By the arrest, detention and assassination of ministers, the party's civil servants, trade unionists and by the blind massacre of defenceless men and women, the authors of these insane acts of robbery, violence, intimidation and assassination of added brutality to their treason.

Never before in the cherished history of our new Ghana have citizens, men and women, been assassinated in cold blood and never have their children become orphans for political reasons. Never before have Ghanaians been shot down because of their political convictions. This is a tragedy of monstrous proportions.

But I know your courage and determination: I see the extent of your indignation against this wanton rebellion. I know that at the appropriate time you will take the initiative to crush it. The party's dynamism will rise up again to save your dignity and personality. As far as I'm concerned, I will do my very best to crush this criminal rebellion.

The integral wings of the CPP, the Farmers' Cooperative Council, the Trades Union Congress, the National Council of Ghana Women, the Young Pioneers, the Workers' Brigade have been established by the party and the spirit that motivates these organisations cannot be destroyed. They now suffer in silence, but they will rise up again and speak. The present rebellion has not only committed treason against the sovereign state of Ghana but has attacked the very foundation upon which all was based and the position of chieftaincy which has been irrevocably enshrined in our Constitution.

In the party's struggle for independence we have had opponents and enemies. Imperialism and neo-colonialism and their agents and stooges have not been our friends. They have tried in many ways to undo what the CPP has done. In all attempts they failed; and even several attempts on my personal life have failed. And so, if today we celebrate our ninth anniversary of independence, we have a lot to be thankful for.

Experience has given us added wisdom to continue the struggle. No one can destroy the socialist gains we have achieved. For no reason other than morbid ambition, inordinate and selfish desire for power, certain officers of my armed forces took advantage of my absence from Accra to subvert and rebel against constitutional authority. This reactionary rebellion sought to perpetrate subversive activities against the lawfully constituted government of Ghana.

What has taken place in Ghana is not a *coup d'etat* but a rebellion and it shall be crushed by its own actions. At the moment you are being suppressed at the point of guns and bayonets and you are made speechless by these same instruments. You are forbidden to hold your rallies and meetings. But I know that even in silence you are determined and resisting. Be assured that I am standing firm behind you. There is a Russian proverb that says one cannot screen the sun by the palm of a hand; nor can I be destroyed by telling lies about me. Very soon I shall be with you again.

The perpetrators of this rebellion have committed an act of high treason. Those soldiers of my army who have taken power in my absence have issued orders that our ninth anniversary of independence, a great national day, should not be celebrated. This shows that they are suppressing you at the points of guns and bayonets. They cannot destroy what we have taken years to build. For what we have achieved is built on rock foundations and is indestructible. Forward Ever, Backward Never. There is Victory for Us.

I am safe and well. I will be with you in due course. Have courage and bear your humiliation and sufferings with fortitude. What has happened is only a phase of our struggle and it shall pass.

Long live the people of Ghana.
Long live the Convention People's Party.
Long live the liberation movement of Africa.
Long live the African continental government that must be.

BIBLIOGRAPHY

'What I Mean By Positive Action', 1949, *Revolutionary Path* (London: PANAF, 1973) pp. 91–95.

'Midnight Speech on Ghana's Independence', 6 March 1957.

'Dawn Broadcast to the Nation: Osagyefo Calls a Halt to Self-Seeking', 8 April 1961.

'Towards Our Goal', Sessional review of the second session of the first Parliament of the Republic of Ghana by Osagyefo the President, 14 September 1962.

'Freedom First', *Africa Must Unite* (London: Heinemann, 1963) pp.50–56.

'Towards African Unity', *Africa Must Unite* (London: Heinemann, 1963) pp. 132–140.

'Continental Government for Africa', *Africa Must Unite* (London: Heinemann, 1963) pp. 216–222.

'Charter of the Organisation of African States', 25 May 1963, *Revolutionary Path* (London: PANAF, 1973) pp. 251-258.

'Address to the National Assembly of Ghana on the occasion of the Ratification of the Charter of the Organisation of African States', 21 June 1963, *Revolutionary Path* (London: PANAF, 1973) pp. 258-275.

'Proposals for a Union Government of Africa', 19 July 1964, *Revolutionary Path* (London: PANAF, 1973) pp. 277–297.

'Society and Ideology,' *Consciencism: Philosophy and Ideology for Decolonisation* (London: Panaf, 1964) pp. 56–77.

'Obstacles to Economic Progress', *Neo-Colonialism: The Last Stage of Imperialism* (London: Thomas Nelson & Sons, 1965) pp. 15–36.

'The Mechanisms of Neo-colonialism', *Neo-Colonialism: The Last Stage of Imperialism*, (London: Thomas Nelson & Sons, 1965) pp. 239–254.

'Peking to Conakry', *Dark Days in Ghana* (London: Lawrence and Wishart, 1968) pp. 9–19.

'24 February 1966', *Dark Days in Ghana* (London: Lawrence and Wishart, 1968) pp.20–32.

'The Big Lie', *Dark Days in Ghana* (London: Lawrence and Wishart, 1968) pp. 75–96.

'Voice from Conakry', 6 March 1966. *Revolutionary Path* (London: PANAF, 1973) pp. 391–393.